S0-BZV-292

Table of Contents

What are the benefits of getting an MBA? Learn what prospective students like you are looking for in an MBA program. Find out what corporate recruiters are looking for. Discover how the job market for MBAs is changing in the 1990s.

What is it like to be an MBA student in a full-time program? What are the courses like, and which ones are required? Learn why you shouldn't worry about the math in these courses, and why some of these courses are really fun. Find out why students at the best schools do actual consulting projects with real companies as part of their coursework.

Every year or so, business schools are ranked in a number of opinion-based magazine surveys. Discover what these rankings really tell about which schools are best. If you go full time, you'll invest over $100,000 (including foregone salary) in your MBA degree, and you can't rely on these magazine surveys to tell you which schools will give you the highest potential return on your investment.

Introducing THE MBA ADVANTAGE–a new market-based approach that ranks business schools by the historical financial returns on MBA degrees from the best schools. Learn why this ranking is very different from the opinion-based magazine surveys.

An in-depth look at the schools that could provide the highest potential payoff on your investment in the MBA degree. Find out which schools have the best programs in finance, marketing, operations management, and consulting–including each school's most recent starting salaries in each of these functional areas.

THE MBA ADVANTAGE

Why it pays to get an MBA

Ronald N. Yeaple, Ph.D.

BOB ADAMS, INC.
Holbrook, Massachusetts

Published by Bob Adams, Inc.
260 Center Street, Holbrook, MA 02343

ISBN: 1-55850-409-5

Printed in the United States of America.

J   I   H   G   F   E   D   C   B

Library of Congress Cataloging-in-Publication Data
Yeaple, Ronald N.
    The MBA advantage : why it pays to get an MBA / Ronald N. Yeaple.
        p.   cm.
    Includes bibliographical references and index.
    ISBN 1-55850-409-5
    1. Business schools—United States—Handbooks, manuals, etc. 2. College choice—United States—Handbooks,
manuals, etc. 3. Master of business administration degree—United States—Handbooks, manuals, etc. I. Title.
    HF1131.Y43   1994
    650'.017'173—dc20   94-3727
                                                                                                  CIP

This book is available at quantity discounts for bulk purchases.
For information, call 1-800-872-5627.

To my wife, Bev

Acknowledgments

My thanks to the many people who encouraged me to develop *The MBA Advantage*, who spent hours discussing ideas for the book, who provided vital information, who read early drafts, and who provided countless suggestions and helpful comments:

First, to my faculty colleagues at the William E. Simon Graduate School of Business Administration at the University of Rochester, particularly Ray Ball, Dan Horsky, Gregg Jarrell, Uday Karmarkar, Stacey Kole, Bill Lawton, Phil Lederer, John Long, Glenn MacDonald, Larry Matteson, Sridhar Moorthy, Paul Nelson, Bill Schwert, Avi Seidmann, Cliff Smith, Ross Watts, and Jerry Zimmerman. My thanks also to Dean Charles Plosser, Associate Deans Ron Hansen, Charlie Miersch, and Dick West, and Assistant Deans Priscilla Gumina and Lee Junkans for their ideas and support for this project. I would also like to thank the many faculty members at other business schools who shared their thoughts with me about how their MBA programs are changing to meet the challenges of the 1990s.

Second, to my MBA students, particularly those whose names appear in the book as authors of research studies that brought into clear focus what prospective students and corporate recruiters are looking for in MBA programs.

Third, to the dozens of Simon School alumni who gave freely of their time to help me understand more fully how the MBA degree can be made even more valuable in the future. In particular, I want to thank Scott Beaudry, Class of '91; Ron Bingham, '90; Suzanne Gray, '91; and Kris Lemke, '88; all of whom joined me in literally hundreds of hours of research and discussion on the value of the MBA.

Fourth, to my agent, Mike Snell, who came forth with excellent advice as the idea for the book began to take shape, and to Bob Adams, my publisher, who saw the potential for this project when it was still in a very early form. I would also like to thank my editor, Brandon Toropov, for his skill in transforming the manuscript into a finished book, and my copy editor, Diane Freed, for her many excellent suggestions and recommendations.

And finally, to my family. To my wife, Bev, without whose love and advice I would have never undertaken this project; to my four children, David, Susan, Jodie and Anne, who asked all the right questions; and to my mother, who taught me early in life about the importance of "stick-to-it-ive-ness"—a very important requirement for an author.

Preface

Every year nearly 300,000 men and women spend $52 each to take the Graduate Management Admissions Test (GMAT) in preparation for applying to business schools. Attending a full-time MBA program is a major decision, requiring an investment of two years and more than $100,000 (including foregone salary). Is it worth it? And what about less expensive alternatives, such as part-time MBA programs and Executive MBA programs. Are they worth it? *The MBA Advantage* is a *complete reference guide for the prospective MBA*, providing the facts and figures to answer these vital questions.

I wrote this book for those who have a real interest in graduate business education:

- Nearly 300,000 men and women who take the GMAT every year and 500,000 more who are seriously thinking about starting an MBA program.

- The additional 200,000 currently pursuing the MBA who wonder from time to time whether it's all worth it.

- Wives and husbands and moms and dads who provide advice, encouragement, and often the cash, to make it possible.

- Thousands of employers searching for managerial talent who are interested in knowing which schools have the best programs in finance or marketing, and in learning what the current starting salaries are at these top schools.

- Faculties and administrations of America's 700 business schools who are looking for an objective way to compare the value of the MBA degree from various schools.

- Finally, nearly one million MBA graduates who wonder how *their* business school is doing against the competition.

The MBA Advantage was written to provide practical information available from no other source:

- How to analyze the decision of whether or not to pursue an MBA degree—for both financial and non-financial reasons—using case studies, checklists and worksheets.

- How to decide between full-time, part-time, and Executive MBA programs, with real-life examples of how to make this choice.

- An overview of the strengths and weaknesses of each of the Top 20 national business schools and the best regional business schools, with specific information on teaching approaches, student lifestyles, and detailed evaluations of each school's programs in finance, marketing, operations management, and consulting—*including each school's starting salaries by functional area.*

- How the Top 20 business schools rank *in terms of financial returns on the MBA degree.* This book is the only published source of information on the potential return on your investment in an MBA at both national business schools and regional business schools.
- How to minimize costs, saving as much as $100,000 while still getting a quality degree.

What are my qualifications to write about these important matters? First of all, I love to teach. I've been a faculty member for the past twenty years at a Top 20 business school. I teach courses in marketing research and the strategic management of technology, and I've had some success with it, having won the Superior Teaching Award four times. In addition to my teaching, I'm also Director of the school's Business Innovation Team, in which faculty and MBA students carry out joint research programs with industry to develop world-class products and services. I've also served as a consultant to more than forty organizations in marketing and new product development.

Prior to becoming a faculty member, I was executive vice president of a $30 million medical products company while still in my early thirties. This accomplishment was due in large part to having obtained an MBA after completing my engineering degree.

Finally, I'm the father of a son and daughter who are currently pursuing MBA degrees, and they have helped me view the decision of whether to get an MBA from many different aspects—financial and non-financial. In fact, the idea for this book originated when my daughter, Susan, asked, "Dad, I'm thinking about getting an MBA. Is it worth it?"

This book is my answer to Susan's question.

—RONALD N. YEAPLE, Ph.D.
Victor, New York

To My Colleagues
at Other Business Schools

This book was written for men and women who are considering investing in an MBA degree. Although rigorous analysis is used throughout the book to develop a number of innovative concepts, the style of the book is meant to be conversational rather than formal.

The major innovations contained in this book are:

- The finding that the popular magazine rankings of business schools do not rank schools according to the historical financial return on the students' investment (chapter 3 and appendix A).

- The development of THE MBA ADVANTAGE, a market-based approach that does rank business schools by historical return on the students' investment (chapter 4 and appendix B).

- The recognition that the popular notion of the MBA degree as providing a fixed "value added" is incorrect; the MBA is really a "value multiplier" of the student's inherent ability (chapter 4).

- Discovery of data that suggests a positive relationship between a school's faculty research and the value of the MBA degree from that school (chapter 14).

- An analysis of factors that may explain why the value of the MBA degree (as measured by the magnitude of THE MBA ADVANTAGE) varies across business schools (appendix B).

- The discovery that the most important factor in determining the value of a business school's MBA degree is the quality of its incoming students (appendix B).

For the convenience of prospective students, business schools are referred to by their common names—the way most prospective students would think of them—rather than by their formal names. Thus the business school at Dartmouth is referred to as "Dartmouth" rather than "The Amos Tuck School." Similarly, the business school at the University of North Carolina is "North Carolina" rather than "The Kenan-Flagler Business School," "UCLA" rather than "The Anderson Graduate School of Management," and "Wharton" rather than "The University of Pennsylvania."

Change favors the prepared mind.

Chapter 1

The MBA Degree: Is It Worth It?

"Dad, I've been thinking about getting an MBA . . . again." My daughter Susan, a desktop publishing specialist in the executive offices of Harcourt General in Orlando, reached into her beach bag and pulled out several business school catalogs.

"I'd really like to have an MBA, but it just seems so expensive. Is it worth it to go full time to a Top 20 school? Would I be better off going part time to a local school and getting the company to pay the tuition? Maybe I could even get into the Executive MBA program at Rollins College, and go to school on alternating Fridays and Saturdays. What do you think? Is it worth it?"

"Is it worth it?" I had been dozing under a beach umbrella. After enduring an usually snowy northeastern winter, my wife, Bev, and I had taken a few days off in Florida between the winter and spring quarters to warm up and shake the winter blahs. We had been joined by two of our daughters, Susan and Annie, both in their twenties.

I teach at a top-ranked business school. We've made the *Business Week* Top 20 rankings, and we're always included in the annual *U.S. News & World Report* Top 25 business schools. Nearly 700 schools offer the Master of Business Administration degree, and we're in the top 3 percent. I should be an expert on the value of the MBA.

Over the years I have reflected on the value of the MBA in my own career. Before becoming a business school professor, I had worked in the medical equipment industry, and my MBA had been a major factor in becoming executive vice president of a $30 million company while still in my early thirties. The MBA had sure helped *me*.

But times change and many people think the value of the MBA has peaked and is in decline. Today the business press is full of articles about MBAs who can't get jobs. Corporate America is cutting back on middle management, the traditional entry route for newly-minted MBAs seeking to climb the corporate ladder. Is there a future for the MBA? Going to business school full time can cost $100,000 or more (including two years of foregone salary). Susan's question was right on the mark: "Is it worth it?"

I decided to find out. This book summarizes what I have learned about the value of the MBA degree in today's market for management talent. In these pages we'll look at the following important questions for prospective students:

- If you invest $100,000 or more to go to business school full time, how long will it take to get your money back? Will you *ever* get it back?
- Does it matter which business school you go to, financially or otherwise?
- How important are business school rankings, such as the *Business Week* Top 20?

- Is one method of business school teaching, such as the case method, clearly superior to other methods? Or doesn't it matter?
- Does it pay to go full time to a regional school instead of a Top 20 school?
- Should you get work experience before going for an MBA?
- What about a part-time program, or an Executive MBA program, as alternatives to going back to school full time? Will the MBA still be valuable?
- Which is better—a research-oriented school or a teaching-oriented school?

Who is a Good Prospect for an MBA?

Before going further, let's get acquainted with four people who, like yourself, are thinking about getting an MBA:

- First, there is Susan, who you've already met. In her late 20s, she is a desktop publishing specialist in the executive offices of a major publishing firm. She has a bachelor's degree in public relations and communications from a small, highly-regarded college. After a couple of years in the rarefied air of the corporate offices assisting vice presidents and other senior managers with their presentations and publications, Susan would like to get on the fast track to becoming a senior manager herself. She sees the MBA as an important step toward her career goals.

- David is thirty-one, married with two young children, and holds a bachelor's degree in electrical engineering from a respected engineering school. Since college, he has worked for an internationally known electronics company as an applications engineer, as a field sales representative, and now as a marketing product manager. An increasing part of his job involves developing sophisticated pricing plans and related competitive strategies for his product line. David feels he needs an MBA to thoroughly understand the product line strategic issues that are the essence of his job.

- Jodie, in her mid-twenties, is an associate editor for a well-known national magazine. She earned her bachelor's degree in communications from a top university. Her husband, Eric, is halfway through medical school, which will be followed by several more years for internship and specialization. Although not essential for her current job, Jodie believes an MBA could be a valuable asset over the long run for developing her professional skills as a manager.

- Anne is in her early twenties and has recently completed her bachelor's and master's degrees in early childhood education. At this point in her career she has no interest in being a business manager. Someday she wants to run her own pre-school, however, and she wonders if an MBA would be of any value in such an entrepreneurial venture.

What are Prospective Students Looking for in an MBA Program?

The best place to start in any business analysis is with the customer. What do the customers of business schools want? What do prospective business school students like you look for in an MBA program?

I teach a course in which teams of second-year MBA students carry out comprehensive marketing studies for local companies. Most of our work has been for *Fortune* 500 companies, and we also do marketing studies for local charities and high-tech entrepreneurial startups.

In the spring quarter of 1990, with competition increasing among the top business schools, we decided to run a marketing study for the school.[1] What are potential MBA students looking for in an MBA program? We sent out a comprehensive mail survey to a nationwide national sample of 1,680 prospective MBA students who had taken the January 1990 Graduate Management Admissions Test (GMAT) and had achieved scores high enough to meet our admissions standards.[2]

We received more than 750 responses. We learned that prospective MBAs prefer:

- small schools over large schools
- an urban campus over a rural campus
- a faculty that is oriented more toward teaching than research
- a school where teamwork and cooperation among students are stressed over competition
- a school that requires them to work fairly hard, not a "country club"

In choosing a business school, prospective students said that the most important attributes are:

- prestige of the school (twice as important as any other attribute)
- quality of teaching
- starting salaries
- net cost, defined as tuition less financial aid

"Closeness to home" was relatively unimportant (contrary to the findings of previous studies[3]), except to the 125 potential part-timers in our response group who ranked it number one. (Perhaps this was because we had directed our questionnaires to GMAT takers who scored in the top 15 percent, and who may have been focusing on top-ranked national business schools rather than regional schools.)

Prospective students get most of their information on schools from *word-of-mouth recommendations* and from *personal contact with the school*, both of which are more important than the *business school rankings* published by *Business Week* and *U.S. News & World Report.*

We were intrigued by the strong showing of *prestige*, which had been rated by the GMAT takers as the number one business school attribute. In a follow-up study, we asked MBA students from a number of schools to help us better understand how the "prestige" of a school is determined.[4] The answer: *"achievements of the alumni"*—cited twice as frequently as *"well-renowned faculty"* and *"name recognition of the school."*

---

1   For more details on this study, see chapter 12.
2   "What Potential Students are Looking For in an MBA Program," William E. Simon Graduate School of Business Administration, June, 1990. This study was developed and carried out by the following team from the Simon School MBA Class of 1990: Ron Bingham, Maureen Blitzer, Chris Carosa, Ted Fagenson, Susan Hermenet, Laurel Izuno, Carolyn Keegan, Abu Moosa, Marianne Quercia, and Jean Tunnell. Special thanks also to Kris Lemke, Simon MBA '88, for her assistance with this project.
3   Stolzenberg, R. and Giarrusso, R., "When Students Make the Selections: How the MBA Class of '87 Picked Its Schools," *Selections*, Graduate Management Admission Council, 1990.
4   "The Decision Process of Choosing an MBA Program," by Ron Bingham, Simon MBA '90; Suzanne Gray, Simon MBA '91; and Kris Lemke, Simon MBA '88; William E. Simon Graduate School of Business Administration, September 1990.

The bottom line: Prospective MBA students know what they are looking for—a small, urban business school that values teamwork and high quality teaching, with a prestigious name that reflects the achievements of the school's alumni.

What Do Corporate Recruiters Look for in an MBA Graduate?

Prospective students constitute only one set of business school customers. An equally important group are the corporate recruiters who ultimately determine the demand and the prices for our products by deciding how many of our graduates they are willing to hire, and how much they are willing to pay them.

In the spring quarter of 1991, one of our student teams did a national survey of 136 corporate recruiters to find out what factors are most important to them in choosing schools at which to recruit MBA students.[5] The most important attributes to recruiters are:

- ability of graduates to apply their MBA education in a practical work setting (number one by a wide margin)
- how often I hear or read about the school
- admissions standards—a proxy for the quality of the students

Surprisingly, other factors such as *communications skills* and *analytical skills* are insignificant in choosing among schools—not because they are unimportant, but because recruiters think that all of the top schools are good at teaching these things.

In a follow-up series of personal interviews with corporate recruiters and senior managers who hire MBAs, I heard the same thing—the top business schools are given comparable ratings in teaching the basics of analysis and communications. "What we are looking for is evidence of leadership, teamwork and creativity, and we expect graduates to hit the ground running when they join our company."

A subsequent mail survey of eighty-nine recruiters and seventy-two alumni in the spring quarter of 1993 by a team of students asked: "Which abilities and skills will be important for your future managers to possess?"[6] The top four from a list of twenty-two attributes were:

- creative problem solving
- cohesive teamwork
- interpersonal skills
- leadership skills

A 1993 *Fortune* article reported on a survey of 202 CEOs of *Fortune* 500 firms: "In 'seeking management talent for your company today,' CEOs cited the following as being 'urgently needed:'

- leadership (cited by 53 percent of the CEOs)
- operations management (28 percent)

---

5   "An Analysis of Recruiters' Perceptions," by Scott Beaudry, Marcy Eisenstadt, Sue Koerner, and Karen Vignare from the Simon MBA Class of 1991; William E. Simon Graduate School of Business Administration, May 1991.
6   "What Businesses Want from Business Schools," by Larry Kleehammer, Juan Lugo, Howard Mulcahey, and Keith Sawyer from the Simon MBA Class of 1994; William E. Simon Graduate School of Business Administration, May 1993.

- marketing (27 percent),
- finance (13 percent)
- oganizational behavior (11 percent)
- accounting (3 percent)" [7]

The bottom line: Corporate recruiters and senior managers expect business schools to teach the fundamentals—finance, marketing, business communications, and technical skills such as statistics—as a matter of course. They believe that the top schools are all good at teaching the fundamentals. The number one attribute in choosing the schools at which they recruit is the *ability of graduates to apply their MBA education in a practical work setting*—they expect graduates to be able to "hit the ground running." When it comes to choosing whom they will hire, corporations are focusing on the *personal* characteristics of graduating MBAs—evidence of *leadership, teamwork and creativity.*

What are the Benefits of Having an MBA?

The surveys were clear. We knew what our customers—recruiters and prospective students—look for in an MBA, but I still didn't know the answer to Susan's question: "Is it worth it?"

Any MBA is a major investment in time. Most good programs require twenty or more courses, each with its own homework, cases, projects and exams. A *full-time* MBA is also a major financial investment of typically $100,000 or more, counting the foregone salary during the two years in business school. Would the degree pay for itself?

At this point, I still wasn't sure. I decided to run some spreadsheet calculations to see if the additional income from getting an MBA at a top school would pay for the cost. (It does, as we shall see in chapter 4.)

In addition to the financial rewards for getting an MBA, there are important *non-financial benefits* that must be considered:

- *Learning:* An MBA is not only a professional degree; it is also a graduate degree. There is immense value in learning for its own sake. It is important personally and professionally to know *how* to learn. According to MIT's Peter Senge, the successful organization of the future will be a "learning organization."[8] If you become more adept at learning than your competition, you will be able to make change work for you, and you will prosper in the rapidly changing economy of the future.

    David, product manager for the electronics company, finds that the rate of change in his product line has become so rapid that product life cycles are now being measured in months instead of years. Moreover, customers want more customization of the product and shorter production runs while still keeping the pressure on pricing. And emerging technologies from small, aggressive competitors continue to challenge the industry status quo.

    How do you deal with so much change? Is there a way to leverage this high rate of change to give his product line an advantage? By learning about the fundamentals of competitive strategy in a dynamic market, David will benefit from an MBA.

7   Richman, L., "CEOs to Workers: Help Not Wanted," *Fortune,* July 12, 1993, p. 43.
8   Senge, P., "The Fifth Discipline: The Art and Practice of the Learning Organization," *Doubleday Currency,* 1990.

- *Lifestyle options:* Even if you don't make a lot more money, the knowledge obtained can open up a wide set of opportunities in entrepreneurship or in management of the arts and other non-profit institutions. With the MBA, you'll have more choices to do what you want to do.

    In today's environment, career options are important, and Jodie wants to develop some options for herself professionally. She is very talented as a writer and editor and has gained excellent experience at the magazine publishing company. Someday she may want to run her own publication. The MBA could help make that option possible.

    These options may become very important later in your career. In recent years, many professionals in large companies have taken the option of early retirement to pursue "the dream"—starting a company, doing consulting, teaching, or volunteering.

- *Credentials:* An MBA is evidence of a commitment to the profession of management. The field of management has become so competitive and demanding that it's no longer possible for most people to wing it and succeed. The MBA shows that you are serious about a career in management, and you've paid your dues.

    Susan enjoys the pace of the executive office. Working with senior executives of a *Fortune* 500 company, she has become an important contributor to the development of plans and strategies. But to fully participate as a member of the management team, she needs the credentials as well as the additional education. An MBA is the right step at this point in her career.

    Another benefit of the MBA is professional security. The MBA is an asset that becomes part of your permanent personal capital. Jobs may come and go, but you'll always have your graduate degree in management.

    In the uncertain world of the '90s, you can't depend on your employer for job security. "Credentials count, and managers should demand them, experts say. . . . All else being equal, the extra credentials can be the difference in who lands a job," stated a Washington headhunter quoted in The *Wall Street Journal.*[9]

- *Fun:* Getting an MBA from a top school can be an exhilarating experience. You get to work in teams with sharp, motivated people from all over the world. You get stretched by the demands of the program, and you surprise yourself by what you can accomplish. You learn how to lead . . . and leadership is an important personal attribute that impresses corporate recruiters.

"But Will I Get a Job?"

The MBA had helped my career immeasurably, but in the early '90s articles claimed that the MBA boom was over. The MBA seemed to be "going out of style." Significantly fewer potential students were showing interest in the MBA. After nearly a decade of steady growth, the number of students taking the Graduate Management Admissions Test (GMAT) in late 1993 was 23 percent below the peak year of 1990.

Nor was there any expectation that the size of the national pool of applicants for MBA education would increase in the near future, for a variety of reasons:

---

9   "Credentials Count," *The Wall Street Journal,* May 29, 1993, p. A1.

- *Discouragement due to downbeat stories in the media:* A constant drumbeat of depressing articles in the national media warned potential students about uncertainties in the MBA job market. Typical was a May 1993 article in The *New York Times* headlined "Business Schools Hit Hard Times Amid Doubt Over Value of the MBA." In the article, prospective MBA student Tracy Ott, a twenty-four year old marketing consultant in New York, asked, "There is a question of whether going to business school is a good investment. . . . The big question I have is, are MBA (schools) really teaching what students need for the '90s?"[10]

- *The economy:* The recession and slow recovery have made prospective MBA students nervous about leaving a good job to go back to school.

- *The downside of the Baby Boom peak:* The demographic peak of the Baby Boomers had passed through the graduate business schools in the late '80s, crowding into the ranks of middle management. The number of twenty-seven-year-olds—the prime age for MBA education—will slowly diminish until after the year 2000.

- *The MBA is not essential for success:* As critics of the MBA have been quick to point out, within the last fifteen years Steve Jobs, Bill Gates, and Michael Dell all built multibillion dollar companies without the benefit of even a bachelor's degree, much less an MBA. Maybe having an MBA is detrimental to creativity. As one wit observed, if Thomas Edison had had an MBA, instead of inventing the light bulb he would have developed a better pricing plan for candles.

- *The demise of middle management:* Overriding all else were stories about the continuing liquidation of middle management by the *Fortune* 500 companies. Almost weekly, articles appeared in The *Wall Street Journal* about pending layoffs of thousands of middle managers at IBM, Kodak, Ford, Procter & Gamble, General Motors, and Du Pont—companies that were the traditional market for hiring the graduates of the top business schools. "Farewell, Fast Track," shouted the cover of *Business Week* in December, 1990.[11] "The old career path no longer exists," warned *Fortune* in early 1993.[12]

The MBA Thrived in the 1980s Despite many Concerns and Criticisms

Stories about the demise of middle management and the MBA are not new. More than twenty years ago, an article in *MBA Magazine* said: "In the mid-1960s . . . the MBA could do no wrong . . . [but] by 1970, the once 'indispensable' MBA was being denounced as arrogant and overpaid. Many MBAs who had called their own tune as late as 1968 were, in 1970, out on the street looking for work."[13]

A decade ago, in 1984, a *Fortune* story entitled "The Recovery Skips Middle Managers" noted that 56 percent of large U.S. companies surveyed had cut middle management in the previous year. "The new corporate fashion calls for fewer levels of authority, with each manager controlling more people, and for participative management, with decisions pushed to lower levels

10 Celis, W., "Business Schools Hit Hard Times Amid Doubt Over Value of MBA," *The New York Times,* May 12, 1993, p. B6.
11 "Farewell, Fast Track," *Business Week,* December 10, 1990, p. 102.
12 Sherman, S., "A Brave New Darwinian Workplace," *Fortune,* January 25, 1993, p. 52.
13 Roscow, J., "Knocking Off the Golden Edge," *MBA Magazine,* August/September 1973, pp. 20-22.

of the company and out into the field. . . . The cliché of the moment is lean and mean."[14] Where would MBAs find jobs?

Similarly, questions about the relevance of MBA education have appeared for more than a decade. In 1979, a *Fortune* article made a strong case for respecting hunches and intuition as well as quantitative analysis in managerial decision making.[15] The complaint that business schools prefer to teach mathematical analysis instead of "soft skills" such as leadership and teamwork has a long history.

In a 1980 *Harvard Business Review* article, "Managing Our Way to Economic Decline," a pair of Harvard Business School professors took their business school colleagues to task for "a preference for analytical detachment rather than the insight that comes from 'hands-on' experience."[16]

A 1983 *Fortune* article entitled "Tough Times for MBAs" criticized business schools for not teaching students the nuts-and-bolts of running a company, and described the plight of Gail Steiger. "She graduated from the University of Chicago business school in the top 10 percent of her class in 1977, has six years' experience in corporate finance—and can't find a job."[17] Sound familiar?

In early 1985, at the beginning of a five-year period during which registrations for the GMAT would *grow* by 25 percent, a *Wall Street Journal* article sounded a premature alarm about declining business school enrollments. "Some educators say that as many as 25 percent of the nation's 600 business schools may be forced to close because of the shrinking pool of applicants. . . . Some schools are considering change as a matter of survival: after explosive growth in the 1970s, the number of MBA applicants is shrinking. . . . Business schools have been blamed for everything from instilling a narrow, short-term view in American managers to preparing students to be chief executive officers rather than entry-level or middle-level managers."[18]

Yet in the decade of the '80s, business schools prospered, graduating upwards of 70,000 MBAs a year, most of whom found good jobs in big companies. Between 1982 and 1992, the number of masters degrees conferred in business and management shot up 28 percent, from 61,000 per year to 78,000 per year.[19] In early 1987, a *Business Week* article carried the headline: "MBAs are Hotter than Ever." "Another boom year for B-schools," the article continued. " . . . the nation's top business schools are being flooded by unprecedented numbers of would-be whiz kids. 'We're going nuts here, we have so many applicants to deal with,' says Eric Mokover, admissions director at UCLA's B-school. . . . 'Many firms won't hire you unless you've got an MBA.'"[20]

The MBA wasn't perfect, but companies were still buying.

The Future of the MBA Job Market

In the decade of the '90s, there *are* new factors at work that will permanently reduce the proportion of middle managers in American companies:

- *Lean organizations:* To compete in world markets, U.S. companies have *had* to become lean. An MIT study of the automobile business found that the concept of 'lean

---

14 Main, J., "The Recovery Skips Middle Managers," *Fortune*, February 6, 1984, p. 112.
15 Rowan, R., "Those Business Hunches Are More Than Blind Faith," *Fortune*, April 23, 1979.
16 Hayes, R. and Abernathy, W., "Managing Our Way to Economic Decline," *Harvard Business Review*, July-August 1980.
17 Fraker, S., "Tough Times for MBAs," *Fortune*, December 12, 1983, p 65.
18 Swartz, S., "Business Schools Revise Programs To Meet Firms' Changing Needs," The *Wall Street Journal*, March 28, 1985.
19 O'Reilly, B., "Reengineering the MBA," *Fortune*, January 24, 1994, p. 40.
20 Byrne, J., "MBAs Are Hotter than Ever," *Business Week*, March 9, 1987, p. 46.

production' was not just a desirable strategy for profit maximization; it was now absolutely essential for corporate survival.[21] Downsizing of large companies will continue.

- *Advanced information technology:* User friendly information systems with on-line databases allow top management to keep track of what is going on throughout the company without the help of layers of middle managers who used to collect data and compile reports for the top brass.

  People at the operating level can tap into the information flow as needed. "(Productivity is increased by) the evolution of information technology to the point where knowledge, accountability, and results can be distributed rapidly anywhere in the organization. . . . Information moves straight to where it's needed, unfiltered by a hierarchy. If you have a problem with people upstream (in the manufacturing process), you deal with them directly, rather than asking your boss to talk to their boss."[22]

- *Flat organizations:* Decentralization of decision making and empowerment of the workforce have reduced the need for supervisors to tell the troops what to do.[23] "The new principle suggests that the people who do the work should make the decisions and that the process itself can have built-in controls. Pyramidal management layers can therefore be compressed and the organization flattened."[24]

- *Cross-functional teams:* Small multidisciplinary teams are challenging and in some cases replacing the archaic functional hierarchies that traditionally provided a safe harbor for middle managers. Self-managing cross-functional teams have cut costs, raised productivity, and sharply reduced time-to-market for new products.[25]

- *Re-engineering the workflow:* Re-engineering—a rediscovery and enhancement of the respected science of systems analysis that seeks to root out every speck of waste by challenging the existing way of doing things—may wipe out twenty-five million jobs in the next few years, many in middle management.[26]

"Will There Be a Job for Me?"

Given these changes in the corporate environment, will there be jobs for the MBAs of the 1990s? Should you seriously consider an MBA? The answer is *yes,* for several reasons:

1. *These changes will occur whether or not you have an MBA:* These changes will affect jobs of all kinds, not just those held by MBAs. The relevant question is not whether you will be affected by these changes, but whether you will be better equipped to deal with the changes *with* an MBA than without one. This is a key point that should be borne in mind throughout this book.

2. *These trends are not new:* Many of these changes—for example, the flattening of the organization and the reduction of middle management—have been under way for

21 Womack, J., Jones, D. and Roos, D., "The Machine That Changed the World," *Harper Perennial*, 1990.
22 Stewart, T., "The Search for the Organization of Tomorrow," *Fortune*, May 18, 1992, p. 95.
23 Dumaine, B., "The New Non-manager Managers," *Fortune*, February 22, 1993, p. 80.
24 Hammer, M., "Reengineering Work: Don't Automate, Obliterate," *Harvard Business Review*, July-August 1990, p. 111.
25 Stewart, T., "The Search for the Organization of Tomorrow," *Fortune*, May 18, 1992, p. 93.
26 Ehrbar, A., "Re-engineering Give Firms New Efficiency, Workers the Pink Slip," *The Wall Street Journal*, March 16, 1993.

more than a decade, during which hundreds of thousands of newly-graduated MBAs have found meaningful, good paying jobs. MBAs are immensely resourceful.

3. *Business schools are revolutionizing their programs:* They are responding vigorously to these changes. New courses, new teaching methods, and new alliances with industry will produce an MBA well equipped for the '90s. Middle management jobs may be on the decline, but the MBA programs of the '90s will be designed to educate entrepreneurial take-charge leaders for the new, highly decentralized organizations of the year 2000.

4. *Small business may become the MBA target market of the '90s:* Small business, rather than the *Fortune* 500, may be the MBA employer of choice in the '90s. During the decade of the 1980s, small business (defined by the government as those employing 500 or fewer) provided most of the job growth. Even in the economic slowdown between 1988 and 1990 big business had a net loss of 500,000 jobs, while small business created 3.2 million new jobs.[27]

MBAs are already heavily involved with small business. For example, the Harvard Business School is usually thought of as the primary supplier of CEOs to the *Fortune* 500. But a recent *Business Week* article on the Harvard MBA Class of 1970 produced some startling survey statistics:[28]

- Of 723 alumni of the Harvard MBA Class of 1970, only four members are CEOs of major companies (*Business Week* Top 1000 firms).

- Of this same class, only 13 percent even work for *Business Week* 1000 firms, while 36 percent are self employed, and the vast majority are entrepreneurs and small-business men and women.

5. *The MBA ought to pay for itself:* "Is it worth it?" Yes indeed. An MBA from a good school should pay for itself in five years or less, as I will demonstrate in chapter 4. But there are major differences in the top schools in terms of the success of their graduates, and these differences can amount to more than $100,000 in just the first few years after graduation.

Furthermore, you may be able to earn a high quality MBA without quitting your job or risking $100,000, as we will see in chapters 8 and 9.

How, then, to choose a good school? In order to intelligently compare schools, you'll need a good understanding of the content of typical MBA programs. Let's drop in at a leading business school to see what MBA programs are all about. What's it like to be an MBA student? What are the courses like? And why are certain courses required while others are electives?

---

27 "Tall Order for Small Businesses," *Business Week*, April 19, 1993, p. 114.
28 "Class Reunion," *Business Week*, June 18, 1990, pp. 162–163.

Chapter 2

Life as an MBA Student

What's it like to be an MBA student in a full-time program? In this chapter we'll spend time with some MBA students at the Martin Graduate School of Business Administration, one of the smallest of the Top 20 schools, to find out.[1]

Three weeks into the first year, the day begins with a half mile hike through the autumn leaves from Boller House, a drafty high rise apartment building on the edge of campus near the Medical Center where most of the first year MBA students live. There's no time for breakfast.

Class—Essentials of Accounting—begins promptly at 8:40 in the school's new state-of-the-art classroom building, Sullivan Hall. There are seventy-five students in this course. The tiers of seats are arranged in a horseshoe pattern so that the students can see each other as well as the instructor. This was done to prompt student-to-student interaction during case discussions, and it worked so well that the first year the new classrooms were used, the professors found it was taking much longer to get through the material because the students were asking a lot more questions.

Professor Kevin King, a bearded professor of accounting with a noticeable accent from his native England, strides in with a stack of handouts. Down comes the projector screen. An article from yesterday's *Wall Street Journal* appears on the screen, and King launches into a quick preview of today's lecture using the article to nail down the point that, by golly, this stuff is relevant! (Martin School professors compete with each other to include the most current material in their lectures; the school tied with Chicago for first place in "currency of classroom material" in the most recent *Business Week* survey.)

But why Accounting? And why Economics at 10:30, and Statistics right after lunch? Why are these courses required in every MBA program while others aren't?

The Basics

There are certain things you have to know if you are going to function successfully as a manager. These are "the basics"—disciplines like Economics and Statistics, and functional core courses like Accounting and Finance. These generally are taken during the first year of the MBA program. In the second year you can choose from a variety of elective courses, such as Finance, Marketing, and Operations Management to prepare you for the specific job you intend to pursue after graduation. But first you have to cover the basics.

Accounting

Accounting is the language of business. *Net sales, cash flow, allocated fixed costs*, and

---

1   The "Martin School" is a fictitious business school that is a composite of several real Top 20 schools.

depreciation are all terms that you will use throughout your professional career. They are the words by which your success as a manager will be measured. You need to know what they mean, how they are calculated, and what assumptions are behind them.

As a manager, you will be concerned with two kinds of accounting: 1) external (or financial) accounting that periodically informs the stockholders and the banks how the business is doing, and 2) internal (or cost) accounting that lets you track and control the day-to-day operations of the business.

When you finish this first course in accounting, you won't be an expert in all the subtleties of accounting and you won't be ready to take the CPA exam, but you will be an intelligent consumer of accounting information—comfortable with the concepts and able to ask the hard questions that managers have to ask.

Economics

Economics is the basic science of business. As physics is to engineering, economics is to the field of management. There are two kinds of economics courses: 1) microeconomics, which deals with economic concepts at the level of the individual firm, and 2) macroeconomics, which describes how the national and world economic systems work. Microeconomics is a required core course in virtually every MBA program, and macroeconomics may be either a required course or an elective, depending on the school.

The core course in microeconomics describes how individual companies do business in a collection of markets, including markets in which they sell their products and services, and markets from which they buy raw materials, production and professional labor, capital assets such as buildings and machinery, and financial assets. Analytical tools are developed in the course to aid managers in understanding these markets and to help them make better business decisions.

Quantitative Methods

If economics is the "physics" of business, quantitative methods is the "calculus," although it's much easier. If you passed high school algebra, you'll be able to handle this course.

The core course in "quant" exists because managers have to make decisions under conditions of uncertainty. They are regularly called upon to make forecasts and estimates of future events—next year's sales, estimated costs for a new product, future returns on investment opportunities in the securities markets—and to make informed decisions based on these estimates. Managers are also expected to analyze why certain events happened—why sales dropped in the third quarter, or why a product is failing to meet its quality objectives in the field. Finally, managers are expected to know how to optimize the performance of their organization, such as how to maximize new orders from a sales force or production from an assembly line.

The quantitative methods course provides a set of analytical tools to resolve such problems. With the availability of powerful spreadsheet programs and user-friendly statistical software for personal computers, the solutions to these problems are achievable with a minimum of mathematical drudgery. Every graduating MBA needs to have a toolbox of these techniques of analysis, as well as a good understanding of their limitations.

Information Systems

Computerized information systems provide the core technology of modern management.

In the late 1980s and into the '90s, a revolution in management has occurred as large corporations have phased out layers of middle management. Computerized information systems have replaced thousands of middle managers who used to collect, analyze, and disseminate information about sales and production. As these large companies have downsized, hundreds of thousands of new jobs have been created in startups and small companies, many of which exploit the power of state-of-the-art computerized information systems.

To succeed in today's highly competitive global markets, managers must understand how computers can help them serve their customers more effectively. And to hit the ground running, graduating MBAs entering the job market are expected to be fully proficient with PC-based spreadsheets and graphic presentation programs.

Organizational Behavior

Organizational behavior deals with how managers get things done in organizations.

In today's organizations, the traditional hierarchy is being challenged by new organizational concepts such as cross-functional teams and highly-decentralized decision making. This raises new questions about decision rights, managerial compensation, and agency issues—the problems of aligning management's interests with those of the stockholders. As companies continue to develop new organizational forms to meet the challenge of competition, it is essential that managers have a clear understanding of basic principles by which people work together.

Communications

Someone once said that finding the right answer to a managerial problem is the easy part—communicating and persuading others to act on this information is the hard part.

Effective managers have always had to have good oral and written communication skills. But as the pace of business decision making increases, managers who are able to quickly organize their thoughts—and who can write and speak clearly and persuasively—have a distinct competitive advantage over those who cannot. The communications course provides coaching and practice in sharpening these important skills.

Finance

The most popular area of concentration in business school is finance. But finance covers a wide range of professional opportunities, from fast-paced, high-paying investment banking jobs on Wall Street to chief financial officer of a manufacturing company.

The core course in finance develops methods for evaluating alternative investments. These could be a new computerized machine tool for your factory or the stock of a new biotechnology company for the investment portfolio of your venture capital firm. Evaluating such investments under conditions of uncertainty is one of the most important decisions that managers make, and you will use the underlying principles from this course again and again throughout your professional career.

Marketing

Companies exist to serve customers, and ultimately these customers determine whether or not the company stays in business.

The core course in marketing analyzes how firms serve their customers. Regardless of the kind of organization—consumer goods, industrial goods, financial services, medical services—success depends on satisfying these customers better than competitors. Marketing managers have a variety of means for reaching and serving customers, including advertising and promotion, new product development, pricing strategies, and distribution channels, but every manager in the company has a stake in understanding how the firm relates to its customers.

Operations Management

Whatever a company produces—automobiles, computers, or services such as portfolio management and medical care—operations management is concerned with the process by which the firm manages physical, financial, and human resources to create and deliver these goods and services to customers.

Over the past decade, worldwide competition has focused intense interest on how firms manage their operations. Not only must the existing product be of outstanding quality at a competitive price, but the process for developing new products must be faster and more effective as product life cycles become shorter and shorter. Excellence in operations management has become an increasingly important factor in the corporate strategies of world-class companies.

The Electives

The core courses develop the underlying principles of management and provide the MBA student with a toolbox containing state-of-the-art techniques and methods for solving problems. In the elective courses, MBAs learn about the specifics of their chosen field, such as how a brand manager in marketing positions a new product or how an investment banker prices the stock of a new company that is about to go public.

Business schools vary in their approach to electives. Many give students freedom to choose any set of electives that fits their individual career strategies, including courses from other schools in the university and from business schools in other countries of the world.

Typical second-year electives for finance majors might include Investment Banking, Options and Futures Markets, and Financial Statement Analysis. Operations management majors might select electives such as Manufacturing and Service Strategies, Manufacturing Control Systems, and Quality Management. In marketing, the most popular electives typically are Marketing Research, New Product Planning and Development, and Advertising and Promotion. Most schools allow second-year students to take joint majors, such as finance and accounting, or finance and marketing.

The final second-year course in many schools is a "capstone course" designed to integrate everything students have learned. Business problems don't present themselves with neat functional labels, such "accounting problems" or "marketing problems." The problem that is initially labeled a "cash flow problem" may in fact be caused by poor product quality, or perhaps by an ineffective advertising campaign. Most real business problems are multidisciplinary and cross-functional. They require simultaneous analysis and solutions across two or more functional areas of the company.

Real Projects with Real Companies

A number of schools are now going beyond the classroom in the second year of the MBA program, and are entering into consulting arrangements with cooperating companies. The students work with real managers on an important business problem—starting up a production line, or doing a marketing research study on a proposed new product. The companies participate because they can hire intelligent, highly-motivated professionals at very low cost, with the expertise of the supervising professor thrown in for free. They also get an advanced, in-depth look at the best of the year's graduating MBA class.

These "projects courses" are generally rated by students as among their most valuable experiences in business school, because this is where they put it all together. To understand why, join us in the executive conference room of a *Fortune* 500 company as a second-year project team from the Martin School prepares to deliver its final report to corporate management.

The Executive Conference Room

The executive conference room at the *Fortune* 500 company's marketing center is filled to capacity. For the past ten weeks, a team of second-year MBAs has been gathering marketing research data on consumer and professional awareness and attitudes toward new surgical techniques for correcting vision problems. Now it's time to present the results. Would surgical techniques such as radial keratotomy and laser sculpturing of the corneas eventually threaten one of company's core businesses, prescription eyeglasses?[2]

This is one of ten strategic studies that the Martin School's second-year MBA students are carrying out for client companies as part of a second-year elective course called the Product Leadership Laboratory. These are real projects—not make-work student exercises, but significant strategic investigations that could influence the company's long-range plans. Although the student teams hold weekly staff meetings with the professor to give periodic progress reports, all of the plans for the projects were developed by the student teams.

Focus Groups

A few weeks earlier, behind one-way glass in a rented marketing research suite at a nearby mall, second-year MBA Barbara Johnson had led a focus group of eight consumers who wore either eyeglasses or contact lenses in a guided discussion of attitudes about eyeglasses, contact lens and surgical procedures to permanently correct vision problems. Each consumer was paid $10 for attending the half-hour focus group. The consumers were asked to fill out a brief confidential demographic questionnaire. They were informed that an audio tape would be made of the discussion, and that other members of the project team were observing from behind the one-way glass.

After a brief warm-up discussion over cookies and soft drinks, the serious questions began: What did they like and dislike about wearing glasses? What about contact lenses? Had they ever heard of radial keratotomy? Would they ever consider a surgical procedure like this to eliminate the need to wear glasses or contacts? If so, how much would they be willing to pay for the surgery? Had they ever heard of laser sculpturing of the corneas to correct vision? Would they consider this? Would they prefer this to radial keratotomy . . . ?

At the end of the discussion, Barbara shook hands with each of the participants and thanked them for their help. As the last participant walked through the door back into the mall, Barbara

---

2 To protect the confidentiality of this study, the scope and the findings are not discussed, and the names of the client and the students have been disguised. Radial keratotomy is an outpatient surgical procedure in which precise radial cuts are made in the corneas (under local anesthesia) with a diamond blade to slightly alter its shape. Laser sculpturing is a new computerized treatment in which ultra-thin layers of the cornea are selectively removed to modify the optical characteristics of the cornea.

slipped into the small room behind the one-way glass where her teammates waited. "Boy, that was scary! I was sure I would run out of questions and they wouldn't talk. But once they loosened up, the time just flew by. Actually, it was fun—I'm ready to do it again!"

An hour later, Jim Myers led another focus group. The same questions were asked in as neutral a way as possible to avoid biasing the answers. Behind the one-way glass, the rest of Jim's team and a marketing product manager from the client company watched and listened, drank Pepsi, and made notes.

And still another focus group, and another—through the afternoon and into the early evening. Each team member led at least one of the focus groups. Between focus groups, hurried meetings were held to critique and fine-tune the process.

Telephone Surveys

The following week the five-person team split up. Two members transcribed and summarized the focus group tapes while the remaining three manned a phone bank in which practicing ophthalmologists from all over the United States, Canada, Europe, and Japan were interviewed using a pretested telephone survey the students had developed. Christa Brunner, a multilingual student from Switzerland, provided the language skills needed for many of the European interviews, while Kenichi Kido, a Japanese student, talked with the Japanese doctors. How did these medical practitioners feel about the adoption of these new surgical techniques? Were they using them now for patient treatment? If not, did they plan to? When, and for what kinds of patients? Which companies made the best surgical equipment for these procedures? How much did the equipment cost . . . ?

Next they went into the Medical School Library and then the Management Library to do a computerized search of the companies who made and marketed the surgical equipment for radial keratotomy and laser sculpturing, followed by phone calls to the companies for product literature and financial reports. Who were the major players in this new business? Which of these procedures had FDA approval? How fast were these companies growing? Where were they getting their financing? Were any of the companies candidates for acquisition? At what price?

At last the data collection was finished. What did it all mean? What will we tell the client? As it all started to come together, all those first- and second-year courses in computers, statistics, economics, and marketing strategy began to pay off.

Showtime

Now, after hundreds of hours of discussion and analysis and a week of late nights running statistics in the Martin School Computing Center, the computerized color graphics presentation has been refined and polished, each team member has rehearsed his or her script a dozen times, and twenty copies of the seventy-five-page final report have been assembled. The vice president of marketing enters the executive conference room, shakes hands with each of the team members, pours himself a cup of coffee, and settles into his chair at the head of the table, facing the screen. It's showtime.

Two weeks after the presentation, the phone rang in Barbara Johnson's apartment just as she was leaving for class. It was someone in the personnel department at the client company. The vice president of marketing was impressed with Barbara's handling of the presentation. Could she stop in on Friday afternoon at 2:30 to explore the possibility of an assistant product manager position when she graduates?

Three years later, Barbara is a senior product manager for the company. She loves her job. She travels a great deal and she works very hard—almost as hard as she worked when she was in business school. This year, *she's* going to sponsor an MBA project at the Martin School, and when the students have prepared the presentation and it's showtime in the executive conference room, she's going to shake hands with each member of the team, pour herself a cup of coffee, and settle into the chair at the head of the table, facing the screen.

Chapter 3

The Ranking Game

Let's begin with a quiz. Everyone knows that going to business school full time means a major investment of time and money. Which of the following surveys ranks the leading business schools *in terms of the financial return on the student's investment?*

    a. The 1992 *Business Week* Top 20 business school ranking
    b. The 1993 *U.S. News & World Report* ranking of graduate business schools
    c. The 1993 *Gourman Report* ranking of business schools
    d. None of the above

The right answer is "d." None of these existing national surveys ranks business schools by the financial return to the student.

The Ranking Game: Which are the Best Business Schools?
We love to have things ranked. J. D. Power ranks automobiles. *Consumer Reports* ranks cameras and dishwashers. *Business Week* and *U.S. News & World Report* rank business schools.

These rankings can be helpful. Buying cars and cameras—and MBA degrees—are difficult and complex purchase decisions. As consumers we often have little or no prior experience in buying some of these expensive products. This is particularly true of MBA degrees since people only buy one in their lifetime. We can't draw on our experience when choosing an MBA program—we need expert advice.

Which schools are the best business schools? This is an important question to potential students who are about to invest $100,000 or more in a full time MBA program. All business schools are not the same. Even among the Top 20, *the choice of business school can make a huge difference, as much as $100,000, in financial return within the first five years after graduation*, as we shall see in chapter 4.

In this chapter and the next, we will thoroughly evaluate three different ways to rank business schools to help you choose the best business school:

- The biennial *Business Week* Top 20 business school ranking
- The annual *U.S. News and World Report* ranking of America's best graduate business schools
- A new method, THE MBA ADVANTAGE, which will be developed in chapter 4, quantifies the financial return from attending the various top business schools (see table 3.1).

Table 3.1

THE MBA ADVANTAGE business school ranking as compared to *Business Week* and *U.S. News & World Report*.

———————————— The Best Business Schools ————————————

	MBA ADVANTAGE Rank (1994)	Business Week Top 20 Rank (1992)	U.S. News & World Report Top 25 Rank (1993)
Harvard	1	3	1
Chicago	2	2	9
Stanford	3	7	2
MIT	4	13	6
Yale	5	(NR)	17
Northwestern	6	1	4
Berkeley	7	18	14
Wharton	8	4	3
UCLA	9	16	15
Virginia	10	11	11
Cornell	11	14	12
Michigan	12	5	5
Dartmouth	13	6	8
Carnegie Mellon	14	17	13
Texas	15	(NR)	18
Rochester	16	(NR)	24
Indiana	17	8	20
North Carolina	18	10	19
Duke	19	12	7
NYU	20	15	16

(NR = not rated)

THE MBA ADVANTAGE is defined as the estimated average cumulative post-MBA pay after five years on the job (after subtracting the cost of going to business school), less what incoming students for that school *would* have made if they had not gone to business school and had stayed in their pre-MBA jobs. This is information that every prospective business school student should have.

This is not to say that there is only one way to rank business schools, and that THE MBA ADVANTAGE is right and *Business Week* and *U.S. News* are wrong. Our method *complements* those of *Business Week* and *U.S. News,* filling in important gaps for prospective students.

An investment in an MBA is like an investment in a new house. The appearance and quality of the house are very important, but so are financial issues such as price, real estate taxes, and the outlook for how much the house will sell for at some time in the future. Considering that an MBA degree can cost as much as a house, it's clear that financial evaluations should also be made when shopping for a business school.

Although we will focus initially on evaluating the top nationally-ranked business schools, much of what will be discussed also applies to regional business schools. In fact, these methods of analysis are suitable for choosing *any* business school.

What is meant by the "best" business schools? "Best" can be defined in a number of ways:

- Which schools attract the greatest number of corporate recruiters?
- Which schools are the most enjoyable to attend?

- Which schools have faculty at the leading edge of their fields?
- Which schools have the highest post-MBA starting salaries?
- Which schools have the most successful alumni in your field of interest?
- Which schools provide the highest economic return to their MBA students?

Ultimately, the "best" business school is the school that is best for *you*. Are you interested in marketing or finance? Do you want to work for a *Fortune* 500 corporation or an entrepreneurial startup? Do you want to work in the U.S. or abroad? Based on your prior work experience, what are you really good at? Do you see yourself as a line manager running a large organization, or more as an expert consultant? Keep these questions in mind as we examine the various methods for ranking and choosing a business school. We'll start with the best known ranking, the *Business Week* Top 20.

The *Business Week* Top 20: Measuring Customer Satisfaction

Every two years, in late October, *Business Week* publishes a cover story entitled "The Best B-Schools," which ranks the Top 20 business schools. In this chapter we shall examine the *Business Week* survey to see how it works and what factors influence the results. Table 3.2 shows the *Business Week* ranking of the Top 20 schools for the past three surveys.

Table 3.2
The *Business Week* Top 20 Rankings for 1992, 1990 and 1988

	1992 Rank	1990 Rank	1988 Rank
Northwestern	1	1	1
Chicago	2	4	11
Harvard	3	3	2
Wharton	4	2	4
Michigan	5	7	6
Dartmouth	6	6	3
Stanford	7	5	9
Indiana	8	15	12
Columbia	9	8	14
North Carolina	10	12	8
Virginia	11	14	7
Duke	12	13	10
MIT	13	11	15
Cornell	14	16	5
NYU	15	17	18
UCLA	16	10	16
Carnegie Mellon	17	9	13
Berkeley	18	19	17
Vanderbilt	19	(NR)	(NR)
Washington U.	20	(NR)	(NR)

(NR = not rated)

The biennial *Business Week* Top 20 rankings of business schools are the most influential of the several business school surveys on the market, and the most controversial, for reasons

that will become apparent. The *Business Week* rankings are actually a statistical combination of two independent surveys:

- One survey measures the "customer satisfaction" of graduating MBA students from each school within a few weeks of graduation.
- The other survey measures how corporate recruiters rate the schools as a source of fresh managerial talent for their companies.

Business Week characterizes its Top 20 ranking as a customer satisfaction survey. It does not claim to rank business schools on the financial return from getting an MBA from these schools.

Who Cares About Business School Rankings?

The *Business Week* Top 20 rankings have captured the most attention since they began in 1988. But business school rankings are not a recent phenomenon, and competition among business schools for high rankings is not new.

As early as January 1981 when informal business school rankings by deans and professors were dominated by Harvard, Stanford, and Chicago, The *Wall Street Journal* quoted Northwestern's business school dean Donald Jacobs as saying, "You're darn tootin' we want to be Number One in our field! What's wrong with that?"[1]

In October 1985 The *Wall Street Journal* reported that Dean Jacobs had achieved his goal: A poll of 134 of the largest industrial and service companies in the country ranked Northwestern as their choice for producing the best MBA graduates. Wharton finished second, Harvard third, and Stanford finished a distant ninth.[2]

In November 1988 *Business Week* published its first comprehensive survey of 1,245 graduating MBA students and 112 corporate recruiters to determine the best business schools. Once again, Northwestern came in first, Harvard second, and traditionally highly-ranked Stanford and Chicago far behind at ninth and eleventh.[3]

For some schools, the effects from the first *Business Week* article were dramatic. In the year following the *Business Week* survey, fifth-ranked Cornell—which had been completely left off a *U.S. News & World Report* Top 20 ranking in 1987—saw its applications jump 50 percent. At eighth-ranked University of North Carolina at Chapel Hill, the number of companies recruiting on campus increased by 30 percent.[4]

The reaction of the business schools ranged from amusement to outrage. A Cornell administrator, writing tongue-in-cheek in *The Chronicle of Higher Education*, accused American higher education of "creating a public-relations machine that would make P. T. Barnum blush" and chided his business school colleagues for letting *Business Week* and other magazines take over the evaluation of academic quality.[5]

---

1   Klein, F., "Getting Ahead: Northwestern's School of Business Scrambles Onto the Fast Track," The *Wall Street Journal*, January 20, 1981.
2   MacKay-Smith, A., "Survey Says Top Business Schools May Not Be Top Business Schools," The *Wall Street Journal*, October 11, 1985.
3   Byrne, J., "The Best B-Schools," *Business Week*, November 28, 1988, pp. 76-80.
4   Fuchsberg, G., "Surveys to Rank Business Schools Wield Big Clout," The *Wall Street Journal*, November 29, 1989, p. B1.
5   Schmotter, J., "Colleges Have Themselves to Blame", *The Chronicle of Higher Education*, August 16, 1989.

Eleventh-rated Chicago, on the other hand, decided not to fight the ratings. In response to student complaints, Chicago—the originator of hard-edged quantitative business analysis—began adding instruction on "soft skills," such as leadership and nonverbal communication, to its traditional fare of statistics and microeconomics. Academics at other business schools snickered when *Business Week* headlined a November 1989 article, "Chicago's B-School Goes Touchy-Feely."[6] But the students loved the new additions, and Chicago's *Business Week* rank soared from eleventh place in 1988 to fourth in 1990.[7]

The Business Week *Guide*

Encouraged by the success of the 1988 magazine survey, *Business Week* Associate Editor John Byrne, who first conceived of the idea of the *Business Week* rankings, published a 186-page soft cover book in 1990 that greatly expanded on the information contained in the original magazine article. Entitled *A Business Week Guide: The Best Business Schools*, the book became required reading for anyone considering a full-time MBA program. When the magazine survey was repeated in 1990 and 1992, the soft cover *Guide* was updated and re-issued.

The latest edition of the *Guide*, published in the spring of 1993 and based on the 1992 survey, contains a wealth of new information on more than sixty of the best business schools in the U.S. and Europe. Based on 4,712 completed surveys from the Top 20 Class of 1992, this soft cover book is a bargain at $14.95 and is must reading for anyone thinking seriously about investing in an MBA.

Good News About Jobs for MBAs

The good news from the 1993 edition of the *Guide* is that the great majority (86 percent) of the 1992 graduates of the *Business Week* Top 20 schools had job offers by graduation, and the rest found jobs within three to six months after graduation.[8] The average number of offers at graduation was 2.2, and during the four-year period from 1988 to 1992—spanning the recession of 1990—the average starting pay at the Top 20 schools increased almost 28 percent, to $63,500.[9,10] Despite the economic malaise, the graduating MBA continued to do well in the early 1990s.

While it is appropriate to raise questions about the methodology by which *Business Week* establishes the actual business school rankings, it is also important to acknowledge the great contribution that John Byrne and his editorial colleagues at *Business Week* have made by focusing attention on the quality of business education. Students and the companies that hire them ultimately determine the success of business schools. *If business schools fail to recognize students and employers as customers that must be satisfied, they cannot succeed.*

How Does the Business Week *Top 20 Ranking Method Work?*

As noted previously, the *Business Week* Top 20 rankings are a statistical combination of separate surveys of graduating MBA students (graduate rankings) and corporate recruiters (corporate rankings). According to the 1993 edition of the *Guide*, the 1992 survey was compiled from

---

6 Greising, D., "Chicago's B-School Goes Touchy-Feely," *Business Week*, November 27, 1989, p. 140.
7 Byrne, J., "The Best B-Schools," *Business Week*, October 29, 1990, pp. 52-56.
8 Byrne, J., *A Business Week Guide: The Best Business Schools*, 3rd edition, McGraw-Hill, 1993, p. 60.
9 Ibid., p. 29.
10 Byrne, J., *A Business Week Guide: The Best Business Schools*, 1st edition, McGraw-Hill, 1990, p. 25.
   Byrne, J., *A Business Week Guide: The Best Business Schools*, 3rd edition, McGraw-Hill, 1993, p. 57.

4,712 questionnaires returned by graduates (a 78 percent response rate) and 199 questionnaires returned by corporate recruiters (a 57 percent response rate).[11] These two components—the graduate rankings and the corporate rankings—are then statistically combined to create an overall *Business Week* Top 20 ranking.

In the next section we'll explore how the *Business Week* Top 20 ranking is determined, and consider some of the limitations of the methodology. For those who want the details, appendix A contains a comprehensive analysis of the *Business Week* Top 20 method.

Limitations of the Business Week *Survey Method*

1. *Instability:* One of the most serious limitations is the volatility of the graduate rankings from survey to survey. *The graduate rankings show virtually no agreement from survey to survey.* Schools that were at the top in 1990 might stay near the top in 1992, or they might plummet down the list (see table A.2 in appendix A). For example, in 1990 the graduates ranked Virginia number 16; in 1992 it was ranked number 2. Chicago went from number 20 in 1988, to number 1 in 1990, to number 10 in 1992. The *average* change for each school from 1990 to 1992 was seven positions on the graduate rankings.

   In fact, in 1992 the true volatility in the graduate rankings was worse than this. One school, Carnegie Mellon, plunged from number 4 in 1990 to number 31 in the 1992 graduate survey—enough to knock it right off the *Business Week* Top 20. The volatility was so bad that *Business Week* had to dilute its 1992 graduate survey data by 50 percent with old data from previous surveys in order for the overall Top 20 rankings to make sense.

   The reason for this volatility is that in any year the graduate ranking of a school may be damaged by a temporary dispute between the students and the administration, or it may be inflated by a dean who gives the graduating students a forceful cheerleading speech—just before the questionnaires arrive—about how the value of their new MBA degree will be influenced by the school's standing on the *Business Week* Top 20.

2. *The volatile graduate rankings drive the overall Top 20 rankings:* To compound the importance of the volatility of the graduate rankings, it was found statistically that *virtually all of the changes in overall* Business Week *Top 20 rankings from survey to survey are caused by changes in the very volatile graduate rankings.* The changes in the corporate rankings are small to begin with, and the changes that do occur in the corporate rankings from survey to survey have little effect on the overall Top 20 rankings.

3. *Size:* While the corporate rankings do not affect *changes* in Top 20 rankings very much, they are important in getting the school initially positioned on the overall Top 20 list. An analysis shows that the corporate rankings are strongly influenced by the size of the MBA class. *Large schools are more highly ranked than small schools—the*

11 Byrne, J., *A Business Week Guide: The Best Business Schools*, 3rd edition, McGraw-Hill, 1993, pp. 345, 347.

bigger, the better. In fact, in 1992 the Top 10 corporate rankings correlated almost perfectly with the size of the school (see figure A.2 in appendix A).

This makes sense. A corporate recruiter is more likely to prefer schools where he or she can interview a large number of potential employees. But this isn't necessarily good for individual students at these large schools who may face a lot more competition from their many classmates for these job openings.

4. *Urban location:* Even among the smaller schools, *recruiters prefer schools that are located in urban areas* (Stanford, MIT, Carnegie Mellon) over those located in more rural places (Dartmouth, Cornell). (Again, this shows clearly in figure A.2 in appendix A.) Is this because the urban schools turn out better students, or is it because city schools are easier to get to during the winter recruiting season?

5. *Halo effect:* Several years ago, one of my colleagues, Professor Shlomo Kalish, sent out a mail survey asking 128 corporate recruiters to rate a list of fifteen business schools. As expected, Harvard and Stanford got the highest ratings. Princeton also got a respectable rating—but Princeton doesn't have a business school.

This is an example of the halo effect. *The prestige of the affiliated university carries over to the business school.* It's not surprising that seventeen of the *Business Week* Top 20 business schools are associated with Top 25 universities (as ranked in a separate poll of the best universities by *U.S. News & World Report*).

The bottom line: The *Business Week* Top 20 ranking is an opinion survey. Its introduction in 1988 was of immense value because it focused attention on the importance of satisfying students and corporate recruiters. Yet as we have seen, it is not without limitations, which are discussed in more detail in appendix A.

U.S. News & World Report: A Different Approach to Ranking Business Schools

U.S. News and World Report takes a very different approach than *Business Week* to ranking business schools. Once a year, in late March, *U.S. News* devotes most of an issue to a cover article on "America's Best Graduate Schools."

The *U.S. News* ranks are produced by an entirely different methodology than the *Business Week* rankings. Under the direction of Senior Editor Robert J. Morse, the *U.S. News* rankings are compiled from a complex formula that includes:[12]

- *Student selectivity* (weighted as 25 percent of the total ranking), which is a combination of average GMAT scores, undergraduate grade point averages, and the percent of applicants accepted.

- *Placement success* (30 percent), which is composed of the percentage of graduates employed at graduation, the percentage employed three months after graduation, their median starting salaries excluding signing bonuses, and the ratio of last year's on-campus MBA recruiters to the number of graduates last year.

---

12 "America's Best Graduate Schools," *U.S. News & World Report*, March 22, 1993, p. 59.

- *Graduation rate* (5 percent), the average percentage of students in the past two graduating classes that earned the MBA within two years.

- *Reputation* (40 percent), a combination of results from two independent polls about
business school reputations: a survey of the deans and MBA directors of all 268 accredited business school and a survey of 2,000 CEOs representing a "cross section of the
largest U.S. corporations."

A comparison of the *U.S. News* rankings (see table 3.3) with the *Business Week* rankings
(see table 3.2) shows that the *U.S. News* rankings are more stable from year to year.

Table 3.3

The *U.S. News* Top 25 rankings for 1993, 1992, 1991, and 1990

	1993 Rank	1992 Rank	1991 Rank	1990 Rank
Harvard	1	2	1	2
Stanford	2	1	2	1
Wharton	3	3	3	3
Northwestern	4	4	4	4
Michigan	5	7	10	7
MIT	6	5	5	5
Duke	7	9	7	9
Dartmouth	8	10	8	6
Chicago	9	6	6	8
Columbia	10	8	11	10
Virginia	11	11	9	11
Cornell	12	12	12	12
Carnegie Mellon	13	15	13	14
Berkeley	14	13	15	13
UCLA	15	14	16	15
NYU	16	18	19	18
Yale	17	16	(NR)	(NR)
Texas	18	20	17	24
North Carolina	19	17	14	17
Indiana	20	19	18	16
USC	21	21	21	(NR)
Georgetown	22	(NR)	22	(NR)
Purdue	23	23	20	19
Rochester	24	22	25	23
Vanderbilt	25	25	(NR)	(NR)
Pittsburgh	(NR)	24	22	(NR)
Maryland	(NR)	(NR)	24	(NR)
Penn State	(NR)	(NR)	(NR)	20
Illinois	(NR)	(NR)	(NR)	21
Wisconsin	(NR)	(NR)	(NR)	22
Ohio State	(NR)	(NR)	(NR)	25

(NR = not rated)

Limitations of the U.S. News & World Report *Top 25 Rankings*

Like the *Business Week* rankings, the *U.S. News* method also has some limitations:

1. *How valid is the formula?* The complex calculation of the *U.S. News* ranking is a

statistical stew ("add a little of this, and a pinch of that"), but has it been shown to provide a useful measure of the value of the MBA degree from each school?

2. *Are the schools always honest?* Editor Robert Morse believes that his *U.S. News* ranking is a better measure of the excellence of the schools because 60 percent is determined from objective data (starting salaries, GMAT scores, placement rates) and only 40 percent is based on opinion surveys. But critics have suggested that the business schools—who have much at stake in these rankings—may report these statistics in ways that make them look better than they really are.

3. *Measuring the halo effect again?* The *U.S. News* reputational opinion surveys of the deans and CEOs (which together are weighted as 40 percent of the rankings) may be biased by the same "halo effect" from the prestige of the affiliated universities that we saw previously in the *Business Week* Top 20 Ranking. There is a strong statistical correlation between the ranking of the 1993 *U.S. News* Top 25 business schools and the separate 1993 *U.S. News* ranking of the top universities.[13] Given that the 268 deans and 2,000 CEOs are asked to rate the reputations of all 268 accredited business schools—most of which they never heard of—it's plausible that they tend to give high marks to the business schools associated with universities they know and respect.

4. *Only big companies?* The reputational survey of 2,000 CEOs represents "a cross section of the largest U.S. corporations." But as we saw earlier, almost all of the growth in the economy is in small companies, while large corporations are expected to continue to downsize for the next several years. Small companies may have different interests, such as fewer financial analysts or more line managers with multidisciplinary training. In the future, small companies should also be represented in the reputational survey.

The bottom line: The *U.S. News* survey has limitations. Although it has the advantage of being based in part on objective measures rather than just opinion surveys, because of the halo effect it may be measuring the reputations of the affiliated universities as much as that of the business schools. See appendix A for more details.

Business Week versus *U.S. News*

As we consider these various ranking approaches, let's remember one thing: All of these schools, which are the top 3 percent of the more than 700 business schools granting the MBA, are excellent. The rankings should be kept in perspective. The differences between adjacent schools in the rankings typically are miniscule (for example, in the 1993 *U.S. News* ranking, first-ranked Harvard got a score of 100, while second-ranked Stanford got a score of 99.8, a difference of 2 parts per 1000. Is this difference *real?*). The actual rankings in these two surveys are of less importance than the supporting information provided along with them.

In the next chapter we'll look at a new methodology for comparing business schools, in which there are large differences from school to school. Unlike the *Business Week* Top 20, it will

---

13 "America's Best Colleges," *U.S. News & World Report*, 1993 edition, pp. 26-27.

not be based on opinion surveys. Instead our approach will look at business education as a substantial investment of time and money, and it will compare schools based on the market value added, not only at the time of graduation, but also during the five years in the job market following graduation.

Our new approach is a more objective method of ranking business schools because it is based on what employers are willing to pay the graduates of these MBA programs. These are not merely opinions about which programs are best, but rather are market-based measures of excellence determined by thousands of hiring and promotion decisions.

Chapter 4

Ranking Business Schools by Financial Returns

The decision to obtain an MBA is a major personal investment decision. If you are a prospective student and you decide to give up your job for two years to attend a full-time MBA program, you will invest not only $35,000–40,000 in tuition for the two years, but you will also forego nearly two full years of salary, which may add another $60,000–80,000 or more to the investment. All told, you will invest from $100,000 to as much as $150,000 in your MBA.

To make such an important decision, you need to have some idea what the payoff would be for an MBA degree.[1] You would need to know how long it will take to recover your investment and come out ahead.

As a prospective student, you would also need to know if there is really any difference in the track record of the major business schools in terms of return on investment. While the *Business Week* Top 20 and the *U.S. News & World Report* Top 25 opinion surveys are interesting, they do not evaluate graduate business education as an investment decision. As we shall see in table 4.1, there are major differences in economic return even among the *Business Week* Top 20 schools, and when schools are ranked in terms of return on investment, the ranking is different from those in the *Business Week* and *U.S. News* surveys.

There are many good reasons besides financial gain for going to business school: the knowledge for its own sake, the wider career choices, the security of adding the MBA to your personal credentials, and the fun of meeting and working with outstanding professionals from all over the world. But for the moment, let's focus on the financial returns of getting an MBA in a full-time program at a top-rated school.

The advantage of my ranking method is that it does not involve opinion surveys about which business schools are best. Rather, it measures what employers are willing to pay the graduates of these schools both at the time of graduation and during the first five years on the job following graduation. These are market-based measures, reflecting thousands of hiring and promotion decisions by large and small companies, and therefore are much less likely to be biased than opinion surveys.

THE MBA ADVANTAGE

Is it worth it to go to business school from a financial standpoint? The best way to answer this

---

1 Although some people may be uncomfortable with the idea of viewing education as an investment decision, the concept has a long and distinguished history. See, for example, Nobel laureate Gary Becker's "Human Capital: A Theoretical and Empirical Analysis, with Special Reference to Education," National Bureau of Economic Research, Columbia University Press, 1964.

question is to estimate how much you will earn over the next several years if you go to business school, less the cost of tuition and fees (exclude room and board since you will have living expenses either way). Then estimate how much you will earn over the same period if you don't go to business school. The difference is the additional value acquired by getting the MBA. I call this difference THE MBA ADVANTAGE.

THE MBA ADVANTAGE of a school is defined as the estimated average cumulative post-MBA pay after five years on the job (after subtracting the cost of going to business school), less what incoming students for that school *would* have made staying in their pre-MBA jobs with nominal pay increases (see figure 4.1). This is the best measure of the additional payoff of getting an MBA degree versus staying in the pre-MBA job.

Figure 4.1

THE MBA ADVANTAGE, as estimated for the Harvard Business School Class of 1992, is the cumulative difference in annual pay with and without the MBA through the fifth year after graduation.

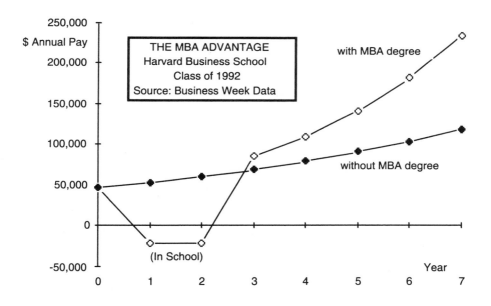

THE MBA ADVANTAGE for the Top Business Schools

In table 4.1, THE MBA ADVANTAGE has been calculated for the Class of 1992 from each of the top business schools, using the method shown in figure 4.1.

Q: How much more will I make over the next seven years if I go to business school?

Table 4.1

THE MBA ADVANTAGE shown here is the estimated, average, cumulative, post-MBA pay of the graduates of each school after five years on the job (after subtracting the cost of going to business school), less what the average incoming students for that school *would* have made staying in their pre-MBA jobs with annual pay increases equal to half the reported growth rate of their post-MBA pay. For alternative ways to calculate THE MBA ADVANTAGE, see appendix B.

	THE MBA ADVANTAGE	Post-MBA Years to Breakeven	1994 MBA ADVANTAGE Rank	1992 *Business Week* Top 20 Rank	1993 *U.S. News* Top 25 Rank
Harvard	$133,647	4	1	3	1
Chicago	110,294	4	2	2	9
Stanford	104,337	4	3	7	2
MIT	102,989	4	4	13	6
Yale	99,882	4	5	(NR)	17
Northwestern	72,500	4	6	1	4
Berkeley	71,298	4	7	18	14
Wharton	70,912	5	8	4	3
UCLA	60,809	5	9	16	15
Virginia	54,200	4	10	11	11
Cornell	45,866	5	11	14	12
Michigan	39,663	5	12	5	5
Dartmouth	37,258	5	13	6	8
Carnegie Mellon	36,782	5	14	17	13
Texas	27,466	5	15	(NR)	18
Rochester	18,683	5	16	(NR)	24
Indiana	11,543	5	17	8	20
North Carolina	7,844	5	18	10	19
Duke	7,506	5	19	12	7
NYU	4,121	5	20	15	16

—————— The Best Business Schools ——————

In table 4.1, THE MBA ADVANTAGE for the *Business Week* Top 20 schools was calculated using *Business Week* data on each school's average pre-MBA pay, average post-MBA starting pay, and average pay after five years on the job.[2] (The fifth year pay for the Class of 1992 was estimated by finding the ratio between the post-MBA starting pay and the fifth year pay for the Class of 1987 for each school, and applying that ratio to the post-MBA starting pay of the Class of 1992 for each school.) The results are dramatic:

- Even among the Top 20 business schools—the top 3 percent of all the business schools in the U.S.—there are major differences in the average payoff for getting the MBA. At the end of five years on the job, the difference in the average payoff between attending Harvard and the lowest ranked schools on this list is over $100,000.

- The ranking of schools based on THE MBA ADVANTAGE is quite different from the *Business Week* and *U.S. News & World Report* rankings. Harvard leads, followed by Chi-

2   Data is from *A Business Week Guide: The Best Business Schools*, 1993 edition, McGraw-Hill. The *Business Week Guide* did not publish complete information needed for these calculations on all of the schools in the 1992 *Business Week* Top 20. There was no published information on pay after five years on the job for Columbia, Vanderbilt, or Washington University, so it was not possible to calculate *The MBA Advantage* for these schools. There was complete information in the *Guides*, however, for Rochester, Texas, and Yale, which had been on the *Business Week* Top 20 in 1988 and/or 1990, so these three schools were included in these calculations.

cago and Stanford (number 7 in the *Business Week* rankings). MIT—ranked number 13 by *Business Week*—is fourth, while Indiana (ranked number 8 by *Business Week*) drops to seventeenth place. Yale, not included at all in *Business Week*'s Top 20, ranks fifth. *Business Week*'s number one school, Northwestern, is sixth.

- Within five years of graduation, the investment in the MBA—tuition and two years without salary—has been recovered at all of the Top 20 schools.

- The calculation in table 4.1 was done using pre-tax salaries. If estimated federal and state income taxes are factored in (20 percent on pay without the MBA; 30 percent on post-MBA pay), it takes an additional year to break even at most of the schools. If present value calculations are made by discounting the future *after-tax* cash flows by 6 percent per year (to recognize the time value of money), ten schools break even within six years of graduation, and all but five schools break even within seven years.

In table 4.1, THE MBA ADVANTAGE was estimated only for the first five years following graduation. This, of course, understates the true lifetime value of getting an MBA.

Limitations of THE MBA ADVANTAGE Ranking Method

As with other methods of ranking business schools, THE MBA ADVANTAGE ranking has some limitations. To begin with, how good is the data? *Business Week* reported an impressive 78 percent response rate for the 1992 graduate survey, with an average of 131 responses per school, thereby tending to minimize non-response bias. Even the supplemental survey sent to 3,683 members of the Class of 1987 (from the twenty-one schools that made the Top 20 in 1988 and 1990) to determine pay after five years on the job produced a respectable 42 percent response rate, with an average of seventy-four respondents per school.[3] Furthermore, one would expect that if non-response bias does exist, it ought to be reasonably consistent across all schools so that comparisons between schools are still useful.

It is important to recognize, however, that reported averages from surveys can be misleading—not everyone who attends Harvard will make over $200,000 in the fifth year on the job, as implied in figure 4.1. The *Business Week* survey sampling process may have reached only the more successful graduates since it may have been difficult to locate those graduates who are not doing well. Those who responded may have inflated their actual earnings. Moreover, the average post-MBA pay of a school is greatly influenced by the kinds of jobs accepted by graduates of that school. A few investment bankers working eighty hours a week on commission and making $1 million a year will distort the averages. And there will always be a few graduates even from the top schools who for one reason or another are unable to find jobs as good as those of their classmates.

In table 4.1, it was assumed that pay without the MBA for each school grew at half the rate that pay with the MBA grew in the post-MBA period (see figure 4.1). To test the sensitivity of THE MBA ADVANTAGE ranking to this assumption, the calculations were repeated for the case in which pay without the MBA grew at a uniform 5 percent a year for all schools, and for the case in which the annual growth rates in pay with and without the MBA were only half the growth

---

3   Byrne, J., *A Business Week Guide: The Best Business Schools*, 3rd edition, McGraw-Hill, 1993, pp. 12, 13, 345, 346.

rates used in calculating table 4.1. Although the dollar magnitudes of THE MBA ADVANTAGE for each school changed significantly with these variations in assumptions, the rank order of schools based on THE MBA ADVANTAGE was virtually unchanged (see appendix B).

If some schools are gaining on their competitors, however, THE MBA ADVANTAGE ranking in table 4.1 may understate the quality of their *current* graduates. This is because the post-MBA fifth year pay used to calculate THE MBA ADVANTAGE is based on the actual fifth year pay of the Class of 1987, as surveyed in 1992. If the current crop of students and/or the quality of teaching at these schools has improved disproportionately since 1987, the post-MBA growth rates for these schools used in calculating table 4.1 might be too low, and THE MBA ADVANTAGE ranking in table 4.1 could understate the true value of the current graduates of these schools. The converse could also be true for schools that are falling behind.

How Fast Would Pay Grow Without *the MBA?*

In calculating THE MBA ADVANTAGE, the growth rate in post-MBA pay is determined by comparing the average fifth year pay of each school with its average post-MBA starting pay. This growth is then assumed to compound at a constant rate over the five years following graduation. But what growth rate is appropriate for the alternative of not going to business school?

In appendix B, we'll show statistically that the quality of a school's incoming students is the most important factor in determining the magnitude of its MBA ADVANTAGE. An assumption of a uniform annual growth in salary without the MBA for *all* schools—say five percent per year is inappropriate. Presumably, Harvard-quality students would see their pre-MBA pay increase faster than five percent even without an MBA.

Instead, we have assumed that pay without the MBA would grow at *half the rate* it would grow with the MBA. In the first five years following graduation, the annual growth rates in post-MBA pay range from 28.8 percent for Harvard to 9.4 percent for Duke. Accordingly, in calculating THE MBA ADVANTAGE in table 4.1, the growth rates for pay without the MBA range from 14.4 percent for Harvard students to 4.7 percent for Duke students.[4]

"Value Added" Versus Value Multipliers

A number of years ago, the dean of a top business school was asked why the starting salaries of his MBA graduates were so much higher than those from lesser schools. His response was, "We look for the very best raw material we can find, filter it, put it in an expensive bottle with a fancy label, and sell it for a high price."

The dean's droll remark embodies the idea of "value added;" that is, repackaging a product to add a fixed increment to its value. It's like saying that an MBA from Harvard is worth an additional $32,000 a year—the difference between Harvard's average pre-MBA pay and post-MBA starting pay in table 4.3—forever.

But our data shows that it doesn't work that way. In the first five years following graduation, the annual growth rates in post-MBA pay range from about 15 percent for schools near the bottom of our list to nearly 30 percent for Harvard (see table 4.4). The MBA from a good school is not a fixed add-on; it's a *multiplier*. The best schools have high multipliers, with post-MBA pay

---

4   To see how THE MBA ADVANTAGE varies with different assumptions about these growth rates, refer to appendix B.

growing about 2.5 times in the first five years, while those further down the list have five-year multipliers of 1.5 to 2.0 times.

From a practical standpoint, what's the difference between value added and value multipliers? Consider the following example: Mike digs ditches for a living, and with a pick and shovel he can add to the length of the ditch at the rate of five feet per hour. He learns that there is a good demand for ditch digging in his area, so he goes out and invests in a back hoe that allows him to dig at the rate of fifty feet per hour. The back hoe is a multiplier of Mike's ability to dig ditches. It multiplies his output by ten times.

The MBA Has No Value By Itself

Without Mike, the back hoe can't dig anything. It adds no fixed increment of value without an operator. Furthermore, in the hands of an inept operator, the back hoe might dig only ten feet per hour. The back hoe takes Mike's inherent talent and skill and multiplies it. That's what an MBA does, too.

Let's consider another example: Eric is a pharmaceutical salesman earning $50,000 per year calling on doctors, and his pay raises average about 6 percent per year. After three years in the field, he decides he would like to be a doctor himself. He quits his job, goes to medical school, and after eight years of education and training, he becomes a very successful orthopedic surgeon. He is soon earning $150,000 a year and his pay is increasing at the rate of 20 percent a year.

For Eric, medical school is a value multiplier. Not only is his pay three times as high as it was before, but it is growing at a much faster rate. Medical school does not add a fixed increment ($100,000) to Eric's pay that is independent of his talent. His success as a surgeon depends on his personal talent and skills. A classmate of his in medical school with less talent but going through the same educational process might not make it as a surgeon. The medical degree has no value without Eric. He can't sell it to somebody else. The medical education *amplifies* Eric's personal abilities. It acts as a multiplier.

The Quality of Incoming Students

The bottom line to this discussion is that going to business school does not add value, it multiplies it. Students with a great deal of talent and drive will get a lot more out of a degree from Harvard or Stanford than those with less ability. In a way, to say that comparisons across business schools must adjust for the quality of incoming students is to miss the point. The admissions offices of the top schools have already done this. They try to accept only those students who in their experience are likely to get the full multiplier advantage that their school offers. They are a vital part of the excellence of the top schools.

In this sense, the competitive game between the top schools is won or lost in the admissions offices. Harvard continues to lead because of the combination of a fine educational program and an outstanding selection of incoming students (as measured by the lofty pre-MBA pay they give up to come to Harvard). If the incoming students don't have what it takes, the rest of the process doesn't matter.

The best way to compare the business schools in terms of financial returns is not to look just at post-MBA starting salaries or even fifth year pay. Instead, look at THE MBA ADVANTAGE column in table 4.1.

There's no need to "adjust" THE MBA ADVANTAGE for incoming student quality, provided *your* pre-MBA pay is reasonably close to the average pre-MBA pay for that school. The "adjustment" for incoming student quality occurs automatically in calculating THE MBA ADVANTAGE because the pay *without* the MBA—which is higher for higher quality students—is subtracted from the pay *with* the MBA. Schools with higher quality incoming students have more subtracted out when THE MBA ADVANTAGE is calculated.

Pre-MBA pay is a useful measure of incoming student quality. If the average pre-MBA pay is $30,000 at one business school and $50,000 at another business school, the quality of students entering the second school, as measured by their pre-MBA performance in the job market, is clearly higher.

While GMAT scores are often used to compare schools on the incoming quality of their students, the GMAT primarily measures the ability to take tests. It has been shown to predict grades in the first year of business school, but does not correlate well with starting salaries or other measures of on-the-job performance.[5] Pre-MBA pay, on the other hand, is an unbiased market-based measure of incoming student quality that is influenced not only by intelligence but also by motivation, personal skills, undergraduate education, the ability to communicate, years of work experience, and whatever else it takes to succeed in the real world. "Top schools . . . rely less on grades and test scores, and operate more on the principle that the best predictor of future performance is past achievements."[6]

How Good is the Data?

The data for our calculations was found in the third edition of the *Business Week Guide* (containing data from the 1992 *Business Week* Top 20 survey), supplemented by data from the first and second editions.[7] In addition to collecting post-MBA starting pay and pre-MBA pay by school on 4,712 MBA graduates of the Class of 1992, *Business Week* also collected—for the first time—current salary data (i.e., fifth year pay) for 1,553 graduates of the MBA Class of 1987 by school, thereby providing a means of comparing post-MBA salary growth across schools.

While none of this data was used by *Business Week* in calculating the *Business Week* Top 20 business school rankings, we will show that it is of great value in estimating the economic value multipliers for each school. The foresight shown by the *Business Week* staff in collecting and publishing this new data is acknowledged with appreciation.

In all of the following value multiplier comparisons of business schools, the *average* pay statistics as published in the *Business Week Guides* will be used throughout. It should be recognized that these averages, like other summary statistics, sometimes can be misleading. For example, since salaries are self-reported by graduates, there may be a tendency for only the more successful graduates to respond to surveys, biasing the averages upward. (Marketing researchers call this "non-response bias.")

However, as noted previously, *Business Week* reported a high response rate for the 1992 graduate survey, as well as for the supplemental survey sent to the members of the Class of 1987 to determine pay after five years on the job.[8] Moreover, one would expect that if non-response

5 Personal communication with William Broesamle, Graduate Management Admission Council, administrators of the GMAT.
6 O'Reilly, B., "Reengineering the MBA," *Fortune*, January 24, 1994, p. 42.
7 Byrne, J., *A Business Week Guide: The Best Business Schools*, 3rd edition, McGraw-Hill, 1993.
8 Byrne, J., *A Business Week Guide: The Best Business Schools*, 3rd edition, McGraw-Hill, 1993, pp. 12, 13, 345, 346.

bias does exist, it ought to be reasonably consistent across all schools, so that rankings of schools are still meaningful.

In addition, the *Business Week* pay statistics include base salaries plus bonuses, which may increase or decrease in subsequent years. Again, if bonuses bias the starting pay statistics upward, this bias should also be fairly consistent across schools; if so, our ranking of business schools will not be affected.

Your Area of Specialization Can Affect Your Post-MBA Pay

A potential bias occurs because of the different areas of functional specialization across schools. Harvard, for example, has traditionally placed about 40 percent of its graduates in consulting and investment banking, both of which pay comparatively high wages.

Since the *Business Week* data was not categorized by area of specialization for either graduates or incoming students, it was not possible to make adjustments across schools for these differences. One can argue that no correction is needed anyway, since part of the value of a Harvard education is that it makes it possible for a large proportion of its graduates to secure high paying jobs in consulting and investment banking.

Moreover, starting salaries *within* the major functional specialties of finance, marketing and consulting, as published in the catalogs of the Top 20 schools, were found to correlate with the overall average starting salaries of these schools as published by *Business Week*. If your heart is set on a job in marketing, your starting pay in marketing is likely to be higher if you go to a school with a high overall starting salary.

Cost-of-Living in Different Regions of the Country

Various regions of the country have differences in the cost-of-living that can influence average starting pay, depending on where each school's graduates accept employment. An unpublished paper by Joseph Tracy and Joel Waldfogel estimates that the cost-of-living differences for MBA graduates can range from about minus 6 percent to plus 11 percent, relative to the average cost-of-living for the country.[9] For large schools with national admissions and placements, these regional cost-of-living differences should tend to wash out in the averages. For regional schools that both accept and place students mostly in the same region, the cost-of-living for that region should be reflected in the average pre-MBA pay, the average starting pay and the average fifth year pay. Since our comparative analysis across schools is based on the ratios of these numbers, the regional cost-of-living will cancel out. There may be, however, a number of schools in the Top 20 that serve a mix of national and regional markets, and for which cost-of-living factors should be borne in mind when looking at these results.

The effect of regional cost-of-living differences on THE MBA ADVANTAGE ranking is discussed in appendix B. There is no significant change in the rankings of the best business schools when cost-of-living adjustments are made.

---

9   Tracy, J. and Waldfogel, J., "The Best Business Schools: A Market Based Approach," unpublished manuscript, Columbia University Department of Economics and Yale University Department of Economics, October 1993.

Defining the Value Multipliers for the Top Business Schools

To estimate THE MBA ADVANTAGE amounts in table 4.1, value multipliers were developed for each business school:

- STARTING SALARY MOMENTUM: The increase in average post-MBA starting pay over the four year period from 1988 to 1992, to show which schools are improving most rapidly in terms of what recruiters are looking for in graduating MBAs.

- MBA STEP UP: The ratio of average post-MBA starting pay to average pre-MBA pay, to determine the average pay increase after two years in business school.

- POST MBA FAST TRACK: The ratio of average pay after five years on the job (fifth year pay) to average post-MBA starting pay, to show the rate at which pay increases in the first five years *after* graduation.

- TOTAL VALUE MULTIPLIER: The ratio of average pay after five years on the job (fifth year pay) to average pre-MBA pay, to indicate the total increase in pay after two years in business school and five years on the job, relative to pre-MBA pay.

- THE MBA ADVANTAGE: As previously discussed, this is the estimated, average, cumulative, post-MBA pay after five years on the job (after subtracting the cost of going to business school), less what students *would* have made in their pre-MBA jobs with annual pay increases equal to half the growth rate of their pay with the MBA. THE MBA ADVANTAGE was estimated from "worst-case" calculations—no scholarships to help pay tuition,

Table 4.2

STARTING SALARY MOMENTUM is defined as the percent growth in starting pay of the top schools over the four-year period from 1988 to 1992.

Average Post-MBA Starting Pay

Rank		1988	1992	Growth (4 yrs.)
1	Berkeley	$45,083	$65,510	+ 45.3%
2	Yale	46,455	66,690	43.6
3	UCLA	45,378	64,540	42.2
4	Columbia	49,397	66,620	34.9
5	Rochester	39,990	53,400	33.5
6	Harvard	64,112	84,960	32.5
7	Northwestern	53,031	70,200	32.4
8	Michigan	43,976	58,110	32.1
9	Wharton	55,183	72,210	30.8
10	Virginia	50,554	65,280	29.1
11	Indiana	38,407	49,070	27.8
12	Stanford	65,176	82,860	27.1
13	Chicago	54,772	68,600	25.2
14	North Carolina	44,941	55,500	23.5
15	Duke	48,740	59,870	22.8
16	Texas	40,115	48,900	21.9
17	NYU	47,037	56,730	20.6
18	MIT	60,680	73,000	20.3
19	Dartmouth	62,681	74,260	18.5
20	Carnegie Mellon	49,109	56,980	16.0
21	Cornell	52,339	59,940	14.5

no income while in school from a part-time job or a summer internship, highest out-of-state tuition for state schools—so these pre-tax numbers should be conservative. Furthermore, THE MBA ADVANTAGE was estimated only for the first five years of post-MBA employment, which understates the true lifetime value of earning an MBA.

STARTING SALARY MOMENTUM for the Top Business Schools

The starting salaries of some schools are growing much faster than others (see table 4.2), as the result of attracting better students and/or through increased recognition by corporate recruiters. A statistical analysis showed that this effect is *not* the result of smaller or low-ranked schools "catching up."

MBA STEP UP for the Top Business Schools

The MBA STEP UP, which is the ratio of post-MBA starting pay to pre-MBA pay, is a measure of the short run value multiplier of each school.

Q: What is the average pay increase after two years in business school?

Table 4.3

MBA STEP UP is the ratio of post-MBA starting pay to pre-MBA pay.

Rank		Pre-MBA Pay	For the Class of 1992 Post-MBA Starting Pay	MBA STEP UP
1	Yale	$38,020	$66,690	+ 75.4%
2	MIT	42,630	73,000	71.2
3	Chicago	40,460	68,600	69.6
4	Vanderbilt	27,900	47,230	69.3
5	Columbia	40,150	66,620	65.9
6	Northwestern	42,950	70,200	63.4
7	Harvard	52,790	84,960	60.9
8	Virginia	40,560	65,280	60.9
9	Stanford	51,570	82,860	60.7
10	Michigan	36,370	58,110	59.8
11	Berkeley	41,050	65,510	59.6
12	Carnegie Mellon	35,730	56,980	59.5
13	Cornell	37,820	59,940	58.5
14	Wharton	45,780	72,210	57.7
15	Rochester	34,430	53,400	55.1
16	Duke	39,060	59,870	53.3
17	Washington U.	31,900	48,200	51.1
18	UCLA	42,740	64,540	51.0
19	Dartmouth	49,700	74,260	49.4
20	Indiana	33,410	49,070	46.9
21	Texas	33,900	48,900	44.2
22	NYU	40,130	56,730	41.4
23	North Carolina	39,990	55,500	38.8

The bottom line: An MBA from one of these schools should immediately increase your pay 50 to 60 percent.

POST MBA FAST TRACK for the Top Business Schools

The actual 1988 starting pay for each of the Top 20 schools (from the first edition of the *Business Week Guide*) was reduced by 5 percent to approximate the 1987 starting pay for each school (MBA starting salaries grew about 5 percent per year during the 1980s). The actual 1992 current pay for each school's Class of 1987 (from the third edition) was then divided by the estimated 1987 pay to get a five-year post-MBA growth factor.

Q: How fast does average pay increase after graduation?

Table 4.4

POST MBA FAST TRACK shows salary growth in the first five years on the job.

		———————— For the Class of 1987 ————————		
Rank		Est. 1987 Starting Pay (0.95 x 1988 Starting Pay)	Actual 5th Year Pay (in 1992)	POST MBA FAST TRACK	Annual Growth Rate
1	Harvard	$60,906	$167,740	2.754 times	28.82%
2	Chicago	52,033	127,350	2.447	25.07
3	Stanford	61,917	144,540	2.334	23.60
4	UCLA	43,109	97,290	2.257	22.57
5	Wharton	52,424	113,790	2.171	21.39
6	Yale	44,133	94,400	2.139	20.94
7	MIT	57,646	122,380	2.123	20.71
8	NYU	44,685	91,070	2.038	19.48
9	Dartmouth	59,547	119,380	2.005	19.00
10	Northwestern	50,379	100,260	1.990	18.77
11	Berkeley	42,829	84,880	1.982	18.65
12	Cornell	49,722	98,490	1.981	18.64
13	Texas	38,109	74,340	1.951	18.18
14	Michigan	41,777	77,200	1.848	16.59
15	Carnegie Mellon	46,654	85,400	1.831	16.32
16	North Carolina	42,694	77,760	1.821	16.17
17	Virginia	48,026	83,060	1.729	14.67
18	Indiana	36,487	62,650	1.717	14.47
19	Rochester	37,990	63,610	1.674	13.75
20	Duke	46,303	66,420	1.434	9.43

The bottom line: Post-MBA pay can compound at 15 to 20 percent annually for the first five years.

TOTAL VALUE MULTIPLIERS for the Top Business Schools

By combining the two-year MBA STEP UP and the subsequent five-year POST MBA FAST TRACK, a TOTAL VALUE MULTIPLIER factor can be calculated for the entire seven-year span from the time you enter business school until you complete five years on the job.

TOTAL VALUE MULTIPLIER = (MBA STEP UP) x (POST MBA FAST TRACK)

Table 4.5
The TOTAL VALUE MULTIPLIER is the factor by which pay increases from pre-MBA pay to the level of pay
earned in the fifth year on the job.

Rank		STEP UP	FAST TRACK	TOTAL VALUE MULTIPLIER	Equiv. Annual Growth Rate
1	Harvard	1.609	2.754	4.432 times	28.16%
2	Chicago	1.696	2.447	4.150	26.76
3	Yale	1.754	2.139	3.752	24.66
4	Stanford	1.607	2.334	3.751	24.65
5	MIT	1.712	2.123	3.635	24.00
6	Wharton	1.577	2.171	3.423	22.76
7	UCLA	1.510	2.257	3.408	22.67
8	Northwestern	1.634	1.990	3.253	21.73
9	Berkeley	1.596	1.982	3.162	21.15
10	Cornell	1.585	1.981	3.139	21.00
11	Dartmouth	1.494	2.005	2.996	20.07
12	Michigan	1.598	1.848	2.952	19.77
13	Carnegie Mellon	1.595	1.831	2.919	19.55
14	NYU	1.414	2.038	2.881	19.29
15	Texas	1.442	1.951	2.813	18.81
16	Virginia	1.609	1.729	2.784	18.61
17	Rochester	1.551	1.674	2.597	17.24
18	North Carolina	1.388	1.821	2.528	16.72
19	Indiana	1.469	1.717	2.522	16.67
20	Duke	1.533	1.434	2.199	14.03

The bottom line: After five years on the job, you should be earning 2.5 to 3.5 times your
pre-MBA pay.

Future Pay for the Class of 1992 for the Top Business Schools
Table 4.6 shows the future pay (in 1997) of the Class of 1992, as calculated by using the TOTAL
VALUE MULTIPLIERS for each school. If MBAs from these schools do as well as their predecessors
did during the recessionary period from 1988 to 1992, the impressive pay in the last column
should be achieved.

Will You Really Make That Much Money?
Although calculated from *Business Week* survey data, the post-MBA salary growth rates of 15 to
20 percent per year shown in these tables may seem high in a period of low inflation and
slow economic growth. As described in table 4.4, these POST-MBA FAST TRACK growth rates
were derived using the actual post-MBA starting salaries for the Class of 1988 and the actual
fifth year pay for the Class of 1987, as published in the first and third editions of the *Business
Week Guide.*[10] In reviewing tables 4.4, 4.5 and 4.6, there may be concern that the
POST-MBA FAST TRACK growth rates and the fifth year pay (actual and estimated) are "just
too high."

---

10 Byrne, J., *A Business Week Guide: The Best Business Schools*, 1st edition, McGraw-Hill, 1990, and 3rd edition, McGraw-Hill, 1993, p. 17.

Table 4.6

Estimated 1997 fifth year pay for the MBA Class of 1992 was calculated by multiplying the actual pre-MBA pay of the Class of 1992 for each school by its TOTAL VALUE MULTIPLIER factor. (For comparison, the actual fifth year pay for the Class of 1987 is also shown.) Because of differences across schools in STARTING SALARY MOMENTUM, the rank order of schools for the estimated 1997 fifth year pay is not the same as that for the 1992 actual fifth year pay.

		For the Class of 1987	——— For the Class of 1992 ———	
Rank		Actual 5th Year Pay (1992)	Actual Pre-MBA Pay	Est. 5th Year Pay (1997)
1	Harvard	$167,740	$52,790	$233,985
2	Stanford	144,540	51,570	193,429
3	Chicago	127,350	40,460	167,896
4	Wharton	113,790	45,780	156,716
5	MIT	122,380	42,630	154,976
6	Dartmouth	119,380	49,700	148,877
7	UCLA	97,400	42,740	145,656
8	Yale	94,400	38,020	142,651
9	Northwestern	100,260	42,950	139,705
10	Berkeley	84,880	41,050	129,811
11	Cornell	98,490	37,820	118,730
12	NYU	91,070	40,130	115,618
13	Virginia	83,060	40,560	112,900
14	Michigan	77,200	36,370	107,381
15	Carnegie Mellon	85,400	35,730	104,303
16	North Carolina	77,760	39,990	101,084
17	Texas	74,340	33,900	95,372
18	Rochester	63,610	34,430	89,411
19	Duke	66,420	39,060	85,881
20	Indiana	62,650	33,410	84,256

How could this happen? There is a possibility that the respondents who provided the *Business Week* data on fifth year pay were not representative of the entire Class of '87. According to the *Guide*, a questionnaire was sent to 3,683 members of the Class of 1987 from the twenty-one schools that made the *Business Week* Top 20 in 1988 and/or 1990, and 1,553 responded.[11] Assuming there are about 6,300 Class of '87 alumni of these schools (21 schools times an average of about 300 graduates per school), the responding sample represented about 25 percent of the '87 alumni.

It's possible that this 25 percent was the most successful segment of the Class of '87 and its pay is therefore biased on the high side. This could mean that the fifth year salaries and the POST MBA FAST TRACK growth rates are overstated in tables 4.1, 4.4, 4.5 and 4.6.

To test the sensitivity of THE MBA ADVANTAGE to slower growth rates of post-MBA pay, calculations were made in which the post-MBA growth rates were cut in half (Harvard's was cut from 28.8 percent to 14.4 percent, Chicago's from 25.1 percent to 12.5 percent, etc.). As in table 4.1, the growth rates without the MBA were half those with the MBA (Harvard's was 7.2 percent, Chicago's was 6.3 percent, etc.). THE MBA ADVANTAGE was extended to six years post-MBA so

---

11 Ibid., pp. 12–13.

that all of the schools would achieve breakeven. The results are shown in table B.3 in appendix B. Note that the rank order of the schools shown in table 4.1 remains the same in table B.3, except that Duke moves ahead of Indiana and North Carolina.

How to Use Value Multipliers: A Business School Example

Now let's apply these value multipliers to a real business school example. Suppose that Susan is earning $35,000 a year in her present job. Let's say that she has been accepted at the University of Virginia, which has an average pre-MBA pay (in 1990) of $40,560 (see table 4.3). When she graduates in two years, she should realize about a 60 percent increase over her pre-MBA pay, to about $56,000 (in table 4.3, the MBA STEP UP for Virginia is 60.9 percent). She might even do a little better because her pre-MBA pay was slightly below the average for Virginia. Furthermore, if she does as well as the average Virginia students have done in recent years, she can expect a salary after five years on the job of $97,000 or more ($35,000 x 2.784; see table 4.5).

If she had been earning $50,000 instead of $35,000, however, she would probably find it difficult to get a 60 percent increase to $80,000, because this is well above Virginia's average post-MBA starting pay of $65,280. But if she was fortunate enough to be accepted at Stanford (pre-MBA pay of $51,570 in 1990), she might be offered $80,000 at graduation, and—if she is as talented and hardworking as her Stanford classmates—she might make $188,000 after five years on the job ($50,000 x 3.751; see table 4.5). Even if she only makes the average fifth year pay that Stanford alums got in 1992, she would earn $145,000 (table 4.6). There are big differences in financial returns on the MBA, even among the top schools.

This brings up an important limitation of the practical application of value multipliers—they should only be applied to pre-MBA salary values that are reasonably close to the averages shown in the tables.

Will These Value Multipliers Change in the Future?

THE MBA ADVANTAGE is a better way to compare business schools because it is based on actual market values—pre-MBA pay, post-MBA starting pay, fifth year salaries—rather than opinions about values. Is it reasonable to project these historical values into the future?

First, since much of our analysis is based on ratios of values (for example, the ratio of pre-MBA pay to post-MBA starting pay), the absolute values are relatively unimportant as long as the historical ratios between them stay the same.

Second, all of this data was collected for the years from 1987 to 1992—a time of recession during which the demand for MBAs slowed markedly. It was also a period of relatively low inflation. Therefore, the ratios we obtained may be conservatively biased. For example, the ratio of post-MBA starting pay (a 1992 number) to pre-MBA pay (a 1990 number) may have been compressed by the slow job market in 1992. Similarly, the growth factor for post-MBA salary growth, which is the ratio of pay after five years on the job (a 1992 number) to starting pay (a 1987 number), may also be on the low side because the recession limited the size of pay raises during this period.

There is no way, of course, to predict changes in these key ratios for individual schools due to competitive activity. As shown in table 4.2, some schools seem to have more MOMEN-

TUM—their starting pay is moving up faster. If in fact these schools are gaining on their competitors, THE MBA ADVANTAGE ranking in table 4.1 may understate the quality of their *current* graduates. This is because the fifth year pay used to calculate THE MBA ADVANTAGE is based on the actual fifth year pay of the Class of 1987, as surveyed in 1992. If the current crop of students and/or the quality of teaching at these schools has improved disproportionately since 1987, the post-MBA FAST TRACK growth rates of these schools in table 4.4 might be too low, and THE MBA ADVANTAGE ranking in table 4.1 could understate the true value of the current graduates of these schools.

Is the MBA Worth It?

As noted in the beginning of this discussion, there are many good reasons besides financial gain for going to business school: the knowledge, the wider career choices, adding to your personal credentials, and the challenge and enjoyment of working with exceptional classmates. This chapter has looked just at the financial returns for getting an MBA in a full-time program at a top-rated school. The key findings are:

- Even among the *Business Week* Top 20 Business Schools—the top 3 percent of all the business schools in the U.S.—there are major differences in the average payoff for getting the MBA. It *does* make a difference where you get your MBA.

- The ranking of schools based on THE MBA ADVANTAGE is very different from the *Business Week* Top 20 and *U.S. News & World Report* business school rankings.

- Yale, Texas, and Rochester belong in the Top 20 business schools, based on the market value of the graduates of these schools.

- Within five years of graduation, the investment in the MBA—tuition plus two years without salary—will be recovered at all of the Top 20 schools. (On an after-tax basis, it takes five to seven years to break even at all of the schools.)

So back to Susan's question from Chapter 1: "Is it worth it?" Yes, an MBA from one of these top schools *is* worth it.

Chapter 5

A Buyer's Guide to the Best National Business Schools

In this chapter, we will describe the key features and advantages of each of the top business schools as listed in table 5.1, noting their strengths, their starting salaries *in each functional area*, and what it's like to be a student at that school.

Table 5.1
The best national business schools, as ranked by THE MBA ADVANTAGE.

MBA ADVANTAGE Rank		Post-MBA Pay Growth Rate	Est. 5th Year Pay (in 1997)	MBA ADVANTAGE (5 years Post-MBA)	Years to Breakeven
		For the Class of 1992			
1	Harvard	28.8%	$233,985	$133,647	4
2	Chicago	25.1	167,896	110,294	4
3	Stanford	23.6	193,429	104,337	4
4	MIT	20.7	154,976	102,989	4
5	Yale	20.9	142,651	99,882	4
6	Northwestern	18.8	139,705	72,500	4
7	Berkeley	18.7	129,811	71,298	4
8	Wharton	21.4	156,716	70,912	5
9	UCLA	22.6	145,656	60,809	5
10	Virginia	14.7	112,900	54,200	4
11	Cornell	18.6	118,730	45,866	5
12	Michigan	16.6	107,381	39,663	5
13	Dartmouth	19.0	148,877	37,258	5
14	Carnegie Mellon	16.3	104,303	36,782	5
15	Texas	18.2	95,372	27,466	5
16	Rochester	13.8	89,411	18,683	5
17	Indiana	14.4	84,256	11,543	5
18	North Carolina	16.2	101,084	7,844	5
19	Duke	9.4	85,881	7,506	5
20	NYU	19.5	115,618	4,121	5

The Concept of the Buyer's Guide

THE MBA ADVANTAGE provides an objective overall ranking of the top schools in terms of the economic benefits of their MBA degree. But how do these top schools compare on a function-by-function basis? Everyone knows that some schools are better in finance; others are better in marketing or general management.

Since many prospective students have a good idea of the functional area they want to concentrate on, this "Buyer's Guide to the Best Business Schools" was compiled to provide quantitative and qualitative information *on the functional areas* of the top schools. If, for example, you know in advance that marketing is going to be your area of concentration, this chapter will highlight the schools that have the best marketing programs.

In using the "Buyer's Guide" information in this chapter, keep in mind the following:

1. All of these schools are outstanding. They represent the top 3 percent of business schools in the United States, and you wouldn't go wrong with any of them.

2. To help you choose the best school to meet your particular career goals, this chapter focuses on the *differences* between the schools. This includes which schools are particularly good in finance or in marketing, which schools are the most flexible in their curriculum requirements, which schools offer hands-on projects courses with companies, and so forth.

3. Starting salaries *by functional area* will be presented for each school where available. The primary sources for this data were the published 1993–94 MBA catalogs and placement reports provided by the various schools, occasionally supplemented by published data from *Business Week,*[1] *U.S. News & World Report,*[2] *The Insider's Guide to the Top 10 Business Schools* by Tom Fischgrund,[3] and *The Official Guide to MBA Programs,* published by the Graduate Management Admission Council.[4]

4. The starting salaries shown will be in the form as provided by the schools. In making comparisons across schools, please be aware of the following limitations of this data:

   • Starting salaries by functional area for some of the best schools—including Harvard, Stanford, and Northwestern—are missing because the schools have chosen not to publish this information.

   • While most schools provide starting salaries that *do not* include signing bonuses or other variable compensation, the *Business Week* survey data used to compute THE MBA ADVANTAGE of each school, collected directly from a mail survey of the Class of 1992, *does* include signing bonuses and other bonuses.[5] The typical signing bonus is about $5,000 and can range from $2,000 to $25,000. Because of this, many of the post-MBA pay figures shown in chapter 4 and appendix B are higher than the numbers shown in this chapter.

   • Some schools provided *mean* starting salaries while others provided *median* starting salaries. Experience shows that the difference is not very great, however—usually within $2,000.

   • Almost all of the salary data shown in this chapter is for the graduating class of

1   *Business Week Guide to the Best Business Schools*, 3rd Edition, McGraw Hill, 1993.
2   "America's Best Graduate Schools," *U.S. News & World Report*, March 22, 1993, p. 58.
3   Fischgrund, T., *The Insider's Guide to the Top 10 Business Schools*, 5th Edition, Little, Brown and Company, 1993.
4   *The Official Guide to MBA Programs*, Graduate Management Admissions Council, 1992.
5   Many schools state outright in their placement reports that signing bonuses are not included, and this statement is noted in the sections on the individual schools in this chapter. A few schools are rather vague, however, about whether they do include signing bonuses (which, of course, would make their starting salaries look higher).

1993. A couple of schools, Chicago and Yale, provided data for the graduating class of 1992.

- The purpose of this chapter is to provide a convenient overview. When you finally choose between two or three schools, you will want to make a detailed study of the schools' catalogs and placement reports, supplemented by campus visits and conversations with alumni and current students.[6]

5. Some prospective students will prefer a business school in a large city that is a major commercial and financial center, while others might desire a peaceful college town environment. Therefore, in addition to comparisons of the academic programs and starting salaries of the top schools, we'll also look at the campus environment (big city versus small college town) and the quality of the classroom facilities of each school.

6. While this chapter was written primarily for prospective students, it may also be of interest to employers who are shopping for exceptional graduates in specific functional areas.

Comparing Starting Salaries by Functional Areas

The graphs in figures 5.1–5.3 show starting salaries by the three most important functional areas—consulting, finance and marketing—for each of the schools that provided placement report data.

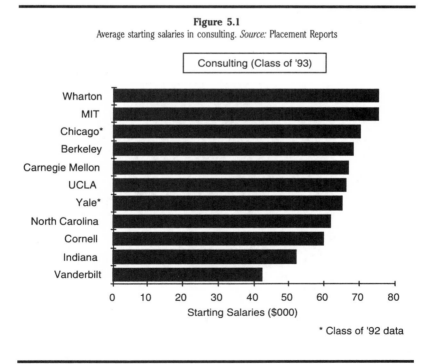

Figure 5.1
Average starting salaries in consulting. *Source:* Placement Reports

Consulting (Class of '93)

Starting Salaries ($000)

* Class of '92 data

---

6 For more details on how students choose business schools, see chapter 12.

Figure 5.2

Average starting salaries in finance. *Source:* Placement Reports

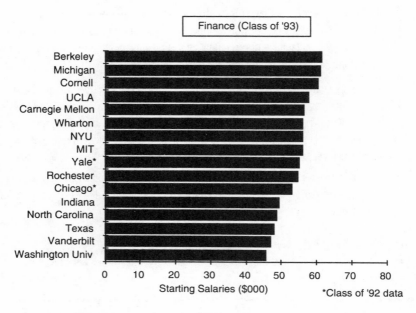

Figure 5.3

Average starting salaries in marketing. *Source:* Placement Reports

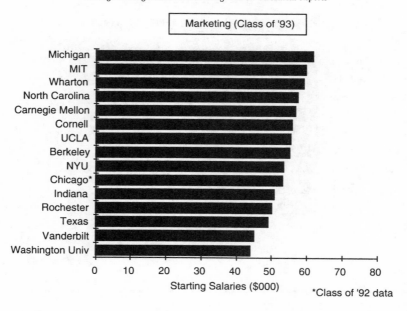

In comparing the starting salaries shown in these graphs, the differences across schools in each functional area are smaller than one might expect, particularly in finance and marketing. For the majority of schools, 1993 starting salaries in finance and marketing were between $50,000 and $60,000 per year.

Other Factors Besides Starting Salaries

This suggests that it is useful to look at other factors besides starting salaries when choosing a business school. The growth of post-MBA pay after graduation is a very important factor, as is the pre-MBA pay that students give up to attend business school. These additional factors are taken into account in the calculation of THE MBA ADVANTAGE for each school. However, there is not sufficient data available at this time to calculate an overall MBA ADVANTAGE figure *for each functional area* in each school; prospective students should inquire about additional factors, such as post-MBA pay growth in their functional area of interest, at schools they are seriously considering.

Table 5.2 was developed to give a qualitative overview of the functional areas of excellence of the top schools. The rating system is like that for fine restaurants and hotels, with five stars for the highest level of quality and performance and one star for the lowest. These functional ratings were based primarily on an analysis of material from the placement reports and catalogs of the various schools, supplemented by published ratings in the media and by the author's personal knowledge about the programs of many of these schools.

Rating System

★★★★★	=	world class program: graduates a large number of students at high starting salaries, or does outstanding research or industrial outreach in this area
★★★★	=	nationally recognized program in this area
★★★	=	very good program, but with lower starting salaries
★★	=	good program, particularly for double majors
★	=	basic program, meets accreditation standards

Table 5.2
Qualitative ratings of the functional areas of the best business schools

Rank		Accounting	Consulting	Entrepreneurship	Finance	General Mgmt	Marketing	Mgmt Info Sys	Operations	Nonprofit
1	Harvard	★★★★	★★★★★★	★★★★★	★★★★★	★★★★★	★★★★★	★★★★★	★★★★★	★★★★
2	Chicago	★★★★★	★★★★★	★★★★★★	★★★★★★	★★★★	★★★★	★★★	★★★	★★★★★
3	Stanford	★★★★★★	★★★★★★	★★★★★★	★★★★★★	★★★★★★	★★★★★	★★★★★★	★★★★★★	★★★★
4	MIT	★★★	★★★★★★	★★★★	★★★★	★★★★	★★★★	★★★★★	★★	
5	Yale	★★★★★★	★★★★★★	★★★★★	★★★	★★★	★★		★★	
6	Northwestern		★★★★	★★★★	★★★★	★★★★	★★★★★★	★★★★	★★★★	
7	Berkeley	★★★	★★★★★★	★★★★★★	★★★★★	★★★★★★	★★★		★★★	
8	Wharton	★★★★★★	★★★★★★	★★★★★★	★★★★★★	★★★★★	★★★★★★		★★★	
9	UCLA	★★★	★★★		★★	★★★	★★★		★★	
10	Virginia		★★★★★	★★★★★★	★★★★★	★★★★★★	★★★★		★★	
11	Cornell	★★★★	★★★★		★★★★	★★★★★	★★★		★★★★	
12	Michigan	★★★	★★★★★★		★★★★★	★★★★★★	★★★★★★	★★★★★★	★★★★★	
13	Dartmouth		★★★★★		★★★★★	★★★★★	★★★★★		★★★	
14	Carnegie Mellon		★★★★★	★★★★★	★★★★★		★★★★	★★★★★	★★★★★★	
15	Texas	★★★★★	★★★	★★★	★★		★★★	★★★	★★	
16	Rochester	★★★★★★		★★★	★★★★★		★★★	★★★	★★★	
17	Indiana	★★★	★★★		★★★	★★★	★★★★		★★★	
18	North Carolina		★★★★★		★★★	★★★	★★★★★		★★★★★	★★★★
19	Duke		★★★★		★★★	★★★★	★★★		★★	★★★★
20	NYU	★★★	★★★★★		★★★★★	★★★	★★★★	★★	★★★	
NR	Columbia	★★★	★★★★★		★★★	★★★	★★★		★★★	
NR	Vanderbilt	★★	★★		★★		★★		★★	
NR	Washington U.									

NUMBER 1: HARVARD

Harvard Business School

Consulting	★★★★★
Entrepreneurship	★★★★★
Finance	★★★★★
General management	★★★★★
Marketing	★★★★★
Nonprofit	★★★★
Operations	★★★★★

Rankings:

MBA ADVANTAGE rank (1994) 1

U.S. News & World Report rank (1993) 1

Business Week corporate rank (1992) 3

Business Week graduate rank (1992) 12

Overview:

The Harvard Business School (HBS) is the best business school in America, based on the economic value of its MBA degree as measured by THE MBA ADVANTAGE. Its mission is to develop general managers, and prospective students are screened on the basis of their potential to become top managers. The program is very competitive, the students work hard, and the average post-MBA pay of Harvard grads—both at graduation and after five years on the job—is the highest of any business school. For prospective students interested in general management, Harvard should be at the top of the list.

Strengths:

- The Harvard Business School is the flagship of the business school fleet—large, stately, perhaps a bit dated in technology, but still the standard against which other schools are compared.

- The HBS is ranked number 1 in THE MBA ADVANTAGE because the post-MBA pay of the average Harvard MBA starts higher and grows faster than that of any other business school. This occurs even though the typical Harvard MBA gives up a higher paying pre-MBA job than the average student at any other business school.

- Harvard graduates are trained for general management. The school's mission is to prepare men and women to consider problems from a broad general-management perspective rather than as functional specialists.

- The HBS looks for prospective students who show evidence of leadership. "The common denominator among these students is an unusual ability to work with others. Top management potential is the only absolute admissions criterion."[7] A few years ago, the HBS dropped the GMAT as a requirement for admissions, focusing instead on the written application and in some cases personal interviews.

- The venerable case method is the primary method of instruction at HBS. Although critics have warned for years that the case method is inefficient and out-of-date, it remains the teaching method of choice in almost all of the courses.[8]

- The first year of the program consists of a series of modular core courses that start and stop at various times during the year. No course waivers are permitted in the first year. In the second year, students are free to choose from among seventy-five electives; there are no formal concentration requirements.

- HBS professors put teaching ahead of research and they work hard at it. Because of the freewheeling nature of case discussions, teaching cases is more difficult for a professor than straight lecturing and requires more preparation time, and the great majority of faculty make the investment.[9]

- There are only four levels of grades at HBS: a "I" (excellent) for the top 10 percent in each class, a "II" (satisfactory) for the middle 80 percent, a "III" for "low pass" (known as a "loop"), and a "IIII" for unsatisfactory. "IIIIs" are rare and are generally given out to students who disrupt the learning process of others. Only about 3 percent of the first year class flunks out, but there is intense pressure to earn "I"s, because the top consulting firms like McKinsey & Co. tend to select from this level. Since 30 to 50 percent of the grade is usually based on class participation, students compete vigorously to say something meaningful during case discussions. Teamwork and cooperation—which are nurtured at other schools—often take a back seat at Harvard when students are competing aggressively for the professor's attention.

- Why do Harvard graduates continue to do so well after graduation? A recent survey of corporate recruiters suggested that all of the top business schools have more or less achieved parity in teaching the technical skills of management—statistics, economics, finance, marketing, accounting—and that differentiation between schools is shifting to the softer skills of creative problem solving, leadership, oral and written presentation skills, and teamwork.[10] To the extent that the case method hones and polishes these softer skills (except, perhaps, teamwork), the Harvard case method may in fact give its students a competitive advantage. The ability to structure messy problems, to de-

---

7   *Harvard Business School MBA Program Catalog*, 1994, p. 6.

8   For discussions of the limitations of Harvard's case method and other issues, see Kiechel, W., "Harvard Business School Restudies Itself," *Fortune*, June 18, 1979, pp. 49–58; Nussbaum, B. and Beam, A., "Remaking the Harvard Business School," *Business Week*, March 24, 1986, pp. 54–70; Kiechel, W., "New Debate about Harvard Business School," *Fortune*, November 9, 1987, pp. 34–38; Byrne, J., "Harvard B-School: An Institution in Need of Reform," *Business Week*, July 19, 1993, pp. 58–65; and Bongiorono, L., "A Case Study in Change at Harvard," *Business Week*, November 15, 1993, p. 42.

9   Several years ago a Harvard professor told me that when he joined the HBS after many years of successful teaching at another top school, his department chairman sat in on the first class he taught at the HBS and the next day gave him a twenty-eight-page memo listing ways he could improve his teaching to bring it up to HBS standards.

10 "What Businesses Want from Business Schools," a marketing research class project carried out by Larry Kleehammer, Juan Lugo, Howard Mulcahey, and Keith Sawyer, all of the Simon School MBA Class of '94.

termine a feasible set of options under time pressure, and to choose and vigorously defend an action plan before a peer group are all useful skills for managers.

- Another possible contributor to Harvard's success might be that the school frequently admits people who are going to be successful anyway—sons or daughters of the founders of family businesses,[11] bright young men and women with the right family and social connections in industry or government, or precocious professionals already identified as fast trackers who are being sent to business school by their companies with the understanding that a brilliant future awaits when they return. While the Harvard MBA undoubtedly adds substantial value, many of these people are destined to make it anyway.[12] As noted earlier, "top management potential is the only absolute admissions criterion" at HBS.

- Another contributor to the success of HBS grads is the army of 34,000 MBA alumni organized into 89 HBS clubs worldwide to advise and help fledgling graduates. Although the majority of HBS alums appear to be associated with small and medium-sized businesses, 20 percent of top three officers of the *Fortune* 500 are HBS alumni.[13]

- Finally, the Harvard Business School is the number one disseminator of academic material to the business community. The *Harvard Business Review* has a paid circulation of over 200,000 and a claimed readership of one million, almost all of whom are senior business managers.[14] While the school's MBA and executive programs generate about $50 million a year in revenue, the school's publishing unit—which produces and markets books, videos, case studies, and the *Harvard Business Review*—was expected to generate about $70 million in revenue in 1993.[15] All of this material goes out over the HBS logo, giving Harvard outstanding brand equity among managers who hire MBAs.

Limitations:

- Like most large schools, the HBS does not excel in overall student satisfaction, as measured by the 1992 *Business Week* Top 20 survey, coming in instead at number 12 of the schools included in the survey.[16] Small schools (e.g., Dartmouth, Virginia, Cornell) are more collegial, and the students tend to give these small schools higher grades on overall satisfaction at the time of graduation.[17]

- Harvard students have a reputation for being highly competitive, a characteristic said to be encouraged by the case method and the grading system. Not everyone would be comfortable in this environment.

---

11 Evidence to support the "small business hypothesis" was found in a 1990 survey of the Harvard MBA Class of 1970—after twenty years, what were the alumni doing? Only 13 percent worked for Top 1000 firms and only four of the 723 alumni of the Harvard Class of '70 were CEOs of Top 1000 firms. The great majority were entrepreneurs or managers in small businesses. See "Class Reunion," *Business Week*, June 18, 1990, pp. 162–163.

12 As shown in appendix B, the average quality of incoming students—as measured either by GMAT scores or pre-MBA pay—is the most significant business school characteristic to explain school-to-school differences in THE MBA ADVANTAGE

13 *Harvard Business School MBA Program Catalog*, 1994, p. 8.

14 Rate Card number 38 and Subscriber Profiles, *Harvard Business Review*, January 1993.

15 Fuchsberg, G., "Harvard Weighs One-Year Version of MBA Program," *The Wall Street Journal*, October 29, 1993.

16 *Business Week Guide to the Best Business Schools*, 3rd Edition, p. 80.

17 See the perceptual maps in appendix A of graduate rankings and corporate rankings versus school size.

- The HBS curriculum is under review and there has been some discussion of offering a one-year MBA as well as the current two-year degree. One possibility that has been discussed is to target the one-year degree at prospective students with substantial work experience, while allowing students right out of college to take the two-year degree.[18] (Currently, all students admitted to the present two-year degree have some work experience.) Reportedly, the one-year MBA has been dropped for the present, according to a recent article in *The Chronicle of Higher Education.*[19] Another proposed change would promote more teamwork by converting up to 25 percent of the first year coursework from the case method to projects courses that would require teams of students to work with outside clients.[20]

- Although most Harvard professors put teaching ahead of research, some put outside consulting ahead of teaching and are never in their offices to meet with students outside of class. The HBS has tried to implement steps to insure faculty availability.

- Finally, the Harvard Business School is not a good choice for those who want to build careers as technical specialists in marketing research, security analysis, and so forth. Harvard's declared mission is to develop general managers.

Harvard does not publish starting salaries in its catalog nor does it distribute a placement report. *U.S. News & World Report* estimated that Harvard's 1992 median starting salary *without* signing bonuses was $65,000.[21] *Business Week* reported that Harvard's 1992 median starting pay *with* signing bonuses was $83,000.[22] Tom Fischgrund, in his 1993 edition of *The Insider's Guide to the Top 10 Business Schools*, states that starting salaries for Harvard's grads in consulting are in the $70,000 to $80,000 range, and investment banking jobs—with starting salaries of $50,000—may triple that number with bonuses and commissions.[23]

Harvard Admissions Statistics (Graduating Class of 1994)[24]

Class size	815	Mean GMAT score	(not required; 640 est.)[25]
Median age	26	Women	29%
Years of work experience	4	International	25%
Percentage with work experience	100%	Minorities	14%

Annual tuition and fees: $21,950

Contact: MBA Admissions, Harvard Business School
             Soldiers Field Road, Boston, Massachusetts 02163
             Telephone: (617) 495-6127

---

18 Fuchsberg, G., "Harvard Weighs One-Year Version of MBA Program," *The Wall Street Journal*, October 29, 1993.
19 Jacobson, R., "Shaking Up the MBA," *The Chronicle of Higher Education*, December 15, 1993.
20 Bongiorno, L., "A Case Study in Change at Harvard," *Business Week*, November 15, 1993, p. 42.
21 "America's Best Graduate Schools," *U.S. News & World Report*, March 22, 1993, p. 58.
22 *Business Week Guide to the Best Business Schools*, 3rd Edition, p. 128.
23 Fischgrund, T., *The Insider's Guide to the Top 10 Business Schools*, 5th Edition, Little, Brown and Company, 1993, p. 93.
24 *Harvard Business School MBA Program Catalog*, 1994.
25 "America's Best Graduate Schools," *U.S. News & World Report*, March 22, 1993, p. 58.

NUMBER 2: CHICAGO

The University of Chicago Graduate School of Business

Accounting	★★★★★
Consulting	★★★★★
Finance	★★★★★
General management	★★★★
Marketing	★★★

Rankings:

MBA ADVANTAGE rank (1994) 2
U.S. News & World Report rank (1993) 9
Business Week corporate rank (1992) 4
Business Week graduate rank (1992) 10

Overview:

The University of Chicago Graduate School of Business is a world class research institution with an exceptionally strong reputation in finance and economics. It has a curriculum that is one of the most innovative and flexible of any major business school. For prospective students interested in finance who would enjoy attending business school in a large, dynamic city that is an international center of commerce, Chicago would be hard to beat.

Strengths:

- Chicago is an intellectual powerhouse. With seven Nobel Prizes in economics in less than twenty years, the Chicago school of free-market economics has won as many Nobels as MIT, Stanford, and Harvard combined.[26] Research at Chicago in business economics, finance, and behavioral science has greatly influenced management education at other schools over the past two decades.

- Chicago is also very perceptive about the changing market for management education. In 1989, it was the first business school to introduce a nontraditional required learning experience for incoming students (the LEAD program) that provides workshops, seminars, and team projects to develop leadership skills. The LEAD program—run by second-year students with input from faculty and corporate sponsors—is another innovation in management education from Chicago that has been adopted by many other business schools.

- As might be expected at a research powerhouse, the Chicago faculty was ranked number 1 in the currency of material used in the classroom, according to the 1992 *Business Week* Top 20 survey, and was ranked number 3 (behind MIT and Rochester) in terms of being at the leading edge of their fields.

---

26 Nasar, S., "Nobels Pile Up for Chicago . . . ," The *New York Times*, November 4, 1993, p. D1.

- As shown in the placement statistics, Chicago specializes in finance, and many consider its curriculum in finance to be the best in the world.

- Chicago was one of the first business schools to offer projects courses in which teams of second-year MBAs work as consultants to companies in the areas of new product development and organizational design.

- The Chicago curriculum is unusually flexible and students.are encouraged to customize their programs. Incoming students are required to take only three core courses (microeconomics, financial accounting, and statistics) plus one functional course (e.g., financial management or marketing management) plus the LEAD program. The remaining courses may be selected from a menu of hundreds of electives.

- Chicago has a network of 29,000 alumni, many of whom are in top level jobs.

- The school's location in Hyde Park, about two miles from the center of the city of Chicago, provides exceptional access to managers and senior executives in many of the world's leading companies.

Limitations:

- Although teaching is taken seriously at Chicago, the university is first and foremost a research institution. As one Nobel laureate remarked recently, "Chicago is downright unpleasant for anyone not totally immersed in research."[27] Overall satisfaction of the graduates is about average (ranked number 10 in the 1992 *Business Week* survey), and students complain about lack of faculty accessibility. This may change however—the new dean, Robert Hamada, was featured in a 1982 *Fortune* article about the best *teachers* in American business schools.[28]

- As a large school (550 students in each class) there is less collegiality between students and faculty than at smaller schools such as Dartmouth and Cornell.

- In view of the school's location near the center of a large city, some students may be uneasy about personal safety, although the university takes many precautions to ensure the safety of students on campus.

Chicago Admissions Statistics (Graduating Class of 1995)

Class size	550	Mean GMAT score	642
Average age	27	Female	21%
Average years of work experience	4	Minorities	6%
Percent with work experience	95%		

Annual tuition and fees: $20,497

---

27 Ibid.
28 Richman, L., "B-School Students' Favorite Profs," *Fortune*, January 25, 1982, pp. 72–79.

Chicago Placement Statistics (Graduating Class of 1992)

Chicago Starting Salaries by Functional Area (Class of 1992; bonuses and commissions excluded[29])

	% of Accepted Offers	Range	Median
Finance	49%	$21,000–$107,000	$53,000
Consulting	21%	$38,000–$100,000	$70,000
Marketing	12%	$37,000–$62,000	$53,000
General management	4%	$41,500–$67,500	$55,000
Control and accounting	4%	$32,000–$60,000	$50,400

Chicago Starting Salaries by Type of Industry (top 10, Class of 1992)

	% of Accepted Offers	Range	Median
Commercial banking	16%	$26,560–$75,000	$55,000
Investment banking/brokerage	15%	$21,000–$80,000	$52,500
Consulting	15%	$42,000–$100,000	$70,000
Accounting (consulting)	7%	$32,000–$85,000	$65,000
Investment management	5%	$36,000–$107,000	$56,000
Household products	5%	$21,600–$59,000	$55,000
Electronics	5%	$40,000–$67,500	$50,400
Pharmaceuticals	5%	$28,500–$60,000	$53,000
Food/beverage/tobacco	5%	$49,000–$56,500	$55,000
Transportation services	4%	$44,000–$55,000	$53,000

Chicago Starting Salaries by Geographic Area (Class of 1992)

	% of Offers	Mean
Chicago	23%	$57,500
Other Midwest	16%	$54,102
New York City	22%	$57,031
Other Mid-Atlantic	8%	$57,484
International	12%	$55,941
West Coast	9%	$55,674
New England	5%	$60,706

Contact: Office of Admissions and Financial Aid
The University of Chicago
Graduate School of Business
1101 East 58th Street
Chicago, Illinois 60637
Telephone: (312) 702-7369

---

29 *Placement Report*, 1991-92, The University of Chicago Graduate School of Business.

NUMBER 3: STANFORD

Stanford University Graduate School of Business

Accounting	★★★★★
Consulting	★★★★★
Entrepreneurship	★★★★★
Finance	★★★★★
General management	★★★★★
Marketing	★★★★★
Operations	★★★
Nonprofit	★★★★★

Rankings:

MBA ADVANTAGE rank (1994) 3
U.S. News & World Report rank (1993) 2
Business Week corporate rank (1992) 7
Business Week graduate rank (1992) 5

Overview:

The Stanford Graduate School of Business attracts exceptionally bright students. Unlike schools that focus on specialized functional skills in finance or marketing, the Stanford program emphasizes broad general management education, and the number one job choice of Stanford grads is management consulting. With strong ties to the entrepreneurial Silicon Valley area, the school promotes a culture that encourages and supports risk taking and new venture formation—and the magnificent Stanford campus is among the most beautiful in the world. Prospective students interested in consulting or high tech general management should put Stanford at the top of their list.

Strengths:

- Stanford attracts perhaps the brightest students of any business school. Although Stanford does not publish its average GMAT, *U.S. News & World Report* estimates that it is as high as 680 which, if correct, is thirty points higher than that of any other business school.[30] This shows up in Stanford's selectivity—for the Class of 1994, there were 4,109 applications for the 359 seats in the class.

- The emphasis of the program is on educating general managers. The first year of the program consists of twelve required core courses which may be exempted by passing written exams so that additional electives can be taken. In the second year, there are no concentration requirements, and students are free to chose any combination of electives, including as many as four courses in other schools of the university. A joint elec-

---

30 "America's Best Graduate Schools," *U.S. News & World Report*, March 22, 1993, p. 58.

tive course with the engineering school puts MBAs in the machine shop with engineering graduate students to design actual new products.

- In addition to the seventy-eight regular faculty members, the school has thirty-two part-time lecturers, some of whom are successful entrepreneurs from nearby Silicon Valley who teach courses in entrepreneurship and the management of technology.

- The starting pay at Stanford is second only to Harvard's, and it grows rapidly after the first year. In a 1992 survey of the Class of 1987, the average pay of those responding was $144,500—again, second only to Harvard.[31]

- In the same survey of the Class of '87, 99 percent of the Stanford alums said they would choose Stanford again—a higher long-term satisfaction percentage than any other business school.[32]

- The beautiful Bay Area Stanford campus—known affectionately as "The Farm"—is a major attraction, as are the incomparable resources of Stanford University, one of the great research universities of the world.

Limitations:
- Many Stanford grads find the Bay Area so attractive they won't leave after graduation; 46 percent of the graduating class of 1993 stayed in California. Recruiters from other parts of the country find it difficult to attract Stanford graduates, and some companies have given up.

- Stanford MBAs also have a preference for small companies—17 percent choose firms having fewer than fifty employees and almost half the class finds employment with companies having fewer than 1,000 employees. This also may have discouraged recruiters from some *Fortune* 500 companies.

Stanford Admissions Statistics (Graduating Class of 1994)			
Class size	359	Mean GMAT score	650-680 [33]
Average age	27	Female	28%
		International	18%
		Minorities	23%

Annual tuition and fees: $20,196

---

31 *Business Week Guide to the Best Business Schools*, 3rd Edition, p. 17.
32 Ibid., p. 15.
33 Stanford does not publish an average GMAT score. Stanford's average GMAT was estimated to be 650 by *Business Week* and 680 by *U.S. News & World Report*.

Stanford Placement Statistics (Graduating Class of 1992)

Stanford Starting Salaries (Class of 1992)[34]

Percent of Positions	Salary Levels
7%	Under $50,000
27%	$50,000–$59,999
20%	$60,000–$69,999
34%	$70,000–$79,000
12%	$80,000 and over
Median Salary:	$65,000

Stanford Placements by Industry (Class of 1993)[35]

	% of Accepted Offers
Management consulting	24%
Investment banking	10%
Entrepreneurs	8%
Financial services	7%
Computer manufacturing	6%
Consumer products	4%
Diversified manufacturing	3%
Media/telecommunications	3%
Foundations/nonprofit/government	2%
Pharmaceutical/medical products	2%
Other manufacturing	7%
Other non-manufacturing	8%
Undecided	16%

Stanford Placements by Geographic Area (Class of 1993)

	% of Accepted Offers
Northern California	37%
International	18%
New York City	13%
Southern California	9%
Other East Coast	8%
Midwest	5%
Southwest	4%
Rocky Mountain	2%
Washington, D.C.	2%
Northwest	1%
South	1%

Contact: MBA Admissions Office
Graduate School of Business
Stanford University
Stanford, California 94305-5015
Telephone: (415) 723-2766

---

34 *The MBA Program Catalog*, Autumn 1994, Stanford University Graduate School of Business.
35 *Career Management Center Report*, November 1993, Stanford University Graduate School of Business.

NUMBER 4: MIT

Sloan School of Management

Consulting	★★★★★
Entrepreneurship	★★★★
Finance	★★★★★
Marketing	★★★★
Information systems	★★★★★
Operations	★★★★★

Rankings:

MBA ADVANTAGE rank (1994) 4

U.S. News & World Report rank (1993) 6

Business Week corporate rank (1992) 10

Business Week graduate rank (1992) 14

Overview:

The Sloan School of Management at MIT is a small business school that benefits greatly from its association with one of the world's finest engineering schools. As former Dean Lester C. Thurow has stated: "The days of an MBA degree in general management are over. . . . Our strategy is to be seen as the best place in the world where technology and management meet."[36] The Sloan School is a superb choice for preparing students, particularly those with engineering backgrounds, for careers in consulting, finance or manufacturing management—and the Boston area is a major cultural and historical center.

Strengths:

- MIT faculty members were ranked number 1 in being at the leading edge of their fields in the 1992 *Business Week* Top 20 survey.

- Consulting is the most popular career option for Sloan graduates, with a median starting salary in 1993 of $75,000 which with a signing bonus can raise first-year pay to as high as $100,000 (see placement statistics). McKinsey & Co. and Booz Allen recruit heavily at MIT, as do a number of other consulting firms.

- One MIT faculty member, Stewart Myers, "wrote the book" on finance. Co-authored with Richard Brealey of the London School of Business, Brealey and Myers' *Principles of Corporate Finance* is the standard finance text in many MBA programs.

- A major revision in the curriculum was introduced in 1993. Traditional concentrations previously required were made optional. The number of required core courses was reduced and compressed into the fall quarter of the first year. In the spring quarter of

---

36 *The Master's Program Catalog 1994-95*, Sloan School of Management, p. 7.

the first year, students can begin on one of four "tracks:" Global Strategic Management in Consulting, Financial Engineering ("rocket science applied to Wall Street"), Financial Management, or Product Development and Management—or they can design their own track. These tracks continue into the second year, with over a hundred electives to choose from. Sloan students can also register to take a limited number of courses at nearby Harvard.

- The Leaders in Manufacturing Program, a special twenty-four-month option with a six-month internship at a sponsoring company, is a joint program of the Sloan School and the College of Engineering. Graduates receive two masters degrees, one in management and the other in engineering.

- Sloan faculty are deeply involved in international management opportunities for teaching and research.

- Boston, across the river from Cambridge, is home to more than fifty colleges and universities and is a major cultural and historical center.

Limitations:
- The facilities at the Sloan School are showing their age and are in need of repair and expansion. They suffer in comparison with the opulence of the Harvard Business School nearby.

- Sixty percent of the incoming students have undergraduate degrees in science or engineering, giving the school a "techie" culture that can make some students with nontechnical backgrounds uncomfortable.

- MIT's main competition is Stanford, which enjoys the advantages of California weather, a beautiful rural campus, and the ambience of Silicon Valley.

- The quality of teaching has been somewhat uneven, particularly in the core courses.

Sloan Admissions Statistics (Graduating Class of 1994)

Class size	225	Median GMAT score	650
Average age	27	Female	27%
Average years of work experience	5	Minorities	13%
International	33%		

Annual tuition and fees: $20,500

Sloan Placement Statistics (Class of 1993)

Sloan Starting Salaries by Top Functional Areas (base salaries only)[37,38]

	% of Accepted Offers	Range		Median
Overall	100%	$40,000-$120,000		$65,000
		25th percentile	75th percentile	
Consulting	34%	$70,000	$75,000	$75,000
Finance	18%	$53,500	$65,000	$55,800
Operations/manufacturing	17%	$60,000	$67,800	$64,800
Marketing/sales	12%	$55,000	$60,800	$59,500

Sloan Starting Salaries by Type of Industry (top 3)

	% of Accepted Offers	Range		Median
		25th percentile	75th percentile	
Consulting	30%	$75,000	$78,000	$75,000
Investment banking	16%	$55,000	$65,000	$57,000
Electronics/computers	15%	$56,700	$64,800	$60,000

Contact: Marilyn Mendel Han
             Director of Admissions
             MIT Sloan School of Management
             The Master's Program, Room E52-112
             50 Memorial Drive
             Cambridge, Massachusetts 02142-1347
             Telephone: (617) 253-3730

---

37 Ibid., p. 70.
38 In 1993, 66 percent of the graduates also received signing bonuses that ranged from $2,000 to $25,000. The average bonus was about $5,000.

NUMBER 5: YALE

School of Organization and Management at Yale University

Consulting	★★★★★
Finance	★★★★
General management	★★★★
Marketing	★★
Nonprofit	★★★★★

Rankings:

MBA ADVANTAGE rank (1994) 5
U.S. News & World Report rank (1993) 17
Business Week corporate rank (1992) . . . . (NR)
Business Week graduate rank (1992) . . . . (NR)

Overview:

The School of Organization and Management at Yale University offers prospective students a small, collegial business school associated with a distinguished Ivy League university. The Yale curriculum is unique in its emphasis on combining non-profit and government management along with the more traditional MBA subjects. For those interested in broad issues of private and public management, the Yale School of Management is hard to beat.

Strengths:

- Organized in 1975, the Yale School of Organization and Management (SOM), started with the enormous advantage of its association with Yale, the third most prestigious university in the country,[39] and the Yale name continues to give it distinction.

- Excellent students (an average GMAT of 647 and five years of work experience) and small size (225 in the entering class) give SOM an intellectual intensity found in few other business schools. The students are very bright, are older and more demanding, and expect a great deal from the school and from the faculty.

- In addition to preparing graduates for positions in private industry, SOM's Master's in Public and Private Management degree is also designed to teach students about the role of government and the interactions that occur between business and government. About 30 percent of the incoming students leave jobs in the public or non-profit sectors to attend SOM, and 15-20 percent of the SOM graduates accept jobs in the public or non-profit sectors after graduation.

- In 1992, SOM graduates received the highest two-year STEP UP (starting pay divided by

---

39 "America's Best Colleges," *U.S. News & World Report*, 1993 Edition, pp. 26-27.

pre-MBA pay) of any of the top schools, 75.4 percent. This is a reflection, perhaps, of the relatively low paying jobs many SOM students give up to attend business school.

- The SOM curriculum contains the usual set of core courses but also includes special courses on soft topics such as organizations, leadership, and institutions. In the second year, students are required to take a two-course sequence in one of the functional areas, such as marketing, and are then free to select courses from other parts of the university. The SOM catalog suggests that second year students consider a wide range of courses taught outside SOM, such as Chinese Politics and Forest Ecotoxicology.

- SOM emphasizes cooperation among students over competition. Grading has three levels, *proficient*, *pass*, and *fail*, and no GPA or class standing statistics are calculated.

- The Yale campus offers SOM students an almost unlimited breadth of resources. The campus is located near downtown New Haven, Connecticut, a New England city situated on Long Island Sound 75 miles from New York City and 135 miles from Boston.

Limitations:

- Despite the abundance of resources from its association with Yale, SOM has been through turbulent times during the last few years as a result of controversial changes made by a previous dean. The school is now in a period of consolidation and rebuilding.

- Like other young, small business schools, the school has relatively few alumni in high places to assist graduating students, although Yale alumni from other schools of the university have been willing to play a mentoring role to students.

Yale Admissions Statistics (Graduating Class of 1995)			
Class size	225	Mean GMAT score	647
Average age	27	Female	36%
Years of work experience	5	International	35%
		Minorities	11%

Annual tuition and fees: $20,220

Yale Placement Statistics (Graduating Class of 1992)

Yale Starting Salaries by Functional Area (Class of 1992)[40]

	% of Accepted Offers (Classes of 1988–1992)	Median (Class of 1992)
Finance	30%	$55,000
Project management, consulting	26%	$65,000
General management	11%	$55,000
Marketing, sales	11%	–
Production, service operations	4%	$52,000
Planning	3%	$100,000
Personnel, public relations	2%	$55,000
Engineering, research	1%	–
Accounting, control	1%	$60,000
Information systems	1%	$47,000
Other	10%	$46,000

Yale Placements by Industry (Classes of 1988–1992)

	% of Accepted Offers
Private Sector Manufacturing	20%
Computers	5%
Consumer products	4%
Pharmaceuticals	1%
Automotive	1%
Electronics	1%
Petroleum	1%
Energy	1%
Food/beverage	1%
Other	5%
Private Sector Non-Manufacturing	60%
Management consulting	16%
Investment banking	13%
Commercial banking	8%
Consulting (other than management)	4%
Real estate	2%
Publishing/printing	1%
Advertising	1%
Communications	1%
Diversified financial	1%
Other	13%
Non-Profit Sector	8%
Hospitals, health care, education, economic development, social work	
Public Sector	6%
Federal government, state and local government, multinational agencies	
Other	5%
Continuing education	

Contact: MPPM Admissions Office, Yale School of Organization and Management
Box 1A, New Haven, Connecticut 06520. Telephone: (203) 432-5932

40 *Yale School of Organization and Management Catalog*, 1993-94.

NUMBER 6: NORTHWESTERN

J. L Kellogg Graduate School of Management at Northwestern University

Consulting	★★★★★
Finance	★★★
General management	★★★★
Marketing	★★★★★
Operations	★★★★
Nonprofit	★★★★

Rankings:

MBA ADVANTAGE rank (1994) 6
U.S. News & World Report rank (1993) 4
Business Week corporate rank (1992) 1
Business Week graduate rank (1992) 3

Overview:

The J. L. Kellogg Graduate School of Management at Northwestern University has been ranked number 1 by students and employers in many business school surveys in recent years. The school is best known for its outstanding program in marketing. Kellogg also places a sizeable percentage of its graduates in consulting. In addition to its regular two-year master's program, the school offers a special one-year program for students who have undergraduate degrees in business. It also offers a joint master's program with the engineering school in manufacturing management. Teamwork is the underlying culture of the Kellogg program, and all prospective students are interviewed prior to admission to assess their potential to work well with others. Prospective students interested in marketing should make Kellogg their first choice, and the school is an excellent choice for consulting and manufacturing management as well.

Strengths:

* Kellogg has been ranked Number 1 in a number of business school surveys over the past decade. Long before the rankings of business schools were front page stories in business magazines, Kellogg had high aspirations. "You're darn tootin' we want to be Number 1 in our field! What's wrong with that?" said Kellogg dean Donald Jacobs in a 1981 *Wall Street Journal* interview.[41] In the 1960s and '70s, Kellogg was not viewed as a serious contender against schools like Harvard, Stanford, and Chicago, but in 1985, a survey of 134 of the largest manufacturing and service companies sponsored by *The Wall Street Journal* ranked Kellogg number 1 for producing the best MBA graduates.[42] Kellogg was singled out as "best value" to employers in terms of what graduates produce in relation to their salaries. When *Business Week* began surveying corporate recruiters and graduat-

---

41 Klein, F., "Northwestern's School of Business Scrambles onto the Fast Track," *The Wall Street Journal*, January 20, 1981.
42 Mackay-Smith, A., "Survey Says Top Business Schools May Not Be Top Business Schools," *The Wall Street Journal*, October 11, 1985.

ing students in 1988, Kellogg was again ranked number 1, a position it continued to occupy through the 1990 and 1992 *Business Week* surveys. Clearly, there is value in holding a degree from the school that has been consistently rated the best in its field.

- Kellogg places great emphasis on teaching quality and on overall student satisfaction, as reflected in the school's number 3 position in the 1992 *Business Week* graduate ranking. Among large schools, Kellogg is unique in having such high student satisfaction (see perceptual map in figure A.1, appendix A).

- In addition to the GMAT and the usual application forms, every candidate for admission at Kellogg is personally interviewed. A senior faculty member commented that in the interviewing process "we look for people who know how to get along with others." Says Dean Donald P. Jacobs, "We look for active, bright, caring people. We don't have loners with sharp elbows for students."[43] This is consistent with the school's emphasis on teamwork.

- Kellogg is on the quarter system, and there are nine required core courses in the first year. Students may substitute electives for core courses that are comparable to courses they have already taken (approximately half of all students waive one or more courses). Kellogg offers majors in seventeen different areas, and almost all students major in more than one area (e.g., finance and marketing). Students are also free to customize their own program and may take as many as all of their electives in other graduate schools of the university.

- In additional to its two-year (six-quarter) master's program, Kellogg also offers a one-year (four-quarter) master's program for students with undergraduate degrees in business. Students in the one-year program enter in June, take a special summer program to complement their undergraduate business degree, and join the second-year class of the regular two-year program in September.

- For students interested in careers in manufacturing, Kellogg offers a two-year joint Master of Management in Manufacturing degree with Northwestern's engineering school. A business outreach program—the Technology Innovation Center—is also associated with this program. This Center includes a commercialization center for new product ideas and an incubator building for housing startup companies.

- Evanston, Illinois, a peaceful residential community of tree-lined streets and Victorian homes, is located on the shore of Lake Michigan twelve miles north of the center of Chicago. Kellogg students have the dual advantages of a quiet suburban campus setting and excellent access by public transportation to one of the world's great financial and commercial centers.

Limitations:

- The Kellogg School is housed in Leverone Hall, a 1972 classroom building that is overcrowded and somewhat dated. A renovated 30,000 square foot expansion scheduled for completion in 1994 will improve this situation.

---

43 *Business Week Guide to the Best Business Schools*, 3rd Edition, p. 65.

- Although Kellogg is highly ranked in surveys of students and employers, the financial return on the degree, as measured by THE MBA ADVANTAGE, is not as high as that of its neighbor school, Chicago, even though its incoming students are of about the same quality (see figures B.4 and B.5 in appendix B).

Kellogg Admissions Statistics (Graduating Class of 1995)[44]

Class size	582	Mean GMAT score	640[45]
Average age	27	Female	31%
Average years of work experience	4	International	26%
Percent with work experience	99%	Minorities	14%

Annual tuition and fees: $19,698

Kellogg does not publish an average starting salary figure. The 1992 *Business Week* Top 20 survey of graduating students reported a median starting pay for the Class of '92 (with signing bonuses included) of $64,750 and a mean starting pay of $70,200.[46] *U.S. News and World Report* estimated the median Class of '92 starting salary (*without* bonuses) at $55,000.[47]

Kellogg Placement Statistics (Graduating Class of 1993)

Kellogg Starting Salaries by Major Function [48]

	% of Accepted Offers	Range
Overall	100%	$25,000–$110,000
Consulting	27%	
Product management	17%	
Corporate finance/sales and trading	15%	
General management	7%	
Operations/production	7%	
Financial analyst	2%	
Investment management/research	1%	
Planning	1%	
Real estate	1%	

Kellogg Salary Ranges by Years of Work Experience Prior to Enrollment

	% of Class	Range
Less than 2 years of work experience	1%	$28,000–$54,000
2-3 years	13%	$30,000–$78,000
3-5 years	72%	$30,000–$102,000
More than 5 years	14%	$25,000–$100,000

---

44 *Kellogg Full-Time Program Catalog*, 1994.
45 Kellogg does not publish an average GMAT score. Kellogg's average GMAT was estimated to be 640 by *Business Week* and 635 by *U.S. News & World Report.*
46 *Business Week Guide to the Best Business Schools*, 3rd Edition, p. 64.
47 "America's Best Graduate Schools," *U.S. News & World Report*, March 22, 1993, p. 58.
48 *Kellogg Full-Time Program Catalog*, 1994.

Contact: Office of Admissions
            J. L. Kellogg Graduate School of Management
            Northwestern University
            Leverone Hall
            2001 Sheridan Road
            Evanston, Illinois 60208-2003
            Telephone: (708) 491-3308

NUMBER 7: BERKELEY

Walter A. Haas School of Business of the University of California at Berkeley

Consulting	★★★★
Entrepreneurship	★★★★
Finance	★★★★
Marketing	★★★★
Information systems	★★★★

Rankings:

MBA ADVANTAGE rank (1994) 7
U.S. News & World Report rank (1993) 14
Business Week corporate rank (1992) 19
Business Week graduate rank (1992) 13

Overview:

The Walter A. Haas School of Business of the University of California at Berkeley offers strong programs in marketing, finance and consulting at a bargain price—$3,612 tuition and fees for California residents and $11,312 for non-residents. The school places 46 percent of its graduates in the Bay Area and 32 percent in international positions in Asia, Western Europe, and Eastern Europe. Haas combines the informality of a small school with the prestige of a major university, and is located in a beautiful campus overlooking San Francisco Bay.

Strengths:

- Finance (32 percent of job placements) and marketing (21 percent) are the two major strengths of the Haas School. The largest categories of hires are marketing product managers (19 percent) and financial analysts (15 percent).

- International placements account for 32 percent of job acceptances, with Asia (15 percent) the favorite destination.

- The cost of attending Haas is exceptionally low. The in-state tuition and fees are an incredible bargain at $3,612 per year. For non-residents, the tuition and fees are $11,312—still very low compared to other top schools—and in many cases students may be able to qualify as California residents for their second year to get the in-state rate.

- A brand new building complex for the Haas School is scheduled to open in December 1994. At a cost of $45 million, the new mini-campus will consist of three state-of-the-art pavilions set around a central courtyard.

- Like Cornell's Johnson School, Berkeley's Haas School is a small business school (class size of 218) located in a major university, so students enjoy the best of both worlds: the collegiality and adaptability of a small school and the resources of an internationally renowned university.

- The curriculum is flexible. Core courses may be waived by taking waiver exams. Haas students may take as many as six electives from other graduate programs at the university. The school does not have rigid concentration requirements—students can design their own program of electives—but a distribution requirement ensures breadth of exposure across disciplines.

- In keeping with the high-tech image of California, Haas offers a concentration on Information Technology Management and a joint program with the College of Engineering on the Management of Technology. The Haas School also has special programs on Entrepreneurship and on Real Estate Development.

- In the second year every student is required to carry out an applied management project—either an original research project or a consulting project with a local firm.

- The Berkeley campus, with its magnificent view across the bay of San Francisco and the Golden Gate Bridge, is exceptionally beautiful.

Limitations:

- Almost half (46%) of all Haas graduates accept jobs in the Bay Area, and another 32 percent take jobs overseas. This leaves fewer than 50 students who take jobs in other parts of the United States, which may not be enough to attract large numbers of corporate recruiters from around the country. Consequently, the Haas School does relatively poorly on national polls of recruiters (it ranked number 19 on the *Business Week* corporate recruiter survey).

- Continuing problems with the California state budget have created a major budget crunch at Berkeley. Some of the best professors at Berkeley have either left or are considering leaving.[49]

Haas Admissions Statistics (Graduating Class of 1995)[50]

Class size	218	Median GMAT score	640
Average age	27	Female	39%
Average years of work experience	5	Minorities	21%
% with work experience	90%	International	27%

Annual tuition and fees: $3,612 (resident); $11,311 (nonresident)

---

49 "Facing 4th Year of Cuts, Berkeley Chancellor Leads Budget Revolt," *The New York Times*, May 12, 1993.
50 Haas School of Business: The MBA Programs Catalog, Fall 1994.

Haas Placement Statistics (Graduating Class of 1993)[51]

Haas Starting Salaries by Functional Areas (Top 10)

	% of Accepted Offers	Range	Average
Overall	100%	$30,000–$100,000	$58,734
Product management	19%	$30,000–$76,000	$55,059
Financial analysis	15%	$50,000–$100,000	$58,675
Consulting (general management)	14%	$43,000–$85,000	$67,969
Investments (sales and trading)	8%	$50,000–$100,000	$63,200
General management	8%	$44,000–$60,000	$53,500
Corporate finance	4%	$65,000–$74,000	$67,500
Consulting (financial and investment)	4%	$55,000–$70,000	$61,667
Consulting (technology)	4%	$45,000–$80,000	$61,000
Information systems	4%	$34,000–$75,000	$52,000
Real estate development	3%	$50,000–$62,000	$55,000

Haas Starting Salaries by Type of Industry (top 10)

	% of Accepted Offers	Range	Average
Consulting	14%	$34,000–$85,000	$65,750
Investment banking/portfolio management	12%	$50,000–$100,000	$62,500
Commercial banking	11%	$40,000–$100,000	$62,600
Consumer products	11%	$48,000–$60,000	$54,583
Computer hardware	9%	$50,000–$75,000	$55,938
Public accounting	7%	$45,000–$85,000	$59,400
Computer software	6%	$45,000–$76,000	$61,000
Telecommunications	8%	$44,000–$65,000	$53,750
Education/non-profit/govt.	5%	$30,000–$60,000	$46,667
Real estate/construction	5%	$50,000–$62,000	$55,900

Haas Starting Salaries by Geographic Area (Top 10)

	% of Accepted Offers	Range	Average
San Francisco Bay Area	46%	$30,000–$80,000	$56,320
Asia	15%	$40,000–$100,000	$65,563
Northeast	10%	$50,000–$100,000	$64,792
Western Europe	9%	$50,000–$85,000	$64,875
Central/South America	4%	$55,000–$74,000	$65,250
Eastern Europe	4%	$52,000–$52,000	$52,000
Northern California	3%	$50,000–$75,000	$59,667
Southern California	2%	$42,000–$62,000	$54,667
Midwest	2%	$45,000–$50,000	$47,667
Pacific Northwest	1%	(Insufficient data)	$54,750

Contact: Fran Hill, Director of MBA Admissions
Haas School of Business
University of California
Berkeley, California 94720
Telephone: (510) 642-1405

---

51 Walter A. Haas School of Business, MBA Placement Report–1993.

NUMBER 8: WHARTON

The Wharton School of the University of Pennsylvania

Accounting	★★★★★
Consulting	★★★★★
Entrepreneurship	★★★★★
Finance	★★★★★
General management	★★★★★
Marketing	★★★★★
Operations	★★★
Nonprofit	★★★★

Rankings:

MBA ADVANTAGE rank (1994) 8
U.S. News & World Report rank (1993) 3
Business Week corporate rank (1992) 2
Business Week graduate rank (1992) 15

Overview:

The Wharton School at the University of Pennsylvania is considered by many to be the best school in finance, and consulting is another major strength. Unlike many top schools that prepare their students exclusively for careers in the *Fortune* 500, Wharton has a long tradition of entrepreneurship among its graduates. For prospective students interested in finance or consulting who have non-technical liberal arts degrees, Wharton should be near the top of their list.

Strengths:

- Finance is Wharton's historical strength. Surveys by both *Business Week* and *U.S. News & World Report* give it the edge over second-ranked Chicago.[52] About 40 percent of Wharton's graduates take jobs in finance, although another 27 percent take high-paying jobs in consulting (see placement statistics).

- Despite the emphasis on finance, 43 percent of Wharton's incoming students have liberal arts backgrounds. Any deficiencies in quantitative skills are corrected in a four-week pre-term at the start of the first year.

- Over the past two years, Wharton has been phasing in a totally new curriculum based on extensive marketing research carried out by the school. The traditional core courses in economics, statistics, accounting, and so forth can be waived based on prior experience or preparation. New required first-year courses in leadership and strategic management are designed to improve "soft skills," and an optional four-week Global Immersion course takes students overseas at the end of the first year. In the second year, students work with companies on actual consulting assignments that are designed

---

52 *Business Week Guide*, 3rd Ed., p. 9, and *U.S. News & World Report*, March 22, 1993, p. 59.

to demonstrate their multidisciplinary skills. Students can pursue majors in more than twenty different functional areas, or they can design their own programs by selecting from 200 elective courses offered at Wharton.

- Wharton has a tradition of graduating aggressive entrepreneurs, including John Sculley, Saul Steinberg, Michael Milken, and Donald Trump. Says Trump, "First they taught you all the rules and regulations. Then they taught you that those rules and regulations are meant to be broken; it's the person who can create new ideas who is really going to be the success."[53] Both Steinberg (who pioneered computer leasing) and Milken (who invented the junk bond) claim that their innovative ideas began as student papers they wrote at Wharton.[54]

Limitations:

- Wharton is one of the largest graduate business schools (second only to Harvard) and also has a large undergraduate business program. It may not appeal to students who prefer a smaller, more collegial school.

- The buildings and other facilities at Wharton are below par for a leading business school. And safety is a concern. Leaving the urban campus near the center of Philadelphia requires reasonable precautions, although a campus van escort service is available to students after hours.

- The entrepreneurial tradition of Wharton extends to the faculty, who are often away on consulting assignments instead of in their offices. Although the faculty is very knowledgeable, particularly about current business practices, teaching quality is rated lower than that of most of the other top business schools.

Wharton Admissions Statistics (Graduating Class of 1994)[55]

Class size	735	Median GMAT score	640
Average age	27	Female	27%
Average years of work experience	4	Minorities	13%
Percent with work experience	99%	International	32%

Annual tuition and fees: $19,928

---

53 Greene, R., "Their Eyes on the Main Chance," *Forbes*, March 9, 1987, p. 69.
54 Ibid.
55 Wharton MBA Program Catalog 1994–95.

Wharton Placement Statistics (Graduating Class of 1993)[56]

Wharton Starting Salaries by Top Functional Areas

	% of Accepted Offers	Range	Median
Overall	100%	$12,000–$112,000	$62,000
Consulting (general management)	27%	$35,000–$120,000	$75,000
Corporate finance	21%	$40,000–$110,000	$55,000
Brand/product management	9%	$12,000–$100,000	$59,000
Financial analysis/treasury	7%	$48,000–$87,000	$57,500
General management	5%	$25,000–$90,000	$58,230
Investments sales and trading	6%	$40,000–$90,000	$55,000
Investment management/research	5%	$50,000–$100,000	$60,000
Strategic planning	3%	$43,000–$110,000	$59,500
Health care consulting	2%	$55,000–$85,000	$70,000
Health care management	1%	$30,000–$90,000	$42,000

Wharton Starting Salaries by Type of Industry (top 10)

	% of Accepted Offers	Range	Median
Consulting	22%	$47,200–$120,000	$75,000
Investment banking/brokerage	16%	$30,000–$95,000	$55,000
Commercial banking	12%	$40,000–$110,00	$55,000
Accounting (consulting)	8%	$35,000–$85,000	$70,000
Household/personal products	4%	$12,000–$100,000	$58,000
Government/not-for-profit	2%	$50,000–$75,000	$55,000
Diversified financial services	2%	$43,000–$80,000	$55,000
Food/beverage/tobacco	2%	$43,000–$70,000	$59,000
Computers	2%	$51,660–$87,000	$56,500
Investment management	2%	$50,000–$85,000	$65,000

Wharton Starting Salaries by Geographic Area

	% of Accepted Offers	Range	Mean
Northeast	43%	$30,000–$110,000	$63,000
International	20%	$12,000–$120,000	$70,000
Mid-Atlantic	17%	$30,000–$110,000	$60,500
Midwest	7%	$33,000–$87,000	$59,000
West	5%	$25,000–$80,000	$67,500
South	5%	$40,000–$75,000	$58,000
Southwest	2%	$50,000–$85,000	$75,000

Contact: The Admissions Office, Graduate Division
The Wharton School
University of Pennsylvania
102 Vance Hall
3733 Spruce Street
Philadelphia, Pennsylvania 19104-6361
Telephone: (215) 898-6183

56 The Wharton School MBA Placement Survey 1993.

NUMBER 9: UCLA

The John E. Anderson Graduate School of Management at UCLA

Accounting	★★★
Consulting	★★★
Entrepreneurship	★★★★★
Finance	★★★★
General management	★★★★
Marketing	★★★★
Operations	★★★

Rankings:

MBA ADVANTAGE rank (1994) 9
U.S. News & World Report rank (1993) 15
Business Week corporate rank (1992) 16
Business Week graduate rank (1992) 11

Overview:

The John E. Anderson Graduate School of Management at UCLA places special emphasis on the balance between theory and practice. Although faculty research is highly valued, the school also requires every student to carry out a practical, hands-on field study with an outside company in the second year. Entrepreneurship is a distinguishing strength of the Anderson School. As with most state-supported schools, the cost of an MBA at Anderson is a terrific bargain. And then there's the beaches and sunshine of Southern California. If the Los Angeles lifestyle appeals to you, UCLA may be your best choice.

Strengths:

- Entrepreneurship is strong at the Anderson School. Evidence of this is its required core course in Operations *and* Technology Management; most programs have a required core course in Operations Management *only*. The Entrepreneurial Studies Center has become a major force for change at the school with both coursework and extracurricular activities for the entrepreneurial student. The Center includes a mentoring program with successful entrepreneurs, a small business consulting service, a venture capital proposal competition, and an entrepreneurs-in-residence program. The student-run Entrepreneur Association has over 400 members, many of whom plan to start their own businesses some day.

- Anderson is on the quarter system. All students must take twenty-four courses, including eleven core courses. Waivers of some of the core courses are permitted based on exams or transcripts, but courses waived must be replaced with other courses.

- In the second year, students can pick and choose from a wide range of electives and can take as many as three electives outside the business school. There is no requirement to declare a major, so students are free to customize their second-year programs.

- An unusual feature of the second year program is a two-quarter management field study project required of every student. Under the guidance of a faculty advisor, teams of three to five students carry out comprehensive consulting assignments for client organizations. The hands-on field study replaces the more traditional Business Policy capstone course found in many MBA programs, and the final report of each field study team satisfies the requirement for a comprehensive exam for the MBA degree. More than 900 organizations have sponsored one or more field studies, including such leading firms as Apple Computer, Ben and Jerry's, Ford Motor Company, Goldman Sachs, Major League Baseball, Mattel, Toyota, Turner Broadcasting, and the Walt Disney Corporation.

- A brand new $74 million seven-building complex for the Anderson School will be completed in 1995. Set in the beautiful Stone Canyon Creek area of the campus, the new complex has been designed to be "the world's finest management education facility."

- Like other state-supported schools, tuition and fees at the Anderson School are an exceptional bargain. Out-of-state residents pay less than $12,000 a year for a first-class MBA program, and under some circumstances may qualify for the $4,026 in-state tuition and fees in their second year.

- The second largest city in the United States, L.A. is home to multi-billion dollar companies as well as thousands of startups. As a major gateway to the Pacific Rim, L.A. is well-positioned for international commerce in the twenty-first century. UCLA is a big city school, and the faculty is not isolated. Professors have the opportunity to get out in the real world and test their theories by working as consultants.

- Finally, there's the L.A. lifestyle . . . the beaches . . . the palm trees . . .

Limitations:

- UCLA suffers from the same budget crunches that other state-supported universities are enduring. The winding down of California's defense industries has made these budget constraints more intense in the past few years.

- Not everyone is cut out for the L.A. lifestyle. Concerns about freeway traffic jams, earthquakes, brush fires, mudslides, the high cost of living and the aftermath of the L.A. riots may discourage the less adventuresome from attending UCLA.

Anderson Admissions Statistics (Graduating Class of 1995)[57]

Class size	370	Mean GMAT score	633 [58]
Average age	28	Female	31%
Average years of work experience	5	International	19%
Percent with work experience	99%	Minorities	19%

Annual tuition and fees: $4,026 (resident); $11,725 (non-resident)

---

57 Anderson 1993 MBA Program Placement Report.
58 For the Class of 1994, as reported in "America's Best Graduate Schools," *U.S. News & World Report*, March 22, 1993, p. 58.

Anderson Placement Statistics (Graduating Class of 1993)

Anderson Starting Salaries by Major Function [59]

	% of Accepted Offers	Range	Mean
Overall	100%	$28,000–$155,000	$59,208
Finance	39%	$30,000–$99,600	$58,100
Marketing	22%	$28,000–$76,000	$54,600
Consulting	16%	$45,000–$85,000	$65,600
General management	11%	$42,500–$155,000	$60,800
Accounting	5%	$41,000–$74,000	$60,700
Entrepreneur	2%	$40,000–$65,000	$55,000
Other (includes operations mgmt. and MIS)	4%	$45,000–$61,500	$56,700

Anderson Starting Salaries by Industry (Manufacturing)

	% of Accepted Offers	Range	Mean
Food/beverage/tobacco	9%	$45,000–$84,000	$63,000
Electronics	5%	$51,000–$75,000	$60,300
Household/personal products	5%	$45,000–$75,000	$59,900
Petroleum/energy	4%	$58,000–$70,000	$61,700
Pharmaceuticals/biotech/health care mfg.	3%	$57,000–$75,000	$64,000
Other manufacturing	8%	$48,000–$70,000	$57,000
Manufacturing subtotal	34%	$40,000–$84,000	$60,500

Anderson Starting Salaries by Industry (Non-Manufacturing)

	% of Accepted Offers	Range	Mean
Financial services	31%	$30,000–$99,600	$56,700
Consulting	18%	$45,000–$85,000	$67,400
Accounting	4%	$41,000–$70,000	$58,500
Entertainment	3%	$45,000–$75,000	$64,800
Computer related services	2%	$55,000–$60,000	$58,800
Hospitality services	2%	$43,000–$60,000	$54,500
Other non-manufacturing	6%	$45,000–$155,000	$55,200
Non-manufacturing subtotal	66%	$28,000–$155,000	$61,400

Anderson Starting Salaries by Geographic Area

	% of Accepted Offers	Range	Mean
West Coast	68%	$28,000–$155,000	$59,900
East Coast	15%	$28,000–$65,000	$54,000
International	9%	$30,000–$85,000	$60,700
Midwest	8%	$40,000–$60,000	$56,000

Contact: John E. Anderson Graduate School of Management at UCLA
MBA Admissions Office, Suite 3371
405 Hilgard Avenue
Los Angeles, California 90024-1448. Telephone: (310) 825-6944

---

59 Ibid.

NUMBER 10: VIRGINIA

Darden Graduate School of Business Administration at the University of Virginia

Consulting	★★★★
Finance	★★★★
General management	★★★★★
Marketing	★★★
Operations	★★

Rankings:

MBA ADVANTAGE rank (1994) 10
U.S. News & World Report rank (1993) 11
Business Week corporate rank (1992) 15
Business Week graduate rank (1992) 2

Overview:

The Darden Graduate School of Business Administration at the University of Virginia—sometimes referred to as the "Harvard of the South"—emphasizes the development of general management skills. Teaching is carried out by the case method and is of outstanding quality, as measured by the satisfaction of graduating students. For those who would like to receive a Harvard-style education in a small, collegial school located in a picturesque college town, Darden should be at the top of their list.

Strengths:

- Darden puts teaching first. Research is not allowed to interfere with good teaching and no faculty member gets tenure if he or she is not a good teacher. Despite the lack of emphasis on faculty research, Darden was ranked number 4 in the currency of material presented in class in the 1992 *Business Week* Top 20 survey. Not surprisingly, the school was ranked number 2 in overall satisfaction of the graduating class in the 1992 *Business Week* survey.

- Although graduates take entry-level jobs in finance, marketing and consulting, the curriculum focuses on general management. Courses and cases are structured to look at "the big picture" as well as the technical functional details.

- Darden is a strong advocate of the case method. The process of analysis gets much attention, and students learn that it is as important to know what questions to ask as it is to know the right answers. As a result of analyzing hundreds of cases in the two year program, students build valuable skills in defending their own decisions and constructively challenging the conclusions of others to develop at the best overall plan of action. The school takes a teamwork approach to case analysis.

- Darden offers the virtues of a small school with the reputation and resources of a large, highly-regarded university. Relations between students and faculty are collegial, and morning coffee and conversation with the faculty is a Darden tradition.

- The first-year curriculum, taken in sixty-student cohorts, is a nine-month-long integrated course, with modules on Accounting, Marketing, Ethics, Quantitative Methods and five other core areas which are phased in and out at various times during the course of the year. There are no waivers from any of these modules.

- In the second year, students take a required course in Strategy, Leadership and Change (to "master the art of strategic analysis and innovative thinking") followed by Directed Study, which involves either a hands-on field study with major firms like Pepsico and British Petroleum, the development of a new case for classroom use, or the writing of an individual research paper of publishable quality. The remainder of the second year is spent on electives in the traditional functional areas of finance, marketing, and so forth.

- The University of Virginia, founded by Thomas Jefferson in 1819, is located in Charlottesville, a picturesque town of 40,000 in central Virginia near the foothills of the Blue Ridge Mountains, about two hours from Washington, D.C. The business school is scheduled to move into a new building in 1994.

Limitations:
- Darden is famous for its heavy first-year workload, reportedly sixty to eighty hours per week. Although most students survive and go on to graduate, the first year is an arduous experience.

- Charlottesville, although in a beautiful rural setting, is rather isolated. The nearest large city is Richmond, seventy-four miles to the East. Faculty have few nearby consulting opportunities to build business contacts who might aid the placement effort, and most recruiters have a long distance to travel to reach the campus.

- Like most state-supported institutions, the University of Virginia is operating under serious budget constraints. The Darden School has launched a major capital campaign to provide resources for future growth and development.

Darden Admissions Statistics (Graduating Class of 1995)

Class size	252	Mean GMAT score	627
Average age	27	Female	33%
% with work experience	99%	International	14%
		Minorities	17%

Annual tuition and fees: $8,655 (resident); $16,055 (non-resident)

Darden Placement Statistics (Graduating Class of 1993)

Class of 1993 Average Starting Salary (excluding guaranteed bonuses): $56,838 [60]

Darden Placement by Functional Area—Darden does not publish a statistical breakdown of Salaries by Functional Area

	% of Accepted Offers
Finance	33%
Consulting	19%
Marketing	15%
General management	11%
Operations	5%
Corporate planning	5%
Other	12%

Darden Placement by Industry —Darden does not publish a statistical breakdown of Salaries by Industry

	% of Accepted Offers
Manufacturing	32%
Food/beverage/tobacco	5%
Consumer goods	5%
Electronics	4%
Transportation	4%
Pharmaceuticals	3%
Other	12%
Services	68%
Consulting	20%
Investment banking	14%
Commercial banking	7%
Financial services	5%
Other	22%

Placement by Geographic Area—Darden does not publish a statistical breakdown of Salaries by Geographic Area

	% of Accepted Offers
Northeast	31%
Mid-Atlantic	23%
West / Southwest	13%
International	12%
Midwest	11%
South / Southeast	10%

Contact: Office of Admissions
            The Darden School
            University of Virginia
            P.O. Box 6550
            Charlottesville, VA 22906-6550
            Telephone: (804) 924-7281 or toll free (800) UVA-MBA-1

---

60 Darden 1993 Graduating Class Profile.

NUMBER 11: CORNELL

S. C. Johnson Graduate School of Management

Accounting	★★★★
Consulting	★★★★
Finance	★★★★★
General management	★★★★
Marketing	★★★★
Operations	★★★★

Rankings:

MBA ADVANTAGE rank (1994) 11
U.S. News & World Report rank (1993) 12
Business Week corporate rank (1992) 17
Business Week graduate rank (1992) 4

Overview:

The S. C. Johnson Graduate School of Management at Cornell University is a small business school that combines excellence in teaching, high faculty research productivity, an unusually collegial atmosphere between students, faculty and administration, a flexible curriculum, and the comprehensive resources of a major world-class university. The Johnson School is an excellent choice for prospective students interested in preparing for careers in finance, consulting, marketing or operations management, and who prefer attending business school in a beautiful small town setting.

Strengths:

- Cornell MBA graduates are among the most satisfied with their program of any business school graduates, according to the 1992 *Business Week* Top 20 survey, which ranked Cornell number 4 in overall graduate customer satisfaction.

- Teaching quality is very high, ranking number 3 in both the first-year core courses and the second-year elective courses, according to the *Business Week* survey.

- Faculty research productivity is also very high, as shown in figure 14.1 on page 238. This demonstrates that high research productivity and excellence in teaching can coexist in a business school.

- The Johnson School offers the informality and friendliness of a small school combined with the resources and reputation of Cornell, one of the world's great universities. In the second year, Johnson MBA students are permitted to take as many as five of the twenty courses needed for the MBA in other parts of the university—from art history to zoology. A dual-degree program with the College of Engineering leads to a Master of Engineering and an MBA in five semesters.

- Exceptional flexibility is a major advantage of the Johnson School program. Students may be exempted from taking any or all of the first-year core courses by passing special exemption examinations given during orientation; they can then take more advanced courses in the first year. In the second year, there are no rigid requirements for concentrations in finance, marketing, or other functional areas. Students are encouraged to design their own customized program of electives.

- Collegiality between the administration, the faculty, and the students is a hallmark of the Johnson School. During the first semester, the Dean invites incoming students to his home for an informal dinner. Johnson students comment on the accessibility of the faculty—they're always in their offices.

- The Cornell campus is situated in a beautiful natural setting of hills and waterfalls in the heart of the Finger Lakes Region overlooking Cayuga Lake, away from pressures and grime of big cities. Local residents sport bumper stickers proclaiming "Ithaca is gorges." You can even board your horse at Cornell.

Limitations:

- The relative isolation of Ithaca, New York, which can make attending Cornell so enjoyable, is an impediment for building close alliances with industry. This makes it somewhat difficult to arrange student projects with local companies. The nearest big cities are Syracuse and Rochester, both of which are more than an hour's drive away. This isolation is also a disadvantage for corporate recruiters. New York City is 250 miles to the southeast.

- Malott Hall, the home of the Johnson School, is an older building that is not as up-to-date as the new facilities of many of the other top schools. However, a major building program for the Johnson School is underway.

Johnson Admissions Statistics (Graduating Class of 1994)

Class size	271	Mean GMAT score	640
Average age	27	Female	24%
Average years of work experience	4	Minorities	6%
Percent with work experience	92%		

Annual tuition and fees: $19,500

Johnson Placement Statistics (Graduating Class of 1993)

Johnson Starting Salaries by Functional Area (signing bonuses excluded from these figures)[61]

	% of Offers	Range	Mean
Overall	100%	$37,000–$130,000	$56,500
Finance	35%	$45,000–$130,000	$60,490
Marketing	18%	$37,000–$100,000	$55,573
Consulting	18%	$38,000–$80,500	$59,500
Operations and engineering	9%	$47,000–$58,000	$52,564
General management	6%	$55,000–$60,000	$59,500
Accounting and auditing	5%	$43,000–$57,500	$52,000
Human resources	3%	$48,000–$57,500	$53,000
Real estate	3%	$54,000–$55,000	$54,500
Other	3%	$49,000–$59,000	$54,000

Johnson Starting Salaries by Type of Industry (top 10)

	% of Offers	Range	Mean
Consulting	18%	$38,000–$80,500	$59,500
Commercial banking	12%	$52,000–$80,000	$57,500
Investment banking	12%	$50,000–$125,000	$68,000
Financial services (non-banking)	9%	$50,000–$130,000	$63,500
Consumer products	9%	$55,000–$60,000	$57,000
Electronics	8%	$38,000–$58,000	$51,500
Pharmaceuticals	6%	$55,000–$60,000	$57,000
Chemicals, energy, petroleum	5%	$48,000–$57,500	$49,250
Industrial products	5%	$42,500–$60,000	$51,500
Accounting and auditing	4%	$43,000–$60,000	$49,500

Johnson Starting Salaries by Geographic Area (top 5)

	% of Offers	Range	Mean
New York City	34%	$45,000–$100,000	$57,500
Midwest	13%	$45,000–$60,000	$54,500
New England	12%	$38,000–$130,000	$60,500
Mid-Atlantic	10%	$40,000–$75,000	$55,500
International	10%	$48,000–$125,000	$78,000

Contact: Office of Admissions
             Johnson Graduate School of Management
             Cornell University
             315 Malott Hall
             Ithaca, New York 14853-4201
             Telephone: (607) 255-2327 or toll free (800) 847-2082

---

61 *Placement Report 1993*, Career Services Office, S.C. Johnson Graduate School of Management.

NUMBER 12: MICHIGAN

The Michigan Business School of the University of Michigan

Accounting	★★★
Consulting	★★★★
Finance	★★★★
General management	★★★★★
Marketing	★★★★★
Operations	★★★★

Rankings:

MBA ADVANTAGE rank (1994) 12
U.S. News & World Report rank (1993) 5
Business Week corporate rank (1992) 6
Business Week graduate rank (1992) 9

Overview:

The Michigan Business School of the University of Michigan has a highly innovative curriculum that requires first-year students to carry out seven weeks of on-site process re-engineering studies at leading companies all over the country. The marketing program at Michigan is first rate, with excellent median starting salaries. The Midwest college town setting and the attractions of Big Ten sports are added inducements.

Strengths:

- The new Michigan MAP (Multidisciplinary Action Project) is a highly innovative multidisciplinary project experience that takes place in the second semester of the first year. Teams of students spend seven weeks on-site at sponsoring companies all over the country, carrying out consulting assignments to re-engineer key business processes under the general supervision of faculty coaches. At the end of the on-site visit, the teams submit detailed written reports to senior management that include specific recommendations for improving the processes under study. In 1993, over 400 first-year students worked on sixty different projects at forty-eight sponsoring companies.[62] Dean B. Joseph White considers this experience similar to that of medical students attending rounds in a hospital with experienced physicians.[63]

- Marketing—with 24 percent of the placements and higher median starting salaries than finance—is stronger at Michigan than at most other business schools.

- Michigan has a flexible curriculum. Waivers are available for most of the required core courses based on prior study and professional experience, or by passing a waiver exam.

---

62 *The MBA Newsletter*, July, 1993, p. 7.
63 Sheridan, J., "A New Breed of MBA," *Industry Week*, October 4, 1993, p. 16.

In the second year, students can focus in one functional area or can customize their program from 130 electives. In addition, they can take up to ten hours in other graduate programs in the university.

- Michigan runs a series of non-degree executive short courses (one to five weeks in length) that were rated best in the country in a recent *Business Week* survey.[64] Executives are a demanding audience for business school faculty, and teaching executives is a great way for faculty to learn about the issues facing senior executives. Michigan uses the materials from their successful executive programs to continually improve their regular MBA program.[65]

- The University of Michigan provides the resources of a major research university. The buildings and classroom facilities for the business school are modern and comprehensive, not to mention football at Michigan Stadium, the nation's largest open-air college arena.

- The campus setting combines the natural friendliness of Midwesterners and the charm of Ann Arbor—a true college town located about twenty-five minutes from the Detroit metropolitan airport.

Limitations:
- Because the school is not located in a major center of commerce (i.e., New York, Chicago, or Boston), students interested in banking and investment management may feel at a disadvantage. About half of all Michigan grads accept jobs in the Midwest.

- A few students with prior work experience have grumbled about the MAP program, claiming that they didn't come to business school to spend seven weeks in a factory again.

Michigan Admissions Statistics (Graduating Class of 1994)

Class size	420	Mean GMAT score	621
Median age	26	Female	24%
Percent with work experience	96%	Minorities	29%
		International	15%

Annual tuition and fees: $19,964 (non-resident); $13,314 (resident)

---

64 *Business Week's Guide to the Best Executive Education Programs*, McGraw Hill, 1993, p. 14.
65 *The Michigan 1994 MBA Catalog*, p. 20.

Michigan Placement Statistics (Graduating Class of 1993)

Michigan Starting Salaries by Top 10 Functional Areas (Class of 1993)[66]

	% of Offers	Range	Median
Overall	100%	$15,000–$127,000	$60,622
Corporate finance (mfg.)	16%	$45,000–$86,000	$58,250
Consulting (service)	11%	$28,600–$115,000	$75,000
Product management (mfg.)	11%	$49,600–$105,000	$65,000
Marketing (sales/retail: service)	8%	$54,000–$100,000	$62,600
Corporate finance (service)	8%	$42,000–$99,000	$53,000
Commercial banking	6%	$43,000–$80,000	$63,400
Investment banking	5%	$50,000–$116,000	$80,000
General management	4%	$52,000–$85,000	$65,100
Marketing (sales/retail: mfg.)	4%	$40,000–$80,100	$52,100
Strategic planning (mfg.)	3%	$51,000–$127,000	$64,000

Michigan Starting Salaries by Type of Industry (top 10)

	% of Offers	Range	Median
Consulting	15%	$42,000–$115,000	$71,750
Automotive	14%	$42,000–$86,000	$54,900
Consumer goods	13%	$48,000–$84,000	$62,600
Chemicals	8%	$46,000–$78,000	$60,000
Computers	8%	$37,000–$105,000	$60,500
Commercial banking	6%	$15,000–$80,000	$60,000
Financial services	6%	$28,600–$100,000	$61,500
Investment banking	5%	$50,000–$116,000	$75,000
Public accounting	4%	$38,000–$70,000	$51,750
Telecommunications	3%	$45,000–$95,565	$57,350

Michigan Starting Salaries by Geographic Area (top 5)

	% of Offers	Range	Median
Midwest (mfg.)	28%	$37,000–$92,000	$56,100
Midwest (service)	20%	$28,000–$115,000	$56,750
Northeast (service)	13%	$38,000–$116,000	$75,000
Northeast (mfg.)	12%	$46,000–$99,000	$62,600
West (mfg.)	9%	$36,750–$105,000	$62,850

Contact: Judith A. Goodman
             Assistant Dean for Admissions
             Michigan Business School
             The University of Michigan
             Ann Arbor, Michigan 48109-1234
             Telephone: (313) 764-5139

---

66   1993 MBA Placement Report, The Michigan Business School.

NUMBER 13: DARTMOUTH

The Amos Tuck School at Dartmouth College

Consulting	★★★★
Finance	★★★★
General management	★★★★★
Marketing	★★★
Operations	★★

Rankings:

MBA ADVANTAGE rank (1994) 13
U.S. News & World Report rank (1993) 8
Business Week corporate rank (1992) 12
Business Week graduate rank (1992) 1

Overview:

The Amos Tuck School at Dartmouth College is the most collegial of the top business schools, with top-rated teaching quality and a very close-knit relationship among the students and between the students and faculty. The quality of the incoming students—as measured by GMAT scores and pre-MBA pay—is excellent. The curriculum focuses on general management rather than functional specialization, and the greatest number of jobs are found in consulting and financial services. For prospective students interested in a general management curriculum taught by outstanding teachers in a beautiful Ivy League liberal arts college setting, Tuck may be their best choice.

Strengths:

- Tuck is a teaching-oriented business school. MBA teaching has first priority; as the catalog points out, Tuck has no Ph.D. program to distract the faculty. This strategy of maximizing student satisfaction has been successful—Tuck was ranked number 1 in overall satisfaction of graduating students in the 1992 *Business Week* Top 20 survey, and number 2 (behind Stanford) in *Business Week's* 1992 survey of satisfaction of graduates who had been on the job for five years.[67]

- The emphasis is on general management. Tuck believes that students should avoid functional overspecialization at the expense of broad, integrative learning. In the second year of the program, students are free to choose from among fifty electives, and there are no requirements for a functional concentration in finance, marketing, and so forth.

- The first year of the program contains the usual core courses found in most MBA programs (there are no waivers) plus a pair of integrative projects courses where students carry out consulting assignments for actual business clients.

- Although Tuck is a small school, it has a very active alumni group. In 1992 the alumni donated $1.5 million, and 62 percent of the alumni participated in the giving program,

---

67 *Business Week Guide to the Best Business Schools*, 3rd Edition, 1992, p. 29, 15.

the highest percentage of any graduate business school. Tuck alumni go out of their way to support the school by interviewing applicants, working with students on class-room projects, and helping graduates launch their careers.

- Tuck attracts students of excellent quality. The average GMAT score of the incoming class is 650, about the same as MIT's and Harvard's. Tuck students give up high-paying jobs to attend business school—typically about $50,000, just below the pre-MBA pay of Harvard and Stanford (see chapter 4).

- Tuck is easily the most collegial of all the top business schools. Founded in 1769 and a member of the Ivy League, Dartmouth views itself as the quintessential liberal arts col-lege, and this tradition carries over to the Tuck School. First-year students live in dorms on campus adjacent to the classroom buildings. The students and faculty are an ex-tremely close-knit group, associating not only in class but also socially after hours and on weekends. Teamwork and cooperation are stressed.

- Hanover is a charming rural New England college town situated on the Connecticut River on the border between New Hampshire and Vermont, about two hours by car from Boston. Outdoor life is extremely popular and the athletic environment is very supportive—no one is cut from intramural sports teams. The campus is close to many ski areas and the White Mountains of New Hampshire are nearby.

Limitations:
- Although the students are first rate and overall satisfaction with teaching quality is tops, these advantages have not translated into a high MBA ADVANTAGE rank. One would ex-pect Tuck to rank much higher than number 13. The reasons for this are not clear but there are several possibilities:

  1. The students are already earning significantly higher-than-average salaries when they come to Tuck, so they have to capture very high paying post-MBA jobs to receive a high MBA ADVANTAGE (recall that the MBA ADVANTAGE measures the cumulative *dif-ference* in pay between going to business school and not going to business school). Tuck students do get high paying jobs upon graduation, but the school's two-year MBA STEP UP—the ratio of post-MBA starting pay to pre-MBA pay—is relatively low, ranked number 19 among the top schools, and the growth rate of post-MBA pay in the first five years on the job is only about average, at number 11 (see chapter 4).

  2. As shown in chapter 14, there is statistical evidence of a positive association between faculty research and the magnitude of THE MBA ADVANTAGE—schools with high fac-ulty research activity tend to provide their students with a high MBA ADVANTAGE. Perhaps the relative lack of emphasis on faculty research at Tuck, compared to many other business schools, is in part a cause of the school's lower-than-expected "value multiplier" ranking.

  3. The isolation and small size of the school may make it less rewarding for corporate recruiters to travel to the campus for interviewing. Tuck was ranked only number 12 on the *Business Week* recruiter survey, far below what the quality of the students (as measured by GMAT scores and pre-MBA pay) would predict.

- In spite of these concerns, Tuck is an excellent school. Graduating students just may have to work harder to get the top flight jobs they deserve.

Tuck Admissions Statistics (Graduating Class of 1994)[68]

Class size	183	Mean GMAT score	650
Average age	27	Female	28%
		International	23%
		Minorities	9%

Annual tuition and fees: $19,950

Tuck Placement Statistics (Graduating Class of 1993)

Tuck Starting Salaries by Major Function [69]

	% of Accepted Offers	Range
Finance	40%	$50,000–$75,000
Consulting	30%	$50,000–$95,000
Marketing	13%	$50,000–$65,000
General management	7%	$40,000–$75,000
Planning	4%	$40,000–$75,000

Tuck Placements by Major Industry

	% of Accepted Offers	Range
Financial services	38%	$50,000–$75,000
Consulting	22%	$50,000–$95,000
Consumer products	8%	$53,000–$65,000
Pharmaceutical/health care	5%	$56,000–$70,000
Electronics	2%	$54,000–$64,000

Tuck Placements by Geographic Area

	% of Accepted Offers	Range
Middle Atlantic	45%	$50,000–$80,000
New England	27%	$40,000–$90,000
Midwest	8%	$50,000–$75,000
West	5%	$50,000–$95,000
Europe	4%	$54,000–$75,000
Other International	9%	$40,000–$75,000

Contact: Admissions Office, The Amos Tuck School
Dartmouth College
100 Tuck Hall
Hanover, New Hampshire 03755-9030. Telephone: (603) 646-3162

---

68 The Tuck School MBA Program Catalog, 1993-1994.
69 Ibid.

NUMBER 14: CARNEGIE MELLON

Graduate School of Industrial Administration at Carnegie Mellon University

Consulting	★★★★
Finance	★★★★
Marketing	★★★★
Information systems	★★★★★
Operations	★★★★★

Rankings:

MBA ADVANTAGE rank (1994) 14
U.S. News & World Report rank (1993) 13
Business Week corporate rank (1992) 9
Business Week graduate rank (1992) 23

Overview:

The Graduate School of Industrial Administration (GSIA) at Carnegie Mellon University is best known for the application of state-of-the-art computerized quantitative analysis to the functional areas of finance, consulting, and operations management. GSIA is an excellent choice for students with undergraduate degrees in math, science, or engineering who would like to accelerate their careers by leveraging the rapidly expanding power of computerized management information systems.

Strengths:

- Carnegie Mellon is famous as a "quant" school. Two semesters of calculus are required before entering, and 57 percent of the incoming students have undergraduate degrees in either engineering (38 percent), science (10 percent) or math/computers (9 percent). Only 2 percent have a liberal arts background.[70]

- Research plays a dominant role at GSIA. Three Nobel prize winners began their academic careers at the school, and current MBA students benefit greatly from the tradition of intellectual excellence in economics, finance, and organization theory. Faculty pride themselves in presenting new material in class long before it is available in textbooks.

- Carnegie Mellon is a world class pioneer in applying computers to management problems. It was the first business school in the world to acquire a computer in the late 1950s, and it continues to lead in the application of computers in manufacturing management and securities analysis. For example, the MBA elective course in Financial Analysis and Security Trading (FAST) includes a trading room equipped with the same high-powered workstations, real-time data feeds, and market analysis software used by

70 *The Master's Program Catalog, 1994-94*, Graduate School of Industrial Administration, Carnegie Mellon University.

major Wall Street firms, enabling GSIA students to actually try out trading strategies in stocks, bonds, and options.

- The computerized "management game" is another GSIA innovation played by all students in the second year. Teams of five to seven students negotiate their company's financing with bankers from the Pittsburgh area and their labor contracts with representatives from local unions. The game is highly competitive—GSIA students compete through the school's international computer network with business students in Tokyo, Mexico City, and Sweden. Like the real world, it demands effective multidisciplinary decision-making under pressure.

- Instead of semesters or quarters, the curriculum is organized into seven-week mini-semesters (four per academic year) to enable the students to take a wider range of courses.

- By taking a full course load during the summer after the first year, it is possible to complete the program in sixteen months, graduating in December of the second year. The tradeoff is the loss of the summer internship, which is very valuable for most students.

- GSIA is a small school (190 in each class) in a small but highly regarded university. Flexibility within the school and between the school and the rest of the university provides many opportunities for students to become involved in multidisciplinary projects.

- In the spring of 1993, GSIA moved into a new facility with state-of-the-art classrooms, seminar rooms, and meeting areas. The Carnegie Mellon campus is located in Pittsburgh, the fifth largest corporate headquarters city in the United States and home base to eleven *Fortune* 500 companies.

Limitations:

- The first-year workload at GSIA is more demanding than at most other top business schools. The seven-week mini-semesters go by at a fast clip and the quantitative orientation of the program means many late nights crunching numbers in the computer center.

- Since most incoming students have degrees in math, science, or engineering, GSIA may not appeal to students with a liberal arts background.

Carnegie Mellon Admissions Statistics (Graduating Class of 1994)

Class size	190	Mean GMAT score	638
International	17%	Female	25%
		Minorities	9%

Annual tuition and fees: $19,600

Carnegie Mellon Placement Statistics (Graduating Class of 1993)

Carnegie Mellon Starting Salaries by Functional Area (only guaranteed annual salaries are reported).[71]

	% of Accepted Offers	Range	Mean
Overall	100%	$40,000–$86,200	$58,401
Finance	28%		$54,926
Consulting	24%		$66,773
Marketing	13%		$56,566
Production/operations	8%		$55,524
Information systems	6%		$54,000
Planning	6%		$52,400
Investment banking	5%		$61,600
Banking operations	5%		$58,500
Other	5%		$55,418

Carnegie Mellon Starting Salaries by Type of Industry (top 10)

	% of Accepted Offers	Mean
Consulting	25%	$65,740
Manufacturing	11%	$55,886
Computer hardware/software	12%	$56,782
Investment banking	7%	$54,556
Other	7%	$52,333
Commercial banking	7%	$63,125
Communications	7%	$57,938
Consumer goods	6%	$50,871
Automotive	6%	$54,057
Chemicals	5%	$56,000

Carnegie Mellon Starting Salaries by Geographic Area (top 6)

	% of Accepted Offers	Mean
Northeast	46%	$59,253
West	18%	$59,802
Midwest	17%	$57,590
International	10%	$56,126
Southeast	8%	$55,535
Southwest	1%	$52,500

Contact: Susan Motz
Director of Admissions
Graduate School of Industrial Administration
Carnegie Mellon University
Schenley Park
Pittsburgh, Pennsylvania 15213
Telephone: (412) 268-2272

---

71 *Employment Statistics 1993*, Carnegie Mellon Graduate School of Industrial Administration.

NUMBER 15: TEXAS

Graduate School of Business at The University of Texas at Austin

Accounting	★★★★★
Consulting	★★★
Entrepreneurship	★★★★★
Finance	★★
Marketing	★★★
Information systems	★★★★★
Operations	★★

Rankings:

MBA ADVANTAGE rank (1994) 15
U.S. News & World Report rank (1993) 18
Business Week corporate rank (1992) . . . . (NR)
Business Week graduate rank (1992) . . . . (NR)

Overview:

The Graduate School of Business (GSB) at The University of Texas at Austin offers very strong programs in information systems management and in accounting. Located in an area of fast-growing technology-based companies, the GSB has a number of innovative research and outreach programs with local firms, including an incubator building for launching new high-tech businesses. The GSB is worth serious consideration by prospective students interested in the management of information systems or the management of high technology firms. To sweeten the offer, the cost of attending is exceptionally low, even for non-residents of Texas.

Strengths:

- Information systems management is a distinguishing strength of the Texas MBA program. Of special interest is Classroom 2000, a computerized technological showcase sponsored in part by IBM to enhance the information systems concentration.

- The GSB teaching philosophy promotes hands-on experience in the field. Since 1992 several leading companies, including Procter & Gamble, 3M, and Motorola, have offered students the opportunity to be an integral part of customer-focused teams working on site with suppliers and retailers as part of the companies' on-going Total Quality Management programs.

- Accounting is another area of leadership for the GSB. A tradition of leadership in this area began in the 1920s when the school hired scholars to produce better accounting textbooks. In addition to the MBA, the GSB also offers a Master in Professional Accounting degree for students interested in public accounting or in accounting specialties such as taxation.

- In the first year, students take a structured set of core courses similar to those at most other business schools. In the second year, however, the program is very flexible. There are no specific concentration requirements, and students choose from among 170 electives according to their specific career interests.

- Much of the research at the GSB is focused on technology management and entrepreneurship. The school is associated with the Center for the Study of Innovation, Creativity, and Capital; another Center for Technology Venturing; and the Austin Technology Incubator, which since its startup in 1990 has nurtured thirty-four fledgling enterprises providing 500 full-time jobs. Each year more than 150 GSB students participate in incubator-related programs involving high-technology firms. The school also operates a Bureau of Business Research in which faculty and students carry out economic research and respond to more than 5,000 inquiries a year from the business community for data and economic information.

- The cost of attending the GSB, $7,340, is extraordinarily low, even for non-residents. This is a high quality program at a bargain price.

- The campus is located in downtown Austin, a high-tech boomtown that was recently rated by *Fortune* as the fifth best city in the country for knowledge-based industries.[72] The area is home to companies like Dell Computer, IBM, Apple, and Motorola. And the weather is great—300 sunny days a year.

Limitations:

- The GSB may have an image problem with some of its corporate customers. In 1992 the school was dropped from the *Business Week* Top 20 rankings after corporate recruiters complained that the quality of graduates was uneven and placement office services for companies were below par. As with most state-supported schools, making improvements under tight state budget constraints will be a difficult problem.

Texas Admissions Statistics (Graduating Class of 1995)[73]

Class size	420	Average GMAT score	634
Average age	26	Female	30%
Average years of work experience	4	International	18%
Percent with work experience	96%	Minorities	18%

Annual tuition and fees: $3,148 (residents); $7,340 (non-residents)

---

72 Labich, K., "The Best Cities for Knowledge Workers," *Fortune*, November 15, 1993, p. 60.
73 *MBA/MPA Employment Profile 1992-1993*, Graduate School of Business, University of Texas-Austin.

Texas Placement Statistics (Graduating Class of 1993)[74]

Texas Starting Salaries by Functional Area

	% of Offers	Range	Mean
Overall	100%	$29,000–$100,000	$49,000
Finance	43%	$28,000–$95,000	$48,000
Marketing	22%	$30,000–$53,000	$49,000
Information systems	16%	$31,500–$65,000	$48,000
Management	15%	$28,000–$100,000	$50,000
Accounting	4%	$30,000–$55,000	$41,000

Texas Starting Salaries by Type of Industry: Manufacturing

	% of Offers	Range	Mean
Computers	9%	$32,000–$69,000	$50,500
Consumer goods	7%	$42,000–$60,000	$51,000
Automotive/transportation	4%	$36,000–$50,400	$43,500
Food and beverage	3%	$42,000–$72,500	$53,000
Petroleum refining	3%	$45,000–$100,000	$62,000
Medical/pharmaceutical	3%	$46,000–$60,000	$52,500
Other manufacturing	1%	$53,000–$75,000	$64,000

Texas Starting Salaries by Type of Industry: Services

	% of Offers	Range	Mean
Consulting	25%	$29,000–$98,600	$51,000
Commercial banking	8%	$28,000–$70,000	$44,000
Investment banking	8%	$30,000–$95,000	$53,500
Transportation	7%	$38,000–$55,000	$46,000
Other services	7%	$28,500–$58,500	$43,500
Public accounting	4%	$30,500–$48,000	$41,000
Financial services	3%	$30,000–$65,000	$43,000
Real estate	2%	$37,000–$75,000	$57,000
Merchandising	2%	$30,000–$52,000	$38,500

Texas Starting Salaries by Geographic Area

	% of Offers	Range	Mean
Southwest	58%	$28,000–$100,000	$46,500
Midwest	12%	$30,500–$60,000	$41,000
Northeast	9%	$28,500–$65,000	$52,000
West	9%	$42,000–$58,000	$48,000
Southeast	6%	$38,000–$57,500	$44,500
International	6%	$45,000–$98,500	$63,500

Contact: MBA Program, Graduate Student Services Office
             Graduate School of Business, CBA 2.316
             The University of Texas at Austin
             Austin, Texas 78712-1172. Telephone: (512) 471-7612

---

74 Ibid.

NUMBER 16: ROCHESTER

William E. Simon Graduate School of Business Administration

Accounting	★★★★★
Entrepreneurship	★★★
Finance	★★★★★
Marketing	★★★
Information systems	★★★
Operations	★★★

Rankings:

MBA ADVANTAGE rank (1994) 16
U.S. News & World Report rank (1993) 24
Business Week corporate rank (1992) 26
Business Week graduate rank (1992) 17

Overview:

The William E. Simon Graduate School of Business Administration at the University of Rochester is a small, leading-edge business school with strengths in finance and accounting. Classes are structured to promote cross-functional teamwork. Simon is an excellent choice for prospective students looking for a small, collegial, team-oriented business school with strong programs in finance and accounting, and a vigorous commitment to state-of-the-art economic analysis of management opportunities.

Strengths:

- The research-oriented faculty are at the leading edge in their fields. Simon was ranked number 2 in "leading-edge knowledge of faculty" and in "use of current research in teaching" in the 1992 *Business Week* Top 20 survey. Three of the top academic journals in finance, accounting, and economics were founded at Simon. Faculty take great pride in presenting new material in class long before it is published in textbooks.

- The small size of the school promotes faculty cooperation and interaction. Simon was ranked number 1 in "cross-functional approach to teaching" in the *Business Week* survey.

- Teaching quality is very high, ranking number 4 in the Top 20 for the second-year elective courses, and number 6 for the first-year core courses in the *Business Week* survey.

- Teamwork is emphasized. Entering students are assigned to five-person study teams chosen to bring together classmates from diverse professional, cultural, and international backgrounds to operate as cross-functional teams.

- Most students choose a double-major (e.g., finance and marketing) for a well-rounded educational preparation for interdisciplinary management responsibilities.
- A state-of-the-art classroom building, completed in 1991, contains nine classrooms with curvilinear seating to promote student interaction and twenty-one conference rooms for use by the study teams, as well as a computing center with eighty personal computers.
- A student designed and managed VISION orientation program is run for entering students by a committee of second-year MBAs in cooperation with twenty-six companies. Its objective is to build such critical management skills as leadership, teamwork, and time management.
- The park-like campus of the University of Rochester is located in a suburban area of Rochester, a medium-sized, high technology city that is home to several *Fortune* 500 international corporations, including Eastman Kodak, Xerox, and Bausch & Lomb.
- Simon offers an accelerated program for students entering in January that allows them to graduate at the same time as the class that entered the previous September.

Limitations:

- As a university, the University of Rochester is not as well known as the parent institutions of most other Top 20 business schools (although it is the home of three other world-class professional schools—the Institute of Optics, the Medical School, and the Eastman School of Music). Thus the Simon School strives to build "brand recognition" for itself without the benefit of a halo effect from the reputation of the University of Rochester.
- The Simon School is young and most of its alumni have not yet reached the peak of their careers. Consequently, the school is not as well known by corporate recruiters as many of the other top business schools.
- Since 1988, the starting pay of Simon grads has grown faster than that of most of the other top schools (see chapter 4, table 4.2). If the Simon School is in fact gaining on the top schools, THE MBA ADVANTAGE ranking may understate the quality of the *current* grads. This would come about because the fifth year pay used to calculate THE MBA ADVANTAGE is based on a survey of the Class of 1987, as surveyed in 1992. If the current crop of students and/or the quality of instruction has improved significantly since 1987, as table 4.2 suggests, the number 16 ranking of the Simon School would understate the true value of the current Simon graduates.

Simon Admissions Statistics (Graduating Class of 1994)

Class size	200	Average GMAT score	620
Average age	26	GMAT range	470–780
Age range	22–34	Female	25%
Average years of work experience	4	International	40%
Percent with work experience	88%	U.S. minority	10%

Annual tuition and fees: $17, 820

Simon Placement Statistics (Graduating Class of 1993)[75]

Simon Starting Salaries by Functional Area

	% of Offers	Range	Mean
Overall	100%	$25,500–$91,000	$52,447
Finance	58%	$35,000–$91,000	$54,518
Marketing	16%	$37,000–$67,666	$49,955
Accounting	12%	$25,500–$45,000	$36,900
Operations management	10%	$36,000–$58,750	$44,609
Information systems	4%	$37,000–$67,000	$47,000

Simon Starting Salaries by Industry (top 10)

	% of Offers	Range	Mean
Commercial banking	29%	$35,000–$80,000	$54,067
Electronics and computers	12%	$40,000–$60,000	$47,137
Investment banking	11%	$50,000–$91,000	$62,571
Financial services	10%	$35,000–$65,000	$52,250
Accounting and auditing	9%	$25,000–$60,000	$38,500
Consumer products	6%	$40,000–$48,000	$43,871
Consulting	5%	$33,000–$74,750	$52,292
Pharmaceuticals	3%	$48,000–$63,000	$54,688
Communications	3%	$38,000–$48,500	$44,907
Food, beverage, tobacco	3%	$37,000–$65,000	$49,250

Simon Starting Salaries by Geographic Area

	% of Offers	Range	Mean
Northeast	45%	$27,500–$91,000	$54,890
Mid-Atlantic	36%	$25,500–$70,000	$44,551
South	7%	$40,000–$65,000	$52,667
International	6%	$45,000–$75,000	$56,679
Midwest	4%	$36,000–$49,000	$40,400
West	2%	$38,500–$57,500	$50,333

Contact: Priscilla Gumina
Assistant Dean for MBA Programs
William E. Simon Graduate School of Business Administration
University of Rochester
Rochester, New York 14627
Telephone (716) 275-3533

75 *Placement Report 1993*, William E. Simon Graduate School of Business Administration.

NUMBER 17: INDIANA

Graduate School of Business at Indiana University

Accounting	★.★★
Consulting	★★★
Finance	★★★
Marketing	★★★★
Operations	★★★

Rankings:

MBA ADVANTAGE rank (1994) 17
U.S. News & World Report rank (1993) 20
Business Week corporate rank (1992) 8
Business Week graduate rank (1992) 6

Overview:

The Graduate School of Business at Indiana University is a teaching-oriented business school located at a Big Ten university in a picturesque Midwest college town. If this sounds appealing, you'll also appreciate knowing that Indiana has a nationally-recognized program in marketing, an innovative first-year curriculum, a top-notch placement office—and low tuition, even for out-of-staters.

Strengths:

- At Indiana, teaching is very important. Indiana is one of the few top business schools to give promotions and tenure on the basis of outstanding teaching as well as successful research.[76] Professors are expected to be in their offices every day, and the results show up in student satisfaction. In the 1992 *Business Week* Top 20 survey, Indiana was ranked number 6 in overall satisfaction of the graduating class.

- Marketing is a strong program at Indiana. About 28 percent of the graduates take jobs in marketing, and the starting pay is slightly higher than in finance.

- The cost of this quality program is a bargain—$6,823 in tuition and fees for Indiana residents and $13,303 for non-residents.

- In the fall of 1992, Indiana introduced a revolutionary new first-year curriculum of integrated multidisciplinary core courses taught by teams of four or five professors, with one grade at the end of each semester, and no waivers. The emphasis is on intensive integration of the core material as an alternative to the more traditional set of unrelated

---

76 *The New MBA Catalog 1993-94*, Graduate School of Business, Indiana University, pp. 18, 20.

core courses found in some schools. Students work in study groups that emphasize team building and cross-disciplinary cooperation in tackling complex business problems.

- The second year is flexible. Electives are offered as half-semester modules, and students can either pursue traditional majors (finance, marketing, etc.) or they can design their own second year program, selecting some or even all of their electives from other graduate programs in the University.

- The placement office at Indiana is exceptionally competent. In 1992-93, 220 companies conducted over 3,300 MBA interviews on campus, and many students have more than twenty interviews on campus each recruiting season.[77]

- Bloomington, Indiana, is a quaint college town of 60,000 located about forty-five minutes from Indianapolis. Students who prefer small towns over big cities will love the quality of life in Bloomington. Indiana University offers Big Ten basketball and football, and the music school has performances almost every night.

Limitations:

- In addition to the MBA program, the School of Business also has about 2,000 under-grads in business who share the building and the faculty with the graduate program. Unlike many top schools, the focus is not exclusively on the MBA program, which can be distracting at times.

- Although charming, Bloomington is somewhat isolated from the centers of commerce. Faculty have fewer opportunities to consult (which means they may have fewer industry contacts), there are not as many opportunities for student projects with local companies, and corporate recruiters have more distance to travel.

Indiana Admissions Statistics (Graduating Class of 1994)

Class size	300	Average GMAT score	610
Average age	26	International	18%
Female	28%	U.S. minority	11%
Percent with work experience	95%		

Annual tuition and fees: $13,303 (non-resident); $6,823 (resident)

---

77 Ibid., p. 34.

Indiana Placement Statistics (Graduating Class of 1993)[78]

Indiana Starting Salaries by Functional Area (signing bonuses not included in these figures):

	% of Offers	Range	Mean
Overall	100%	$30,000–$80,000	$49,678
Marketing and advertising	28%	$37,800–$67,000	$50,490
Corporate finance	24%	$31,500–$79,000	$50,420
Management and consulting	21%	$30,000–$80,000	$52,060
Commercial and investment banking	11%	$38,000–$66,000	$46,800
Information systems and operations	6%	$36,000–$56,000	$47,796
Human resources	4%	$45,000–$57,250	$50,036
Other (incl. accounting and real estate)	6%	(insufficient data)	

Contact: MBA Program
Graduate School of Business, Room 254
Indiana University
Tenth and Fee Lane
Bloomington, Indiana 47405-1701
Telephone: (812) 855-8006

---

78 Ibid., p. 35.

NUMBER 18: NORTH CAROLINA

The Kenan-Flagler Business School at the University of North Carolina at Chapel Hill

Consulting	★★★★
Finance	★★★
General management	★★★
Marketing	★★★★
Operations	★★★★

Rankings:

MBA ADVANTAGE rank (1994) 18
U.S. News & World Report rank (1993) 19
Business Week corporate rank (1992) 11
Business Week graduate rank (1992) 8

Overview:

The Kenan-Flagler Business School at the University of North Carolina at Chapel Hill gives teaching first priority. The case method is used in most of the courses, and the curriculum maintains a real-world orientation, enhanced by a second-year mandatory projects course with real companies as clients. The school's graduates have landed jobs paying above-average starting salaries in three functional areas—marketing, consulting, and operations management. To top it off, the tuition is very low, even for out-of-staters, and the setting of the Chapel Hill campus is delightful.

Strengths:

- Kenan-Flagler is a teaching-oriented school. The professors are there to teach, and applied faculty research is encouraged as the means for developing fresh concepts for the classroom.

- The case method is the preferred teaching approach at Kenan-Flagler. Real world business experience improves teaching of cases, and the dean—the retired president of Sara Lee Corporation—and a number of the professors have extensive backgrounds in business. Faculty members are encouraged to consult with companies in order to stay in touch with the needs of practicing business managers.

- The Kenan-Flagler program is a terrific bargain. The tuition and fees for a state resident are only $2,325 per year. Out-of-staters pay only $9,575, and in some cases out-of-staters can qualify as residents in the second year.

- The first year is made up of seven-week modules for the thirteen core courses. Students work in assigned study groups of five or six students selected for diversity of experience. Waivers of the core courses are not permitted.

- There are no fixed concentration requirements. In the second year, students are allowed to customize their programs by selecting from a wide range of electives offered not only at the business school but also at other departments of UNC-Chapel Hill and at nearby Duke University. The second year does require one year-long global strategy course which includes a ten-day management simulation game.

- Every second-year student also takes the twenty-four-week MBA practicum course in which teams of students, guided by a faculty advisor, work on comprehensive business problems for actual companies or non-profit organizations. Working with the managements of the client organizations, the student teams gain experience in applying their new skills and knowledge to broad, ill-defined multidisciplinary problems. The projects are concluded with oral and written presentations to the client managements.

- Chapel Hill, a picture-perfect college town, is located at the edge of North Carolina's Research Triangle in a magnificent setting the residents describe as "the southern part of heaven." Students report that the quality of life is outstanding.

Limitations:
- Like other state schools, Kenan-Flagler's plans for growth and new facilities are sometimes constrained by state budget considerations.

- Kenan-Flagler's low rank of number 18 in THE MBA ADVANTAGE ranking is caused in part by its relatively low two-year STEP UP–the ratio of post-MBA starting pay to pre-MBA pay. The school's STEP UP of 38.8 percent is the lowest of the twenty-three schools analyzed (see chapter 4, table 4.3). Post-MBA pay growth in the first five years following graduation is also low compared to the other top schools. It is not clear why this is the case. Perhaps companies in the Southeast, which is where many of the school's graduates have accepted employment in the past, are not as quick to raise pay or give promotions as in other sections of the country.

Kenan-Flagler Admissions Statistics (Graduating Class of 1995)[79]

Class size	190	Mean GMAT score	625
Average age	27	Female	26%
Average years of work experience	4	International	12%
Percent with work experience	99%	Minorities	12%

Annual tuition and fees: $2,325 (resident); $9,575 (non-resident)

---

79 *The MBA Program 1993-1994 Catalog*, Kenan-Flagler Business School.

Kenan-Flagler Placement Statistics (Graduating Class of 1993)

Kenan-Flagler Starting Salaries by Major Function[80]

	% of Accepted Offers	Range	Average
Overall	100%	$30,000–$85,000	$55,057
Marketing/sales	23%		$57,216
Consulting	21%		$61,800
Corporate finance	13%		$51,221
Manufacturing/operations	10%		$56,180
Investment banking	9%		$50,364
Investment management	8%		$45,667
General management	6%		$58,750
Strategic planning	4%		$53,040
Commercial banking	3%		$40,667
Other	3%		$61,333

Kenan-Flagler Placements by Geographic Area

	% of Accepted Offers	Average
Southeast	33%	$51,703
Northeast	25%	$58,186
Midwest	17%	$54,685
Mid-Atlantic	10%	$63,000
International	8%	$51,200
Far West	4%	$52,550
Southwest	3%	$47,000

Contact: Anne-Marie Summers
            Director of Admissions
            The Kenan-Flagler Business School
            The University of North Carolina at Chapel Hill
            Chapel Hill, North Carolina 27599-3490
            Telephone: (919) 962-3236

---

80 Ibid.

NUMBER 19: DUKE

The Fuqua School of Business at Duke University

Consulting	★★★★
Finance	★★★★
General management	★★★★
Marketing	★★★★★
Operations	★★

Rankings:

MBA ADVANTAGE rank (1994)	19
U.S. News & World Report rank (1993)	7
Business Week corporate rank (1992)	14
Business Week graduate rank (1992)	7

Overview:

The Fuqua School of Business at Duke University has a strong reputation in the field of marketing. Although only twenty years old, the Fuqua program has become a top contender among the leading business schools. Ideally located on the campus of Duke University in North Carolina's Research Triangle region, Fuqua's modern facilities and completely revised curriculum make this school the choice of many prospective students interested in marketing.

Strengths:

- Marketing is the number one choice of Fuqua graduates. Every year 25 to 30 percent enter careers as marketing managers.

- In 1992, the curriculum was completely overhauled. The fourteen-week semesters were replaced with seven-week "terms" for more flexibility. Core courses meet twice a week for two and one quarter hours each to permit extra class time for extended case discussions and outside speakers. Core courses may be waived in order to take more electives by either passing an exemption exam or producing evidence of prior coursework in that subject.

- A year-long, first-year Individual Effectiveness course is devoted to communications skills, computer competence, and the like. An intensive, week-long Integrative Learning Experience is held at the beginning of each of the four semesters in both years. It involves topics such as team building, career planning, diversity in the workplace, quality management, and strategic management simulations.

- There are no formal concentration requirements and students can customize their programs in the second year by selecting electives that meet their career goals.

- Among the electives are four-month practicums in marketing, operations management and small business management. In recent marketing practicums, teams of students have worked on comprehensive multidisciplinary consulting projects for such clients as Ford, IBM, General Electric, Hallmark, NutraSweet, and a number of high-tech startups. In 1993, a student team worked with Ford Motor Company to develop a marketing plan for the company's electric automobile, and travelled to Ford headquarters in Michigan to give a final presentation to the vice president of marketing for North America.

- The strikingly modern physical facilities for the Fuqua School, located in a wooded area on Duke's beautiful West Campus, consist of three interconnected buildings designed expressly for management education. Duke University is respected as one of the finest universities in the country, and its top-rated basketball team is well known to most sports fans.

- Durham, the home of Duke University, is located in North Carolina's famous Research Triangle. The Raleigh-Durham area was recently ranked number 1 in the country in a *Fortune* article on the "Best Cities for Business."[81]

Limitations:

- The relatively low rank of Fuqua—number 19 on THE MBA ADVANTAGE—occurs because the post-MBA pay of Fuqua grads was found to grow more slowly in the first five years of post-MBA employment than that of graduates from any of the other top schools (see chapter 4, table 4.4). This could be due to the following:

1. Fuqua has a higher proportion of marketing placements than most other schools. The rate of growth of pay in marketing may be less than that in finance and consulting, which can be heavily affected by commissions and performance bonuses. The calculated post-MBA pay growth rate of 9.4 percent for Fuqua is consistent with the rate of pay raises in the large corporations that tend to hire marketing majors.

2. Fuqua is a young school, established in 1970. If it is still in the process of catching up to the top schools, THE MBA ADVANTAGE ranking may lag the quality of the current grads. This could come about because the fifth year pay used to calculate THE MBA ADVANTAGE is based on a survey of the Class of 1987, as carried out in 1992. If the current crop of students has more work experience and/or the quality of instruction has improved significantly since 1987, the number 19 ranking of Fuqua may understate the true value of the current Fuqua grads.

Fuqua Admissions Statistics (Graduating Class of 1995)[82]

Class size	325	Median GMAT score	630
Average age	27	Female	27%
Average years of work experience	4	International	14%
Percent with work experience	97%	Minorities	13%

---

81 Labich, K., "The Best Cities for Knowledge Workers," *Fortune*, November 15, 1993, p. 50.
82 *1993-94 MBA Program Catalog*, The Fuqua School of Business.

Annual tuition and fees: $19,800

Fuqua Placement Statistics (Graduating Class of 1993)

Fuqua Starting Salaries by Major Function[83]

	% of Accepted Offers	Range
Marketing	24%	$30,000–$75,000
Consulting	18%	$38,000–$80,000
Finance	16%	$42,000–$60,000
Investment banking	16%	$40,000–$90,000
Manufacturing/operations	10%	$40,000–$64,000
Commercial banking	3%	$44,000–$55,000
Health services/hospital management	3%	$28,000–$60,000
Real estate	2%	$55,000–$86,000
Advertising/sales	1%	$53,000–$57,000
Human resources	1%	$50,000–$52,000

Fuqua Placements by Geographic Area

	% of Accepted Offers	Range
Northeast	39%	$30,000–$80,000
South	30%	$28,000–$75,000
Midwest	14%	$47,000–$75,000
Southwest / West	11%	$28,000–$75,000
International	6%	$30,000–$90,000

Contact: Office of Admissions
             The Fuqua School of Business
             Duke University
             Durham, North Carolina 27708
             Telephone: (919) 660-7705

---

83   Ibid.

NUMBER 20: NYU

Leonard N. Stern School of Business at New York University

Accounting	★★★
Consulting	★★★★
Finance	★★★★★
General management	★★★
Marketing	★★★
Information Systems	★★

Rankings:

MBA ADVANTAGE rank (1994) 20
U.S. News & World Report rank (1993) 16
Business Week corporate rank (1992) 13
Business Week graduate rank (1992) 16

Overview:

The Leonard N. Stern School of Business at New York University offers a highly-regarded program in finance taught by faculty with both solid academic credentials and "street smarts" from working or consulting in New York City, one of the leading financial centers of the world. Stern has a new core curriculum, a magnificent new facility, and a renewed dedication to teaching quality. For prospective students interested in Wall Street, Stern ought to be high on their list.

Strengths:

- Finance is number one at the Stern School. Two-thirds of the students concentrate in finance, and many stay on in New York City to work for major banks, brokerages and consulting firms.

- In 1992, Stern moved into a new eleven-story $68 million Management Education Center at Washington Square in New York City's Greenwich Village. Classrooms and other facilities are state-of-the-art, providing Stern an advantage over Columbia, its New York City rival.

- Members of the finance faculty at Stern have a reputation for "street smarts" as well as impressive academic credentials, and many have real world experience in the financial community. In addition to 200 full-time faculty, Stern has 120 adjunct faculty from the business world. The evening course in Options Trading may be taught by someone from Wall Street who trades options during the day.

- In recent years, Stern has focused attention on teaching quality as well as research. According to Stern's in-house newsletter, "In 1990, faculty voted unanimously to apply equal weight to teaching and research in making tenure decisions."[84] This led to a major

---

84 *Stern Business*, Summer 1992, p. 14.

overhaul of the first year core curriculum, and contact hours per course (between students and faculty) were increased by 33 percent.

- First-year core courses may be waived by students who have taken an equivalent undergraduate course. In the second year, students are required to declare a major in one or more functional areas, such as finance or marketing. The school offers more than 200 elective courses.

- Students who are interested in getting hands-on experience take the second-year Management Advisory Project course that stretches over the fall and spring semesters. In this course, students perform consulting projects for such firms as American Express and Sony Corporation. Students may also volunteer for the Urban Business Assistance Corporation, a student consulting group that helps women and minorities launch new businesses.

- A major strength of Stern—particularly for finance majors—is its location in New York City, a world leader in everything from finance to fashion. The NYU Campus, located in the heart of Greenwich Village, is near old-world delicatessens, brownstones, and boutiques.

Limitations:

- For many years, NYU's business school was primarily considered a night school, lacking the social and intellectual status of its Ivy League neighbor, Columbia. The Stern School, with its impressive new facility, is working hard to change that image.

- Not everyone loves New York. The city is expensive, noisy, and pushy, but glamorous and exciting as well.

- Why doesn't Stern do better than number 20 on THE MBA ADVANTAGE ranking? An analysis of the tables and graphs in chapter 4 and appendix B shows that Stern graduates do fine on post-MBA salary growth, almost 20 percent per year in the first five years following graduation. But graduates do relatively poorly on the two-year STEP UP—the ratio of post-MBA starting pay to pre-MBA pay—realizing only a 41 percent STEP UP, second from the bottom of the list for the top schools. Perhaps many NYU grads from the New York area return to the companies they were with before they started their MBA, and find it difficult to negotiate as large a post-MBA pay increase as those who start fresh with a new firm.

Stern Admissions Statistics (Graduating Class of 1994)[85]

Class size	400	Mean GMAT score	616
Median age	26	Female	30%
Years of work experience	2–8	International	32%
		Minorities	9%

Annual tuition and fees: $18,228

---

85 The Stern School of Business MBA Program, 1992-93 Catalog.

Stern Placement Statistics (Graduating Class of 1993)

Stern Starting Salaries by Major[86]

	% of Accepted Offers	Range	Mean
Overall	100%	$32,000–$100,000	$56,162
Finance	66%		$56,012
Marketing	21%		$53,274
Management	6%		$55,430
Information systems	4%		$48,950
Accounting	2%		$50,190
Economics	1%		$64,855

Stern Starting Salaries by Functional Area

	% of Accepted Offers	Mean
Finance	40%	$55,587
Marketing/sales	20%	$54,268
Consulting	13%	$59,986
Accounting/control	4%	$55,853
Information systems	4%	$57,499
Research	4%	$56,387
Operations	2%	$51,833
Human resources	1%	$56,833
Planning	3%	$55,750
Other	9%	$56,328

Stern Starting Salaries by Major Industry (Manufacturing)

	% of Accepted Offers	Mean
Consumer products	6%	$53,752
Chemicals/pharmaceuticals	5%	$58,075
High technology/electronics	5%	$55,965
Food and beverages	3%	$59,422

Stern Starting Salaries by Major Industry (Non-Manufacturing)

	% of Accepted Offers	Mean
Commercial banking	15%	$54,851
Investment banking/corporate finance	12%	$55,968
Sales and trading	11%	$55,512
Consulting	9%	$60,714
Other diversified financial services	5%	$57,437
Insurance	4%	$57,769
Accounting/auditing	4%	$54,000
Entertainment/leisure	2%	$50,000
Communications	2%	$61,700
Computer services	1%	$51,325

Contact: Office of Graduate Admissions, Stern School of Business
New York University, Management Education Center, 44 West Fourth Street
New York, New York 10012-1126. Telephone: (212) 998-0600 or toll free (800) 272-7373

---

86 Leonard N. Stern Placement Report, Class of 1993.

NOT RANKED: COLUMBIA

Columbia Business School

Accounting	★★★
Consulting	★★★★
Finance	★★★★
Marketing	★★★
Operations	★★★

Rankings:

MBA ADVANTAGE rank (1994) . . . . (NR)[87]

U.S. News & World Report rank (1993) 10

Business Week corporate rank (1992) 5

Business Week graduate rank (1992) 18

Overview:

The Columbia Business School is best known for finance. It also has the advantage of being located in Manhattan just minutes by subway or cab from the world's greatest concentration of leading banks and brokerage houses. Many of the courses at Columbia are taught by adjunct faculty from the New York financial community. Prospective students interested in finance or consulting who would like to work in the New York area could get a head start by attending Columbia.

Strengths:

- Columbia is a great place for people who love New York City. Situated on the Upper West Side of Manhattan, the Columbia University campus is an academic village with tree-shaded lawns and brick walks in the midst of New York's noise and hustle. Book-stores, ethnic restaurants, and open air fruit markets surround the school.

- The one hundred full-time faculty are supplemented by eighty-five adjunct faculty, many of whom are senior managers at major banks or Wall Street brokerage houses. One of Columbia's strengths is the mix of theory (from the full-timers) and street smarts (from the adjuncts).

- Columbia is known for finance. Nearly 70 percent of the second-year students concen-trate in it, although many also double-major in other subjects. Most of the recruiters who hire at Columbia represent financial services companies or consulting firms.

- In 1992, the school revised its curriculum around four major themes: globalization, total

---

87 The Columbia Business School was not ranked by THE MBA ADVANTAGE due to a lack of data on fifth year pay for Columbia graduates. Because it was ranked as a top business school by both *U.S. News & World Report* and *Business Week*, it was selected to be included in this summary of national schools.

quality management, ethics, and human resource management. It is possible to exempt out of some of the core courses by taking waiver exams, but these courses must be replaced with electives.

- An unusual feature of Columbia's curriculum is that it runs twelve months a year, and it is possible to enter the MBA program at three times during the year—in September, January, or May.

- Manhattan offers special advantages: students can take a cab to interview at leading corporations, faculty can consult with top companies to test their theories in the real world, spouses are likely to have jobs to choose from, and 10,000 Columbia alums in the New York area are nearby to give a hand to new grads who want to stay in the city.

Limitations:

- Although Columbia goes out of its way to attract students from other areas, 42 percent are from the New York City area.

- While New York City is Columbia's greatest asset, not everyone would enjoy living there. Like other large cities, New York has its share of crime and decay.

- The facilities at Columbia are in poor condition. Uris Hall, a worn out 1960s-era concrete building, is not competitive with the modern facilities available at most leading business schools. The dean has undertaken a major fund drive and has already raised $65 million toward a $100 million goal, but a new building is not expected in the immediate future.

Columbia Admissions Statistics (Graduating Class of 1995)[88]

Class size	450	Mean GMAT score	630
Average age	27	Female	28%
Typical years of work experience	2-4	International	29%

Annual tuition and fees: $20,050

---

88 *Columbia Business School Catalog,* Fall 1993.

Columbia Placement Statistics (Graduating Class of 1992)

Columbia does not publish starting salaries in its catalog nor does it distribute a placement report. *U.S. News & World Report* indicated that Columbia's 1992 median starting salary *without* signing bonuses was $55,000.[89] *Business Week* reported that Columbia's 1992 median starting pay *with* signing bonuses was $65,000.[90] Tom Fischgrund, in his 1993 edition of *The Insider's Guide to the Top 10 Business Schools*, states that the range of starting salaries at Columbia is $40,000 to $90,000 with a median of just over $55,000, exclusive of year-end and signing bonuses.[91]

Contact: Office of Admissions
            Columbia Business School
            105 Uris Hall
            Columbia University
            New York, New York 10027
            Telephone: (212) 854-1961

---

89 "America's Best Graduate Schools," *U.S. News & World Report*, March 22, 1993, p. 58.
90 *Business Week Guide to the Best Business Schools*, 3rd Edition, p. 128.
91 Fishgrund, T., *The Insider's Guide to the Top Business Schools*, 5th Edition, Little, Brown and Company, 1993, p. 45.

NOT RANKED: VANDERBILT

Owen Graduate School of Management at Vanderbilt University

Consulting	★★
Finance	★★★
General management	★★★.
Marketing	★★★
Operations	★★

Rankings:

MBA ADVANTAGE rank (1994) . . . . (NR)[92]

U.S. News & World Report rank (1993) 25

Business Week corporate rank (1992) 20

Business Week graduate rank (1992) 19

Overview:

The Owen Graduate School of Management at Vanderbilt University is a young school with a growing national reputation, located in the rapidly developing Sunbelt region of the Southeast. This research-oriented school is respected for its programs in finance, marketing, consulting, and human resources management. Owen's small size fosters an informal and cooperative attitude among the students and faculty, and the city of Nashville offers economic growth, low living costs, and a mild climate.

Strengths:

- Owen is a school on the move. Starting salaries have grown substantially in the past five years, and Owen's two-year STEP UP—the ratio of starting pay to pre-MBA pay—is 69.3 percent, exceeded only by Yale, MIT, and Chicago (see chapter 4, table 4.3).

- Owen is a small, collegial school with an incoming class size of only 190. The average number of students in any classroom is typically about thirty-five, which encourages discussion and interaction among students.

- The research-oriented faculty stay on top of their fields. The school was ranked number 3 in currency of materials used in the classroom in the 1992 *Business Week* Top 20 survey.

- Owen has been alert to new opportunities for its grads. For example, it has staked out a niche in the curriculum for services marketing, one of the fastest growing areas of the economy.

---

92 The Owen School was not ranked by THE MBA ADVANTAGE due to a lack of data on fifth year pay for Owen graduates. Because it was ranked as a top business school by both *U.S. News & World Report* and *Business Week*, it was selected to be included in this summary of national schools.

- The school believes in hands-on experience as part of the learning process. In the Integrative Applied Projects elective, teams of students carry out multidisciplinary studies for local firms. The students also run a consulting service called the Owen Business Projects Group that specializes in developing business plans for startups and small companies.

- The MBA curriculum is conventional, with ten required core courses in the first year and mostly electives in the second year, many of which can be taken in other graduate programs of the university. Students can waive individual core courses through waiver exams so that they can take more electives.

- Owen students find jobs in a wide variety of functional areas. About a third take jobs in finance, which pay somewhat more than marketing (23 percent of the placements) or consulting (16 percent). Eleven percent of the Class of '93 accepted jobs in human resource management, a higher proportion than at any other top business school.

- The placement office publishes a comprehensive annual recruiter's guide, complete with student pictures and mini-resumes, that is sent to 5,000 potential employers.

- The Owen School occupies a modern facility, completed in 1982, that houses classrooms and all other functions of the school under one roof.

- Nashville, the historical home of country music, is a medium-size city with a mild climate. Long recognized as a center of banking and finance, Nashville is participating in the vigorous growth of the Sunbelt and is now the corporate home of more than sixty companies specializing in managed health care.

Limitations:

- Organized in 1969, Owen is a young school. It has fewer alums in high-level jobs to give a helping hand to new grads than many other business schools.

- Starting salaries are lower than for other top schools, reflecting in part the lower cost-of-living in the Southeast, where 62 percent of the graduates accept employment.

- Although Nashville is located in the fast-growing Sunbelt, it is still less convenient for many corporate recruiters to reach than the major cities of the Northeast and Pacific Coast.

Admissions Statistics (Graduating Class of 1994)

Class size	190	Mean GMAT score	607
Average age	26	Female	27%
Average years of work experience	3.6	International	20%
% with work experience	83%	Minorities	17%

Annual tuition and fees: $18,600

Owen Placement Statistics (Graduating Class of 1993)

Owen Starting Salaries by Functional Area [93]

	% of Accepted Offers	Range	Mean
Overall	100%	$30,000–$102,000	$49,100
			Median
Marketing/sales	23%		$45,000
Investment banking	17%		$50,000
Consulting	16%		$42,300
Human resources	11%		$42,500
Corporate finance	9%		$47,000
Management	8%		$51,000
Commercial banking	7%		$39,500
Manufacturing	6%		$40,000
Accounting	3%		$37,000

Owen Starting Salaries by Geographic Area (U.S. placements only)

	% of Accepted Offers	Median
Southeast	62%	$43,000
Midwest	16%	$49,400
Northeast	11%	$45,000
Southwest/West	11%	$42,500

Contact: Admissions Office
              Owen Graduate School of Management
              Vanderbilt University
              401 Twenty-first Avenue South
              Nashville, Tennessee 37203
              Telephone: (615) 322-6469 or toll free (800) 288-OWEN

---

[93] *MBA Recruiter's Guide, 1994*, Owen at Vanderbilt "Profiles."

NOT RANKED: WASHINGTON UNIVERSITY

John M. Olin School of Business at Washington University in St. Louis

Consulting	★★
Finance	★★
Marketing	★★★
Operations	★★★

Rankings:

MBA ADVANTAGE rank (1994) . . . . (NR)[94]

U.S. News & World Report rank (1993) . . . . . . (NR)

Business Week corporate rank (1992) 18

Business Week graduate rank (1992) 24

Overview:

The John M. Olin School of Business at Washington University in St. Louis is a small, up-and-coming Midwest business school with a very large endowment. Although its faculty has a strong commitment to research, the school also highly values hands-on consulting projects courses with local companies. Olin's suburban campus in St. Louis, the corporate home of a dozen *Fortune* 500 companies, provides convenient access to the senior managements of many nationally-known firms.

Strengths:

- With a class size of only 158 incoming students, Olin is the smallest of the nationally-ranked MBA programs, providing the opportunity for informality and collegiality.

- Although Olin is small, it is one of the wealthiest schools. Its endowment of over $60 million places it among the top business schools, and its alumni have contributed since 1985 at the rate of more than $1 million per year.

- Many schools now offer projects courses where second-year students perform consulting assignments (with faculty guidance) for local companies. But Olin goes one better—the students can get paid up to $750 for their efforts. These "practicum" studies have been carried out for more than a dozen leading companies, including Apple Computer, Monsanto Chemical and Mallinckrodt Medical, and students also participate in unpaid consulting projects for local charitable organizations. The school plans to expand this kind of hands-on learning experience.

- The first-year curriculum consists of core courses that range in length from as little as

---

94 The Olin School was not ranked by THE MBA ADVANTAGEdue to a lack of data on fifth year pay for Olin graduates. Because it was ranked as a top business school by *Business Week*, it was selected to be included in this summary of national schools.

two weeks (for Introduction to Calculus) to fifteen weeks (for Microeconomics for Managers). It is possible to waive a core course to substitute a more advanced course by taking a proficiency exam, and the school will consider petitions to transfer in as much as nine credits from other accredited programs.

- The second year is very flexible. Although most students concentrate their second-year electives in one or two areas, there is no requirement to declare a formal area of concentration. Up to fifteen credit hours may be taken in other graduate-level courses in the university, even foreign language and law courses.

- The facilities are first-rate. In 1986, the school moved into a new state-of-the-art building with a modern computing center and a laboratory for experimental studies in consumer behavior.

- Washington University is located in a suburban part of St. Louis, site of the famous Gateway Arch and home to twelve *Fortune* 500 companies.

Limitations:
- As a small up-and-coming business school, Olin is not as well known to corporate recruiters as most of the other top schools, which may explain why Olin's starting salaries are somewhat lower. Almost half of the 1993 graduating class accepted offers in the St. Louis area.

- Like several other top schools, Olin has an undergraduate business program as well as executive and doctoral programs, so the faculty has other teaching responsibilities besides the MBA program.

Olin Admissions Statistics (Graduating Class of 1993)[95]

Class size	158	Mean GMAT score	602
Average age	26	Female	30%
Percent with work experience	80%	Minorities	15%

Annual tuition and fees: $16,750

95 *MBA Catalog, 1993-94*, Olin School of Business.

Olin Placement Statistics (Graduating Class of 1993)

Olin Starting Salaries by Top 10 Functional Areas[96]

	% of Accepted Offers	Range	Mean
Overall	100%	$23,500–$77,300	$44,400
Consulting	26%	$34,000–$49,000	$41,300
Corporate finance	15%	$41,000–$59,000	$50,400
Marketing	11%	$23,500–$65,000	$42,000
Operations management	9%	$45,000–$62,000	$53,300
Product management	7%	$43,000–$56,000	$48,800
Commercial banking	7%	$34,000–$55,000	$41,400
Investment banking	5%	$30,000–$47,000	$36,250
Corporate planning	4%	$45,000–$52,000	$49,500
Corporate accounting	4%	$25,500–$42,000	$35,500
Sales	4%	$28,000–$77,300	$49,500

Olin Starting Salaries by Geographic Area

	% of Accepted Offers	Range	Mean
St. Louis	47%	$25,500–$65,000	$42,200
Other Midwest	25%	$23,500–$62,000	$45,600
South	13%	$32,000–$48,000	$44,100
Northeast	9%	$30,000–$55,000	$45,500
West	3%	(insufficient data)	
International	3%	(insufficient data)	

Contact: MBA Admissions
John. M. Olin School of Business
Washington University
Campus Box 1133
One Brookings Drive
St. Louis, Missouri 63130-4899
Telephone: (314) 935-7301 or toll free (800) 622-3622

96 *Placement Report, MBA Class of 1993*, Olin School of Business.

Chapter 6

Regional Business Schools: Are They Worth It?

The Top 20 business schools we have analyzed so far compete for the best students in a national and international market. Their graduates are placed in managerial positions all over the country and around the world.

Chances are, you may also be considering one of the hundreds of regional business schools around the country that serve local markets for graduates and employers. The Top 20 have the capacity to only accept about 10 percent of the 70,000 students that begin the MBA every year. *The great majority of MBA degrees are awarded by regional schools.*

Does It Pay to Go Full-Time to a *Regional* MBA Program?

For most people, it pays to go full time to a Top 20 school, as shown by the estimated values of THE MBA ADVANTAGE in table 4.1 on page 30. But it's also clear from this table that the size of THE MBA ADVANTAGE drops rapidly as you go down the list, and by the time you get to school number 20, you'll just about break even on your investment in the first five years after getting the degree.

A simple extrapolation of that decreasing trend shows that below the Top 20, THE MBA ADVANTAGE seems to disappear. One of the major reasons for this is that prospective students who are admitted to the Top 20 schools frequently forego good jobs—the average pre-MBA pay for the Top 20 was over $40,000 in 1990.[1] For these prospective students who already have good jobs, the MBA has to add a lot of value to pay for itself.

Does it pay to go full time to a *regional* school? Under certain conditions, the answer is yes, but not for everybody.

In this chapter we'll explore the conditions under which you may be better off attending a regional business school by addressing the following questions:

- First of all, what would you be giving up in order to spend two years in a full-time regional MBA program? Under what conditions would it make more sense to go part time?

- Second, what are your non-financial reasons for going to business school?

- Third, when considering different schools, how important are the various teaching methods, such as the "case method?"

---

1 Byrne, J., *A Business Week Guide: The Best Business Schools*, 3rd edition, McGraw-Hill, 1993, p. 56.

- Finally, what are some other important considerations when choosing a regional school?

Let's take these questions one at a time.

What Are You Giving Up to Go to Business School?

The biggest cost in going to business school full time is not the tuition, but rather the cost of giving up your salary for two years. There's also some risk involved since you may not find exactly what you want when you graduate. But if you are unemployed, or in a low-paying job with few opportunities for advancement, the "opportunity cost" of going to business school full time is very low.

Recall that THE MBA ADVANTAGE is the difference between what you would make over the next seven years if you go to business school versus what you would make over this period if you *didn't* go. If your current employment is paying little or nothing, then you don't have to make a fortune after receiving your MBA degree in order to generate a positive MBA ADVANTAGE—that is, to have the MBA pay for itself.

If, on the other hand, you currently have an excellent job with good prospects for promotion and advancement, it may not pay to give it up to attend a regional school full time. Instead, you should seriously consider either a part-time MBA or an Executive MBA. Either might be obtained at a regional business school with no loss of salary, and your employer may even pay the tuition.

Consider David's situation, for example, who we met in chapter 1. You will recall that David has a degree in electrical engineering and is married with two small children. He was recently promoted to a very promising job as a marketing product manager for a prominent electronics company. David has several years of impressive work experience in sales and marketing, and his GMAT score is high enough to get him into any regional business school and many of the Top 20 schools.

But it does not make sense for David to give up his excellent job to go full time to any business school—he's already on the fast track. He needs the knowledge and the credentials of the MBA, but it would be a poor career strategy to give up his present job. His company is progressive and changing rapidly, so his job might not be there when he returns in two years. Furthermore, it would be a real hardship on his family for David to give up two years of salary.

Instead, David is completing his MBA part time at a local regional school. His employer has given him permission to take a few hours off every week to take courses offered only during the day. And, of course, the employer picks up all of the tuition costs.

Under what conditions does it make financial sense to attend a *full-time* regional business school program? Let's look at four case histories:

- *Getting back into the job market:* Shirley has been a full-time homemaker for the past several years. Although she has a liberal arts degree, she feels that she has few marketable skills in today's job market. She is considering enrolling in a full-time two-year MBA program at a good regional school. Tuition will be $14,000 per year. Upon completion of her MBA, she believes she can get a job in sales that will pay $40,000 the first year, with annual increases of 10 percent.

   Because Shirley feels that her present skills are not marketable, her "opportunity costs" are zero. Although she will invest $28,000 in her MBA, she will recover this cost in her first year on the job. At the end of five years on the job, she will have earned a total of $216,204. Since the alternative of not working has a financial value of zero, her MBA ADVANTAGE from going full-time to a regional MBA program is $216,204—more than twice THE MBA ADVANTAGE earned by the average full-time student at Stanford! (see table 4.1 on page 30).

The reason her MBA ADVANTAGE is so high is not because of a high post-MBA salary, but because her opportunity cost is so low. In cases like Shirley's, the value of a *full-time* regional MBA program is very high.

- *Upgrading from a clerical to a professional job:* Paul has a degree in history and currently works as a stockroom clerk in a manufacturing firm for an annual salary of $25,000. His annual raises average about 5 percent. If he obtains an MBA, he can become an inventory analyst at a starting salary of $45,000, with 10 percent raises.

  If he quits his job to take the same full-time MBA program as Shirley, with tuition at $14,000 per year, it will take Paul until the fourth year to break even, and his MBA ADVANTAGE at the end of five years in the new job will be $43,179.

  But if Paul goes to school *part-time* for three years and gets his employer to pick up the tuition, he breaks even immediately and by the *fourth* year in his new job, his THE MBA ADVANTAGE will total $84,107.[2] This occurs even though he is delayed by one year in starting the higher paying job.[3] Clearly the part-time MBA is a better deal for Paul.

- *Adding credentials to a professional degree:* Bill is a recent engineering graduate making $35,000 a year, with the prospect of 5 percent annual raises. If he obtains an MBA, he may be eligible for promotion to product manager at $50,000 per year, with expected raises of 10 percent annually.

  If he quits his engineering job to go full-time to the same regional school as Shirley and Paul, at a tuition of $14,000 per year, he will not break even until the sixth year in his new job. His MBA ADVANTAGE will be $7,715 in the hole at the end of five years.

  Bill will be much better off keeping his job and working hard to get his MBA part time in three years, with the company paying for the tuition. At the end of four years on the new job, his MBA ADVANTAGE will be $57,417—not as much as Paul's, because Bill's pay as an engineer without the MBA would also be very good. But the *part-time* program for Bill is still a better deal, considering that it does not entail the risk of quitting and then trying to find a job after he gets the MBA.

- *Recovering from a layoff:* Peter has a degree in optics and has been employed by a major defense contractor on a secret high-powered laser project for the past several years. He was making $45,000 and has had 5 percent annual raises in recent years. With the decline in defense spending, Peter was laid off along with most of the other

---

2 Three years is about the minimum time in which someone can get a part-time MBA, taking two courses at a time. Stretching out the time for completion to five or six years greatly reduces the economic rewards for getting an MBA because it postpones the higher income stream from the new job.

3 THE MBA ADVANTAGE is calculated at the end of *four* years post-MBA in this part-time example so that it can be compared at the same end point in time to the five-year MBA ADVANTAGE from going *full time*.

engineers and scientists at his company, and there are few if any jobs available that can use his experience in high-powered lasers. He could settle for a technician's job in a nearby consumer goods company that would not make full use of his education and experience, and would only pay $25,000 per year with 5 percent raises. The consumer goods company does not pay part-time tuition for MBA degrees. He is married and his wife has a good job, so he would prefer not to move to another city to attend a Top 20 school.

Peter has decided to start on an MBA. His objective is to market high technology products. He did well on the GMAT, and a nearby regional business school has offered a 50 percent scholarship provided he attends full-time, reducing its $14,000 annual tuition in half to $7,000 per year. After studying the school's placement report, Peter estimates that with an MBA from this school he will start at $55,000, with 10 percent annual increases.

Peter has two choices:

1. He can take the $25,000 job—which does not make full use of his education and experience—and attend the regional school part-time, paying his own tuition for three years. Upon graduation he would quit the consumer goods company. THE MBA ADVANTAGE for this option would be $102,517 at the end of *four* years in his new job, at which time he would be making $73,205 per year.

2. He can go full time to the regional school. His MBA ADVANTAGE at the end of five years post-MBA would be $118,230 and in the fifth year he would be earning $80,526. (Even if Peter had to pay the full tuition, his MBA ADVANTAGE for the full-time program would be about $2,000 more than for the part-time program.)

For Peter, going full time to the regional school is the better choice.

The bottom line: If you currently have an excellent job with a good company but need the extra knowledge and credentials of an MBA, attending a good regional school part time makes more sense than quitting your job to go to a regional school full time. On the other hand, if you are in a marginal job—or if you're unemployed—then a full-time MBA program at a good regional school could give your career a real boost.

What are Your Non-financial Reasons for Getting an MBA?

Financial rewards are not the only reason for getting an MBA. David is getting his MBA for the knowledge and the credentials, and to prove that he is serious about management as a profession. He may also make more money as a result, but money was not the key reason for pursuing the MBA.

Another important advantage of getting an MBA is to open new professional options. Today many professional people have more than one career in their lifetime. The first few years may be spent learning everything you can about an industry in a large, highly-regarded company. Later on, you might move to a smaller company as a senior executive, or become an entrepreneur and create a new startup company. Perhaps you'll take early retirement and become a consultant or a college instructor. The MBA helps, by providing the education and the professional recognition to pursue that dream.

Occasionally, people are interested in making major career changes in mid-career, from engineering to management consulting for example. Rather than an evolutionary series of jobs that build on one's experience in a single field, some people want to virtually start over. They see the MBA as a way to make this happen.

Major career changes are risky, with or without an MBA. The value of the MBA is highest when the graduate can use the MBA to amplify his or her pre-MBA experience (recall our discussion in chapter 4 about the MBA as a multiplier of a person's skills and abilities). In fact, most corporate recruiters at MBA schools probe intensively at a candidate's pre-MBA work experience. They might ask if you have ever hired someone, managed a team, been in sales, or showed leadership in some unusual way. Employers know that the best measure of a prospective employee's future success is that person's past success, regardless of the industry.

If you go to a Top 20 school to change careers, the school's reputation may be so powerful that employers accept that as sufficient evidence of your capability. A degree from a school like Harvard or Stanford may be your ticket to a management consulting job at McKinsey & Co.

But regional schools usually don't have such powerful reputations, even among the companies in their immediate region. Making a major career change by attending a regional business school carries significant risk. You may be able to do it, but it will not be easy.

The bottom line: Getting an MBA from a regional school can be a great way to improve your professional options if you are on an evolutionary career path that builds on your experience. But be cautious about expecting too much from a regional MBA degree if you are committed to a total change in your career.

Are the Different Teaching Methods of Regional Schools Important?

There is sometimes a tendency for business schools, both regional and national, to overstate the value of one teaching method (i.e., the "case method" or the "lecture method") over another. Is there one magic teaching method that is clearly superior to the others?

Let's look at the evidence. The four highest ranked national business schools shown in table 6.1 (based on THE MBA ADVANTAGE shown in table 4.1) all use different teaching methods—and they all turn out exceptionally qualified graduates:

Table 6.1

Teaching methods of the top four schools, as ranked by THE MBA ADVANTAGE

	Size	School Orientation	Teaching Method	Highest Placements
Harvard	Large	Teaching	Case method	Consulting, finance
Chicago	Large	Research	Lecture	Consulting, finance
Stanford	Small	Teaching & research	Combination	Consulting, finance
MIT	Small	Research ("quant")	Lecture & thesis	Consulting, finance

The Harvard business school faculty devote enormous energy to doing a first-rate job in the classroom. But the legendary Harvard case method, in which students analyze 800-1,000 complex business scenarios during their two year program, has been the subject of criticism for many years. In a 1979 article about the Harvard Business School, *Fortune* raised doubts about the case method: "At stake here is Harvard's vaunted 'case-study method.'"[4] In 1986, *Business Week* noted that "the case method approach, Harvard's signature, is drawing attack for teaching only the simplest of ideas."[5] In 1993, *Business Week* criticized Harvard's "near-total reliance on the case-study method of teaching. Because it requires students to debate brief synopses of challenges confronting managers, the method may train managers to perform superficial analyses."[6] Yet despite years of criticism of the case method, Harvard leads our ranking of THE MBA ADVANTAGE, which is the market's valuation of the quality of the Harvard MBA. They must be doing something right.

At the other end of the spectrum, Chicago traditionally has relied heavily on lectures laced with quantitative methods and microeconomic theory. Long an intellectual powerhouse with three Nobel laureates in finance and economics, the Chicago faculty has been quick to point out that cases are an inefficient way to teach the fundamentals of business management. Rather than expect students to learn the fundamentals for themselves by analyzing hundreds of cases, they present the fundamentals in lectures, using the latest findings from the management research literature. But in the late 1980s, the Chicago lecture approach was strongly criticized by students for being "too theoretical," and in recent years cases and projects with companies have been added to provide a more balanced approach.

Third-ranked Stanford emphasizes freedom of choice and is not committed to any one teaching approach. "Professors are free to choose whatever teaching methods suit their personal style and the materials they are using. Some courses use lectures and textbooks, while others involve case discussions based upon the experiences of working managers."[7] Nor does Stanford have the traditional concentrations mandated at some other business schools. "Students are required to take a minimum of fourteen electives, but the choice of how to fill this requirement is open."[8] Freedom of choice works for Stanford. Its post-MBA starting salaries are second only to Harvard's, and it admits only 12 percent of its applicants, the most selective of any Top 20 school.

Finally, MIT—traditionally a small "quant" school favored by engineers who would rather solve equations than write cases—has no constraints on teaching methods. "The faculty uses teaching methods that are appropriate to the material being covered and the students involved. Classroom lectures and discussions, case analyses, and group projects—in addition to the relevant conceptual material—expose students to real problems in ongoing organizations."[9] Information technology provides a common framework for several of the first year core courses at MIT. "With the advent of vastly improved technology, particularly the availability of personal computers, it is believed these subjects should be taught from a common base: the use of information, information technology, and models to support individual and organizational decision making."[10] The MIT degree—an MS rather than an MBA—differs from the teaching approach of other business schools in another dimension. It is the only Top 20 graduate management degree program to require a master's thesis from each student.

---

4   Kiechel, W., "Harvard Business School Restudies Itself," *Fortune*, June 18, 1979, p. 49.
5   Byrne, J., "Remaking the Harvard Business School," *Business Week*, March 24, 1986, p. 54.
6   Byrne, J., "Harvard B-School: An American Institution in Need of Reform," *Business Week*, July 19, 1993, p. 60.
7   *The 1993 MBA Catalog*, Stanford Graduate School of Business, p. 7.
8   Ibid., p. 10.
9   *Sloan Master's Program in Management, 1993 Catalog*, Massachusetts Institute of Technology, p. 10.
10 Ibid., p. 10.

These are all superb schools with preeminent faculties, yet they each have a somewhat unique approach to teaching. Although various teaching approaches may be better suited to each school's traditional area of competence—general management for Harvard, finance for Chicago— the most popular functional areas for placement of the graduates from all four schools are consulting and finance, according to their catalogs. Functional specialization by school does not seem to explain the success of all of these different methods in producing outstanding MBAs. The case method is not better than the lecture method, or vice versa. If this is true of the best of the Top 20 schools, it is also likely to be true of the regional schools you are considering.

The bottom line: The teaching method just isn't that important. What really counts are two things: the quality of the faculty and the quality of the students.

"How Should I Choose a Good Regional School?"

When we ranked the Top 20 national schools by THE MBA ADVANTAGE in chapter 4, we had the advantage of a comprehensive published database of pre-MBA pay, post-MBA starting pay, and fifth year pay after five years on the job. Unfortunately, no such database exists for all the regional business schools in the country.

The most important factor in choosing a regional school is finding one that has an exceptional track record in your functional area of interest. Let's suppose you want to become a financial analyst. Find a school that has a proven track record in developing people like yourself as successful financial analysts. Go beyond what the school says about itself in the catalog. Here's a checklist of what to look for:

- ☐ *Placement:* Start with the school's placement report. How many students got jobs last year as financial analysts? What percent of the financial analysts had jobs by graduation? What were salary range and the average starting salary for these financial analysts? How do these starting salaries compare with those for financial analysts from other schools? What about the quality of the firms that hired these financial analysts? Are there firms on this list that you would like to work for?

- ☐ *Alumni:* Ask for a list of recent alumni who are working as financial analysts, and call them up. How good was the program? Would they recommend it? Would they choose this school again if they had it to do over?

- ☐ *Current students:* The number one source of information for potential students is word-of-mouth, and much of that comes from current students in the program. Arrange with the admissions office to visit the campus and attend a few classes in your field of interest. Ask current students in finance about the quality of teaching. Are faculty members prepared, and are they available outside of class? Are good teachers respected and rewarded by the school? How sharp are your fellow students. Can you learn from them? What is the tradition of the student body. Is there cooperation on team projects or cutthroat competition for grades? Is the dean's office responsive to student concerns? Is the placement office effective?

- ☐ *Internships:* An internship with a company between the first and second year of the MBA program is often the key to an offer of permanent employment with that firm upon graduation. You might even be able to work ten to fifteen hours a week for the company during your second year to keep the relationship going. How successful is the school at finding internships for financial analysts, and with what firms? Are there any you would like to work for?

☐ *Financial aid:* Today business schools are competing vigorously for good students, so it's a buyers' market for students shopping for a business school. Don't be afraid to drive a hard bargain on financial aid—it's expected.

☐ *Pre-MBA salaries:* Ask about the average salaries of incoming students in finance. Look for a school where the pre-MBA salaries are comparable to yours, or maybe somewhat higher. Recruiters are apt to have an average starting salary in mind for financial analysts from your school. If your pre-MBA salary is much higher than that of your classmates, your percentage stepup in post-MBA starting salary will probably be smaller than theirs.

☐ *Faculty research:* The best faculty are those that stay at the forefront of their field by contributing to the research literature. Faculty who do little or no research may not even have any interest in keeping up. To successfully compete in the job market in today's fast moving economy, you need exposure to the latest and best information in your field of study. As a check on the quality of the faculty, make sure the program is accredited by the American Assembly of Collegiate Schools of Business.

☐ *Faculty consulting:* Although most schools display the research credentials of their faculty with pride, you should also inquire about faculty who consult in your field. Consulting is a market test of the applicability of a professor's knowledge to current business problems. Not all professors are interested in consulting since many prefer to develop the basic research in their field. But a well-balanced faculty will also have professors who are experts at applying the latest knowledge to practical business problems. Furthermore, these faculty members are likely to have industry-wide networks that could prove invaluable in helping you find just the right job.

☐ *Managers in your field:* Ask for a list of managers of companies who have hired financial analysts who have graduated from the school. How good is the school's reputation in this field? Where else do they recruit, and how does this school compare with those other schools? Is the school's reputation strictly local? If so, do you plan to stay in the area after you get your degree?

With this kind of research, you will be able to make an intelligent appraisal of the strengths and weaknesses of the regional business schools you are considering. And finally, trust your intuition. The school has to be right for *you*. If you are comfortable with what you see and hear, proceed. But if the chemistry between you and the school isn't right, continue looking.

The bottom line: Choose a good regional school with an established track record of success in your field. Because published comparisons of regional schools are generally not available, you'll have to do the research yourself. Going to business school is a major commitment of time and money, and it pays to do your homework to ensure that you have made the right choice.

Chapter 7

The Best Regional Business Schools

Only about 10 percent of the more than 70,000 students who begin their MBA studies each year enroll in one of the top national business schools. As noted in chapter 6, the great majority of MBA degrees are awarded by regional schools that draw most of their students from the surrounding area, and that place most of their graduates with employers in nearby cities and towns.

In a sense, the distinction between national and regional schools is one of degree. Many of the top national business schools are actually quite "regional." For example, Columbia draws 42 percent of its students from the New York metropolitan area, and the University of Virginia's Darden School draws 37 percent of its incoming class from the State of Virginia. In terms of jobs, Stanford places 37 percent of its students in northern California, Chicago places almost 40 percent of its students in the Midwest, and almost half (46 percent) of Berkeley's grads find employment in the Bay Area surrounding the school.

A more meaningful characterization of regional schools is that most of their students do not receive starting salaries as high as those of the top national schools. As shown in the salary graphs in figures 5.1–5.3 on page 45–46, average starting salaries tend to be lower for schools like Vanderbilt and Washington University at St. Louis, which are near the borderline between national and regional schools.

In the following pages we'll look at a representative sample of the best regional schools. The selection criteria were somewhat arbitrary. Some schools were chosen because they just missed being included in the top national schools, while others were chosen because they represent an excellent choice for students in a geographic region that has few top national schools. The schools are grouped by geographic region of the country, and because they tend not to compete aggressively with each other for students, they are not ranked but rather are listed alphabetically within their region.

The schools chosen as being representative of the best of the regional schools are:

East	South	Midwest	West
Babson	Emory	Illinois	Thunderbird
Case Western	Southern Methodist	Iowa	Univ. of Southern California
Georgetown	Tulane	Michigan State	Univ. of Washington
Penn State	Rollins	Minnesota	
Pittsburgh		Purdue	

As with the individual reviews of the top national schools in chapter 5, these regional school profiles are drawn mainly from the published MBA catalogs and placement reports of the individual schools, supplemented with published information from the media, and from the author's personal knowledge of these schools.

We will use the same rating scale as used with the national schools in chapter 5. Because most of these regional schools will not have nationally ranked programs, there will be few four- and five-star ratings for this group of schools. Distinctions will be made primarily on the basis of information provided in the placement reports and catalogs received from these schools.

RATING SYSTEM

★★★★★	=	world class program: graduates a large number of students at high starting salaries, or does outstanding research or industrial outreach in this area
★★★★	=	nationally recognized program in this area
★★★	=	very good program, but with lower starting salaries
★★	=	good program, particularly for double majors
★	=	basic program, meets accreditation standards

BABSON

Babson Graduate School of Business

Accounting	★★★
Entrepreneurship	★★★★★
Finance	★★★
General management	★★★
Marketing	★★★
Information systems	★★★

Overview:

The Babson Graduate School of Business, located on a 450-acre wooded site in the Boston suburb of Wellesley, Massachusetts, has achieved national recognition for its strong program in entrepreneurship. Founded in 1919 by financier Roger W. Babson, Babson College offers a special opportunity to those prospective MBA students interested in starting their own businesses.

Strengths:

- The Babson Graduate School of Business has been building a niche in entrepreneurship for more than twenty-five years. In 1993, the Babson entrepreneurship program was ranked second in the country by *U.S. News & World Report*.[1] In the 1994 *U.S. News* survey, Babson pulled ahead of Wharton to become the top ranked entrepreneurship program in the country.[2]

- In the fall of 1993, Babson introduced a wholly new two-year MBA curriculum that abolished traditional functional courses in favor of a year-long, modular format. First year discussions and coursework trace the entrepreneurial product life cycle from the invention of a new product or service, through assessing the business opportunity, into building marketing and delivery systems, and finally to the development of a family of related products and services. Functional skills are introduced into the coursework as needed in the context of this program.

- Teaching is the first priority of Babson faculty, as opposed to research. A number of the faculty have significant business experience to bring to the classroom.

- The Business Mentor Program is another Babson innovation. Throughout the first year of the MBA program, groups of five students serve under the guidance of a faculty adviser as consultants to large and small companies in industries such as finance, high technology, and communications to apply classroom learning to real business problems.

- The International Management Internship Program provides 60 second-year students with the opportunity to work abroad for the summer with leading companies in Asia, Australia, Europe, and North and South America. Students work with highly skilled business professionals and receive credit for two graduate courses.

---

1   *U.S. News & World Report*, March 22, 1993, p. 59.
2   *U.S. News & World Report*, March 21, 1994, p. 81.

- For students entering with an undergraduate degree in business, Babson offers an accelerated MBA program that begins in May and can be completed in one calendar year.

Limitations:

- Babson is not as well known by corporate employers as the top national schools, and nearly four-fifths of the graduates find jobs in Massachusetts.

Babson Admissions Statistics (Graduating Class of 1995)[3]

Class size	170	Mean GMAT score	576[4]
Typical years of work experience	4.9	International	14%

Annual tuition and fees: $18,500

Babson Placement Statistics (Graduating Class of 1993)[5]

Babson Starting Salaries by Function (Top 10)

	% of Accepted Offers	Median
Overall	100%	$46,500
Finance	20%	$48,300
Marketing	18%	$43,000
Management/human resources	13%	$55,000
Sales	10%	$41,000
Systems/information systems	7%	$51,000
Accounting/auditing/tax	7%	$53,500
Engineering	7%	$51,000
Consulting	6%	$53,000
Analysis/research	5%	$48,500
Production/operations	3%	$46,000

Babson Placements by Geographic Region (Class of 1993)

	% of Accepted Offers
Massachusetts	79%
International	8%
Northeast	7%
Midwest	2%
Southeast	2%
West	2%

Contact: Office of Graduate Admission
            Babson Graduate School of Business
            Babson Park, Massachusetts 02157-0310. Telephone: (617) 239-4317

---

3   Babson MBA Salary Survey, 1994.
4   From *U.S. News & World Report*, March 22, 1993, p. 59.
5   Babson MBA Salary Survey, 1994.

CASE WESTERN RESERVE

Weatherhead School of Management at Case Western Reserve University

Accounting	★★★
Consulting	★★★
Finance	★★★
General management	★★★
Marketing	★★★
Information systems	★★
Operations	★★★★

Overview:

The Weatherhead School of Management at Case Western Reserve University is a small, highly innovative business school that offers a very personalized program through the development of individual learning plans for each student, supplemented by a mentoring program with senior executives. Weatherhead's highest starting salaries are in the area of operations management, and most of the students find employment in the Midwest. Weatherhead is a fine choice for prospective students looking for a small, highly-personalized MBA program.

Strengths:

- The Weatherhead program has been at the forefront of adapting its MBA program to meet the demands of today's technology-intensive global economy. The most unusual feature of the new program is the guided development by each student of a personalized learning plan based on his or her prior experience, professional strengths and weaknesses, and career interests. This plan then becomes the framework for selecting coursework and measuring progress during the two-year program.

- Another unusual feature of the Weatherhead curriculum is the voluntary mentor program, in which students pair up with senior executives in the Cleveland area to learn about the aspects of various jobs and to develop networks for internships and permanent employment.

- In addition to its regular two-year MBA curriculum, Weatherhead also offers a one-year (twelve-month) MBA for students with recent undergraduate degrees in business. Students on this accelerated program enter in June and graduate the following May. The advantage is a substantial savings in time and money without a year of lost salary.

- The core courses in the first year may be exempted for those who took similar courses as an undergraduate. In the second year, students take a pair of required "perspectives" courses that are team-taught by faculty from throughout the university to provide broad outlooks on topics such as global management and the role of technology. Second-year students also choose a functional area of concentration (three courses) from among ten functional areas, or they can design their own specialized concentration.

- The campus is located in University Circle, a 500-acre park-like setting in a suburb of Cleveland, Ohio—home to the world-renowned Cleveland Orchestra and the headquarters of twenty-nine *Fortune* 500 companies.

Limitations:

- Like most regional schools, Weatherhead is not as well-known by corporate employers as the top national schools, and over three-quarters of the graduates find employment in the Midwest.

Weatherhead Admissions Statistics (Graduating Class of 1995)[6]

Class size	233	Median GMAT score	590
Age range	22–43	Female	30%
Typical years of work experience	4	Minorities	12%
Percent with work experience	84%	International	39%

Annual tuition and fees: $16,700

Weatherhead Placement Statistics (Graduating Class of 1993)[7]

Weatherhead Starting Salaries by Function

	% of Accepted Offers	Mean
Overall	100%	$44,775
Finance	26%	$44,500
General management	23%	$46,373
Marketing	14%	$44,057
Accounting	11%	$40,000
Law	9%	$53,267
Information systems	7%	$36,750
Operations	7%	$54,500

Weatherhead Starting Salaries by Major Industry

	% of Accepted Offers	Mean
Consulting	28%	$45,284
Manufacturing	18%	$45,786
Banking	10%	$39,400
Health care	9%	$49,600
Government	7%	(NA)
Consumer goods	5%	$47,500
Other	16%	$40,580

---

6   *Weatherhead School of Management MBA Catalog, 1994.*
7   Ibid.

Weatherhead Placements by Geographic Region (Class of 1993)

	% of Accepted Offers
Midwest	77%
East	10%
International	7%
South	4%
West	2%

Contact: Terri L. Justofin
Director, Marketing and Admissions
Weatherhead School of Management
Case Western Reserve University
10900 Euclid Avenue
Cleveland, Ohio 44106-7235
Telephone: (216) 368-2031 or toll free (800) 723-0203

GEORGETOWN

Georgetown University School of Business

Consulting	★★★★
Finance	★★
General management	★★★★
Marketing	★★★★
Nonprofit (government)	★★★★★
Global business	★★★★★

Overview:

The Georgetown University School of Business is a great choice for prospective students interested in the relationship between government and business. The Washington location and the proximity of Georgetown's School for Foreign Service offer unique resources for the study of government and business in both domestic and international areas.

Strengths:

- The MBA program at Georgetown is organized around four main themes—global business, ethics, business-government relations, and management communication. Its close association with the Washington community gives the school a unique perspective on the relationship between government and business in both domestic and international matters.

- Led by a dean with an MBA from the University of Virginia, a Ph.D. from Wharton, and years of experience as a partner with the elite consulting firm McKinsey & Company, Georgetown's aim is to become a leading school for the education of international general managers.

- The School of Business offers a joint program with the School of Foreign Service (Bill Clinton's alma mater) for selected students to earn a certificate in International Business Diplomacy in addition to their MBA degree.

- Although the school attracts bright students (the mean GMAT score is 617), the program is not particularly quantitative, making the curriculum somewhat more palatable for those with liberal arts backgrounds (more than half the class). In keeping with its global perspective, it emphasizes foreign language skills. However, 78 percent of the incoming students have foreign language proficiency and/or have lived or studied abroad.

Limitations:

- The Georgetown MBA program is very young, begun in 1981 and accredited in 1988. The program has not been in existence long enough to build a strong alumni body, and it is not yet well known by many corporate recruiters. Nevertheless, the starting salaries in consulting, marketing and general management are comparable to those of many of the top national schools.

Georgetown Admissions Statistics (Graduating Class of 1994)[8]

Class size	163	Mean GMAT score	617
Mean age	26	Female	28%
Typical years of work experience	4	Minorities	11%
Percent with work experience	90%	International	25%

Annual tuition and fees: $19,850

Georgetown Placement Statistics (Graduating Class of 1992)[9]

Georgetown Starting Salaries by Function (Class of 1992)

	% of Accepted Offers	Mean
Overall	100%	$52,644
Consulting	29%	$54,423
Marketing	22%	$53,389
Finance	20%	$44,625
General management	20%	$51,375
Law	7%	$75,750
Other	2%	$36,667

Georgetown Placements by Major Industry (Class of 1992)

	% of Accepted Offers
Consulting	21%
Manufacturing (consumer goods)	21%
Computer hardware and software	15%
Manufacturing (other)	8%
Law	8%
Commercial banking	6%
Investment banking/securities	6%
Communications	4%
Financial services	2%
Other	10%

Georgetown Starting Salaries by Geographic Region (Class of 1992)

	% of Accepted Offers	Mean
Middle Atlantic	48%	$50,348
International	15%	$55,000
Northeast	15%	$57,143
Midwest	10%	$59,000
West	10%	$57,100
South	2%	$46,500

Contact: MBA Admissions Office, 105 Old North, School of Business
Georgetown University, Washington, DC 20057-1008. Telephone: (202) 687-4200

8 Georgetown MBA Catalog, 1993-94.
9 Ibid.

PENN STATE

The Smeal College of Business Administration at The Pennsylvania State University

Consulting	★★★
Finance	★★
Marketing	★★★
Operations	★★★★

Overview:

The Smeal College of Business Administration at The Pennsylvania State University is a small business school that has access to the resources of a large research university. Located in the wooded mountains of central Pennsylvania, the Smeal College offers well-regarded programs in manufacturing and operations management, and in industrial marketing. For prospective MBA students who would enjoy the splendid outdoor setting of Penn State, there is an additional benefit—very low tuition.

Strengths:

- The Smeal College offers strong programs in materials-handling logistics and in industrial marketing. It is also known for a two-semester, team-taught business communications course that stresses written and oral communications skills.

- Teaching methods at Smeal are diverse, consisting of lectures, cases, problem sets, and computer simulations. Study groups are formed in many courses to build teamwork skills.

- Recently the first-year core courses were re-scheduled in seven-week blocks for greater flexibility than under the school's old semester system. In the second year, students can concentrate in traditional areas (dual majors are common) or can work with their faculty adviser to develop a customized set of electives, taking up to two electives from outside the college.

- A special manufacturing option is available for students with undergraduate degrees in engineering to educate future managers in the applications of advanced manufacturing technology to the increasingly competitive global environment.

- As in other state-supported schools, tuition is a bargain, even for out-of-staters.

- The Penn State campus—with 40,000 students and 2,800 faculty—is located in State College, PA. A low-stress small town set in the beautiful wooded mountains of Central Pennsylvania, it has abundant opportunities in the nearby forests and parks for camping, hiking, fishing, skiing, and even hang gliding.

Limitations:

- State College is located right in the middle of Pennsylvania, with Philadelphia 150 miles to the east and Pittsburgh 120 miles to the west. Although the area is beautiful, corporate recruiters often find the location difficult to reach, particularly during the winter recruiting season.

Smeal Admissions Statistics (Graduating Class of 1994)[10]

Class size	150	Mean GMAT score	585 [11]
Mean age	26	Female	28%
Mean years of work experience	3	Minorities	20%
Percent with work experience	83%	International	20%

Annual tuition and fees: $5,088 (residents); $10,176 (non-residents)

Smeal Placement Statistics (Graduating Class of 1993)[12]

Smeal Starting Salaries by Function

	% of Accepted Offers	Mean
Overall	100%	$44,281
Finance	22%	$43,345
Consulting	20%	$52,000
Marketing	14%	$41,467
Logistics	12%	$40,917
Other (sales, purchasing, planning)	32%	$49,140

Smeal Placements by Major Industry

	% of Accepted Offers	Mean
Financial	22%	$42,750
Consumer products and services	17%	$51,330
Consulting	14%	$52,000
Manufacturing	12%	$37,133
Other (energy, education, logistics)	10%	$45,000
Telecommunications	10%	$44,500
Government	8%	$41,800
Automotive	7%	$46,250

Contact: MBA Program
The Smeal College of Business Administration
The Pennsylvania State University
106 Business Administration Building
University Park, Pennsylvania 16802-3000
Telephone: (814) 863-0474

---

10 The Smeal College MBA Catalog, 1993-94.
11 Smeal does not publish a mean GMAT score. The value estimated by *Business Week* was 580 and by *U.S. News and World Report* was 590.
12 Smeal College Placement Report, 1993.

PITTSBURGH

Joseph M. Katz Graduate School of Business at the University of Pittsburgh

Accounting	★★★
Finance	★★★
Health administration	★★★★
Information systems	★★★★
Marketing	★★★
Operations	★★★

Overview:

The Joseph M. Katz Graduate School of Business offers a unique eleven-month fully ac-credited MBA program, giving prospective students the opportunity of earning an MBA in one calendar year. Inasmuch as the opportunity cost of foregone salary is the dominant cost of going to business school for many students, the Katz one-year program offers the potential for signifi-cant cost savings. In addition, while the tuition is over $21,000 for out-of-staters, it is incurred for only one year. For prospective students in a hurry (or who want to minimize their opportunity costs), the Katz MBA program deserves a careful look.

Strengths:

- The underlying theme of the new Katz MBA curriculum is "adding value to organiza-tions." The eleven-month program, from mid-July to mid-June of the following year, is a dramatic embodiment of this theme. Students save the cost of a second year's tuition and gain an extra year's earning power on the job, and still earn a fully accredited MBA degree.

- Several dual degree programs are offered in combination with the eleven-month MBA, including both an MBA and a Master of Health Administration in two years, and an MBA with a Master of International Business, also in two years. In the time it takes to get an MBA at most schools, the graduates of the Katz School can earn two master's degrees.

- Project courses with local and international companies are among the most popular electives at the Katz School. Teams of students work with major firms such as USX, Bethlehem Steel, Barclay's Bank, and Eastman Kodak Company under the guidance of experienced faculty to solve actual corporate problems.

- The Katz School is housed in a modern glass-sided building on the Pitt campus, ten minutes from the center of Pittsburgh.

- The city of Pittsburgh, famous for its Golden Triangle business district at the confluence of the Allegheny, Monongahela, and Ohio Rivers, is a major financial and commercial center and is home to eleven *Fortune* 500 companies, as well as the Steelers football team and the Pirates baseball club.

Limitations:

- Cramming a full MBA program into eleven months puts pressure on both the faculty and the students. According to *Business Week*, teaching quality is below average, and many Katz MBAs report that the workload is intense.

- With a mean GMAT score of 603, Katz students are as bright as those in some nationally-ranked MBA programs, yet the starting salaries, in the low- to mid-forties, are well below those of the Top 20 schools. It may be that the market has yet to accept that a one-year MBA is truly as valuable as a more traditional two-year MBA.

Katz Admissions Statistics (Graduating Class of 1995)[13]

Class size	301	Mean GMAT score	603
Average age	27	Women	31%
Typical years of work experience	4	Minorities	10%
		International	31%

Tuition and fees: $12,897 (in state) for the one year of study; $21,651 (out-of-state) for the one year of study

Katz Placement Statistics (Graduating Class of 1993)[14]

Katz Starting Salaries by MBA Concentration

	% of Accepted Offers	Mean
Overall	100%	$43,000
Finance	38%	$42,623
Marketing	16%	$45,650
MBA/Master of Health Administration	9%	$31,950
Operations	6%	$47,290
MBA/Master of International Business	6%	$45,184
Accounting	4%	$42,300
Human resources	4%	$35,417
Information systems	3%	$45,333

Katz Placements by Geographic Region

	% of Accepted Offers
Pennsylvania	43%
International	18%
Midwest	16%
Northeast	12%
South	5%
West	1%

13 The Katz School MBA Catalog 1994-1995.
14 Ibid.

Contact: Kathleen Riehle Valentine
Director of Admissions
The Joseph M. Katz Graduate School of Business
276 Mervis Hall
University of Pittsburgh
Pittsburgh, Pennsylvania 15620
Telephone: (412) 648-1700

EMORY

Emory Business School at Emory University

Accounting	★★
Consulting	★★★
Finance	★★★★
General management	★★★
Marketing	★★★★
Operations	★★

Overview:

The Emory Business School at Emory University is a small, collegial school located in one of the fastest growing cities of the Sunbelt. Emory has been unusually innovative in establishing ongoing projects with top corporations. Although most students currently find employment in the Atlanta area, Emory has the potential to become a nationally ranked top school.

Strengths:

- The Emory Business School is one of the smallest business schools, with an incoming class of only 126 students. Emory has one of the best faculty-to-student ratios, with one faculty member for every six students. To take advantage of the small size and collegiality of the school, the faculty has chosen not to divide up into formal academic departments; rather, multidisciplinary activities by faculty and students are strongly encouraged.

- Emory has reached out to its key corporate customers by setting up a Customer Business Development Track. Initiated in 1991 with the encouragement of the CEO of Procter & Gamble, the new program integrates a summer practicum at P&G with a team-taught multidisciplinary class in the fall semester. In 1992, Coca-Cola joined the track, and Motorola joined in 1993. This experimental new approach to teaching combines real-world hands-on field experience with classroom discussion of the field experiences.

- Emory students are also involved with volunteer projects to help Atlanta's poor, and in marketing projects with major corporations such as United Parcel Service, BellSouth, and Budget Car Rental, with final presentations to the CEOs of these companies. The prize for the top marketing project is $5,000, which students often donate to charity.

- First-year core courses may be waived by taking waiver exams during orientation week, allowing students to substitute electives for the waived courses. In the second year, students are free to take electives in the traditional concentrations, or they can set up customized programs to meet their career objectives.

- In addition to the regular two-year MBA, Emory also offers a one-year MBA for students with undergraduate degrees in business and significant work experience. In the one-year program, students enter in June for an intensive series of summer courses and workshops and then join the regular second year class in the fall to graduate in May.

- While the curriculum at Emory is demanding, it is not a "quant" school. Most of the incoming students are not engineers—49 percent have liberal arts degrees and 26 percent have undergraduate degrees in business.

- One of Emory's major assets is the city of Atlanta, which combines southern grace with urban sophistication. Over 450 of the *Fortune* 500 have headquarters or offices in Atlanta.

Limitations:

- Although Emory attracts high quality students (average GMAT score is 620), it has not yet achieved widespread national recognition. In 1993, over half of the graduating class accepted jobs in Atlanta. But more than most other regional schools, Emory has the potential to become a top-ranked national school.

Emory Admissions Statistics (Graduating Class of 1995) [15]

Class size	126	Mean GMAT score	620
Mean years of work experience	4	International	16%
Percent with work experience	90%		

Annual tuition and fees: $17,900

Emory Placement Statistics (Graduating Class of 1993) [16]

Emory Starting Salaries by Function

	% of Accepted Offers	Range
Marketing/sales	26%	$42,000–$60,000
Finance/accounting	22%	$35,750–$70,000
General management	19%	$38,000–$55,000
Consulting	17%	$42,000–$75,000
Investments	12%	$49,000–$62,000
Other	4%	$60,000–$60,000

Emory Placements by Major Industry

	% of Accepted Offers	Range
Banking/financial	23%	$36,000–$70,000
Consumer products	13%	$50,000–$55,000
Consulting	9%	$52,000–$75,000
Food service	9%	$44,000–$51,000
Health care	9%	$42,000–$60,000
High tech/communications	9%	$42,000–$60,000
Transportation	9%	$42,500–$50,000
Public accounting	4%	$35,750–$36,300
Manufacturing	2%	$40,000–$40,000
Other	13%	$38,000–$60,000

15 Emory Business School MBA Program Catalog, 1993-94.
16 Ibid.

The MBA Advantage

Contact: Julie Barefoot
             Director of Admissions
             Emory University
             School of Business Administration
             Atlanta, Georgia 30322-2710
             Telephone: (404) 727-6311

SOUTHERN METHODIST

Edwin L. Cox School of Business at Southern Methodist University

Consulting	★★
Finance	★★★★
Marketing	★★★
Information systems	★★
Operations	★★

Overview:

The Cox School at Southern Methodist University offers unusual opportunities for self-development of its MBA students. The personal assessment and coaching program through the school's Business Leadership Center and the Corporate Mentor program with industry leaders gives students the chance to develop their individual leadership and communication skills and to receive personal advice and counsel from business leaders. The school has been successful in achieving a solid reputation in finance, as shown by the strong starting salaries in this area. The vitality of the Dallas area also makes the Cox School an attractive choice.

Strengths:

- In addition to the regular MBA coursework, the Cox School offers an innovative personal assessment program to develop leadership skills through the school's Business Leadership Center. Each incoming student is provided with an initial personalized assessment of his or her strengths and weaknesses, followed by a two-year program of goal-setting, coaching, tutoring, and self-evaluation to maximize each student's leadership and communication skills.

- Summer internships with top companies are major learning experiences for most MBA students, and the Cox School is unusually successful in finding good internships for its students. In a recent class, 95 percent of the students who wanted internships obtained them with companies like American Airlines, Procter & Gamble, JC Penney, and Johnson & Johnson.

- Another special program for Cox students is the Corporate Mentor program. Nearly 200 Dallas-area business leaders act as personal mentors to several MBA students each year, advising and counseling students as they develop their career plans.

- Although the overall starting salaries of Cox graduates are generally lower than those of most national schools, the starting salaries in financial services and investment banking are comparable to those from the top national schools.

- To encourage students to develop a sense of responsibility to the community as well as to their jobs, Cox invites teams of student consultants to work through the Community Partners program with local non-profit organizations in the areas of arts, education, health, and social service. A recent competition sponsored by Brown Brothers Harriman resulted in a $7,500 award for the best consulting project, with the proceeds donated to charity.

- Dallas, with a metropolitan population of 2.8 million, is one of the Sunbelt's great centers of commerce and finance. In a recent *Fortune* survey, it was ranked number 4 in the country in pro-business attitude.[17]

Limitations:

- Small and regional, the Cox School has less national recognition than many schools with students of comparable quality.
- The MBA curriculum consists of twenty semester courses, of which fourteen are required and six are electives. Although well structured, the second year of this program is less flexible than at many other schools.

Cox Admissions Statistics (Graduating Class of 1994)[18]

Class size	120	Mean GMAT score	610
Average age	25	Female	25%
Average years of work experience	3	Minorities	3%
		International	7%

Annual tuition and fees: $17,012

Cox Placement Statistics (Graduating Class of 1993)[19]

Cox Placements by Major Industry

	% of Accepted Offers	Mean
Consulting	23%	$42,077
Transportation/automotive	11%	$44,306
Service	10%	$43,825
Consumer products/retailing	8%	$39,250
High technology	8%	$39,200
Commercial banking	7%	$46,200
Telecommunications	5%	$45,667
Financial services	5%	$54,333
Investment banking	4%	$55,000
Real estate/construction	4%	$35,833
Health care	4%	$39,833
Advertising/marketing services	3%	$31,500

Contact: Edwin L. Cox School of Business, Graduate Office, Southern Methodist University Dallas, Texas 75275-0333. Telephone: (214) 768-2630 or toll free (800) 472-3622

17 Labich, K., "The Best Cities for Knowledge Workers," *Fortune*, November 15, 1993, p. 64.
18 Information obtained from *Business Week Guide to the Best Business Schools*, 3rd Edition, McGraw-Hill, 1993, pp. 252-255.
19 Cox School of Business Summary of Placement, MBA Class of 1993.

TULANE

A. B. Freeman School of Business at Tulane University

Accounting	★★★★
Consulting	★★★
Finance	★★★
General management	★★
Human resources	★★★
Marketing	★★★
Operations	★★

Overview:

The Freeman School at Tulane University is a small, friendly business school with modern facilities, an intense commitment to a global perspective in management education, and a strong placement record in public accounting. For some prospective students, the New Orleans lifestyle is a special added attraction.

Strengths:

- With 26 percent of its graduates entering public accounting, the Freeman School has one of the largest proportions of students entering this field of any major business school.

- As with most small schools, the emphasis is on cooperation and teamwork rather than competition between students, supporting Freeman's reputation as a friendly place.

- Although the Freeman School is small (118 in the entering class), it has a long history. It was founded in 1914 and accredited in 1916, and is well known in the immediate area. The MBA program was started in 1940.

- The school is not committed to a particular teaching approach, such as the case method. Instead, a wide variety of teaching methods are used at Freeman—group projects, cases analyses, computer simulations, videotape sessions and field assignments.

- One thing that *is* common to all Freeman courses—a strong emphasis on global business.

- An innovative feature of the MBA curriculum is a set of four intensive required "focus modules" given prior to the start of the fall and spring semesters in both the first and second years. In the fall of the first year, the first module concentrates on the functions of an executive in an organization. The second module is on the social environment of business; the third, in the fall of the second year, on total quality management; and the final module focuses on leadership skills.

- The Freeman School is housed in a relatively new building, a seven-story complex completed in 1986 that includes such special features as a computer classroom with forty-four networked laptop computers for hands-on computer instruction and a complete television studio with full production and editing facilities for practicing presentation skills.

- New Orleans, the home of Tulane University, is a special Southern city, with warm weather, a low cost-of-living, jazz, spicy food, and Mardi Gras.

Limitations:

- Although the lifestyle in New Orleans is one of the attractions for attending the Freeman School, the city does not have the same vigorous pro-business climate as many other large cities. Graduates may find it necessary to look beyond the immediate area for top jobs in their fields.

Freeman Admissions Statistics (Graduating Class of 1993)[20]

Class size	118	Mean GMAT score	595
Average age	25	Female	24%
Average years of work experience	3	Minorities	12%
Percentage with work experience	81%	International	33%

Annual tuition and fees: $18,760

Freeman Placement Statistics (Graduating Class of 1993)[21]

Freeman Placements by Function

	% of Accepted Offers	Mean
Finance	22%	$48,311
Accounting, audit, and tax	22%	$32,642
General management	19%	$34,820
Consulting	12%	$48,550
Human resources	9%	$46,680
Marketing	5%	$60,000
Operations	4%	$40,500

Freeman Placements by Major Industry

	% of Accepted Offers	Mean
Public accounting	26%	$37,580
Commercial banking	17%	$46,971
Manufacturing	10%	$44,100
Food Services	8%	$43,100
Consulting	7%	$48,500
Financial services & investment banking	7%	$50,000
Health care	7%	$60,000
Oil and gas	3%	$40,200

---

20 Freeman 1993 MBA Class Profile Report.
21 Freeman 1993 MBA Placement Report.

Freeman Placements by Region (Class of 1993)

	% of Accepted Offers	Mean
South	45%	$36,873
Southwest	15%	$44,333
International	15%	$57,400
Northeast	9%	$52,400
Midwest	5%	$46,600
West	5%	$44,000
Mid-Atlantic	3%	$44,150
U.S. Territories	3%	$33,000

Contact: John C. Silbernagel
            Director of Admissions
            A.B. Freeman School of Business
            Tulane University
            New Orleans, Louisiana 70118-5669
            Telephone: (504) 865-5410 or toll free (800) 223-5402

ROLLINS

Roy E. Crummer Graduate School of Business at Rollins College

Consulting	★★★
Finance	★★★
General management	★★
Marketing	★★★
Operations	★★★

Overview:

The Crummer Graduate School of Business at Rollins College is a small but excellent business school in Winter Park, Florida, a suburb of Orlando. Teaching quality comes first at Crummer, and the school integrates the latest laptop computer hardware and software into its coursework more successfully than many better-known national schools.

Strengths:[22]

- The Crummer Graduate School of Business at Rollins College fits the description of "small but excellent." The parent college, Rollins, was recently ranked number 5 in regional universities of the South in a national survey by *U.S. News & World Report.*[23]

- Although the Crummer School admits only about sixty students per year, it draws them from many parts of the U.S. and overseas—fewer than 30 percent of Crummer's incoming students did their undergraduate work in the state of Florida—thus qualifying the school for consideration as a true regional school.

- Crummer has an unusual approach to hiring faculty. Most business schools hire newly graduated Ph.D.s as assistant professors and hope that in time they will learn to become good teachers. Crummer hires only experienced professors—all with doctorates—and encourages them to write textbooks for their courses rather than scholarly papers for academic journals, thus ensuring that the time spent by faculty on writing will directly enhance classroom performance.[24] More than 70 percent of the faculty have written at least one textbook.

- As at Harvard, the case method is the primary method of instruction at Crummer. But Crummer adds something extra to the case method. Upon entering, every student receives a laptop computer loaded with state-of-the-art software, all of which is included in the cost of the tuition. All students carry their laptops to class, and when they have case discussions, the students can run real-time "what if" studies on their spreadsheets to test the financial results of various strategies as they are proposed during the discus-

---

22 Based in part on "A Special Introduction to the Crummer School," a videotape available from the Crummer School.
23 "America's Best Colleges," *U.S. News and World Report,* 1993 edition, p. 37.
24 Fowler, E., "Business Schools Juggle Tradition and Change," *The New York Times,* as reprinted in the *Democrat and Chronicle,* Rochester, New York, June 25, 1990, p. 24D.

sion. This is an area where Crummer seems to be ahead of Harvard and many other top schools.

- Like several other small schools in major cities, Crummer has established a mentor program to give students the opportunity to receive advice and counsel from local senior managers. Among prominent mentors who have served as advisors to Crummer MBA students are the president of Tupperware, the chairman and CEO of Readers' Digest, the chairman of SunBank, and the Governor of the State of Florida.

- Winter Park is an upscale shopping and residential area with older homes and mature trees. The campus itself is in a park-like setting on the edge of a small lake (one professor is said to commute by boat) and the wooded grounds around the tile-roofed buildings are meticulously groomed. And when the work load gets to be too much, students can unwind at Walt Disney World, Cypress Gardens, or the nearby beaches.

Limitations:

- As a small player on the national scene, Crummer does very well by attracting more than half of its students from areas outside the southeastern United States. Given the impressive growth opportunities in the Greater Orlando area and in the Southeast in general, it's not clear that Crummer should even try to increase its presence in the highly competitive national market.

Crummer Admissions Statistics (Graduating Class of 1993)[25]			
Class size	62	Median GMAT score	600
Average age	26	International	10%
Average years of work experience	3	Percentage with work experience	80%

Annual tuition and fees: $15,440

---

25 Crummer Graduate School of Business Catalog, 1993-94.

Crummer Placement Statistics (Graduating Class of 1993)[26]

The salary range for Crummer graduates was $25,000–$53,000. The average starting salary for students in the Class of '93 who had at least two years of prior work experience was $45,000.

Crummer Salaries by Function (exclusive of bonuses or commissions)

	% of Accepted Offers	Mean
Finance	31%	$43,000
General management	14%	$38,000
Consulting	11%	$45,000
Marketing/sales	11%	$35,000
Operations	9%	$43,000
Information systems	2%	$40,000
Other	22%	(NA)

Contact: Office of Admissions
             Crummer Graduate School of Business
             Rollins College
             1000 Holt Avenue
             Winter Park, Florida 32789-4499
             Telephone: (407) 646-2405

---

26 Crummer Career Planning and Placement Report, August 1993.

ILLINOIS

College of Commerce and Business Administration at the University of Illinois at
Urbana-Champaign

Accounting	★★★★★
Finance	★★
Marketing	★★★
Information Systems	★★★

Overview:

The University of Illinois MBA program in accounting is nationally recognized as one of the best. According to the school's catalog, "More partners in the 'Big Eight' accounting firms are graduates of Illinois than of any other institution."[27] In 1993, the Illinois accounting program was ranked first in the country by *U.S. News & World Report.*[28] In view of the low tuition, even for out-of-staters, prospective MBA students planning to major in accounting should carefully consider the program at Illinois.

Strengths:

- The accounting program at Illinois is very highly regarded. It was ranked number 1 by *U.S. News & World Report* in 1993, and number 2 in 1994, behind Stanford but still ahead of Texas, Chicago and Wharton.[29] Given the outstanding reputations of these other schools, the high ranking of the Illinois accounting curriculum is impressive.

- The business school faculty at Illinois has a distinguished tradition of excellence in research, as has the rest of the university. Among the alumni of the University of Illinois are seven Nobel Laureates and sixteen Pulitzer Prize winners.

- Teamwork is emphasized at Illinois. Students are assigned to study groups in their first year and do many of their assignments as team projects. Nearly half of the incoming students have undergraduate degrees in business.

- The MBA curriculum at Illinois is fairly conventional. The usual core courses are taken in the first year, and the second year is open for electives, except for required courses in Business Policy and Business Law. Students can concentrate in one or more areas, or they can customize their second year programs from a long list of electives. The school has recently introduced new areas of specialization in health care management, agribusiness, and the management of technology.

Limitations:

- The MBA program at Illinois has been expanded in part by admitting younger students

---

27 Illinois MBA catalog, 1994, p. 3.
28 *U.S. News & World Report*, March 22, 1993, p. 59.
29 Ibid., and *U.S. News & World Report*, March 21, 1994, p. 81.

with less work experience. With only two years of experience on average, the Illinois students are among the least experienced of those at any major business school. This may explain the low average starting salary of just under $39,000.

Illinois Admissions Statistics (Graduating Class of 1995)[30]

Class size	253	Mean GMAT score	600
Average age	24	Minorities	13%
Average years of work experience	2	Women	28%
		International	14%

Annual tuition (1993-94): $4,988 (in-state); $10,520 (out-of-state)

Illinois Placement Statistics (Graduating Class of 1993)

Illinois MBA starting salaries and placement statistics for the Class of '93 were not published by the school. However, *U.S. News & World Report* listed the median 1993 starting salary as $38,700.[31]

Contact: MBA Program at the University of Illinois
15 Commerce West
1206 South Sixth Street
Champaign, Illinois 61820
Telephone: 1-800-MBA-UIUC or 1-217-244-7602

---

30 Illinois MBA Profile, Fall 1993.
31 *U.S. News & World Report*, March 21, 1994, p. 81.

IOWA

The Iowa Business School at the University of Iowa

Accounting	★★★
Finance	★★★
Marketing	★★★
Human resources	★★★
Information systems	★★
Operations	★★

Overview:

The Iowa Business School at the University of Iowa has a strong program in finance as well as competent programs in other areas. Midwest friendliness and Big Ten sports will be attractive to many prospective students, as will the very low tuition, even for out-of-staters.

Strengths:
- Located in the middle of the beautiful farm country of the Midwest, Iowa has a very good program in finance and a solid program in marketing. Almost a quarter of the graduates accept jobs in banking, insurance, and financial services.
- Iowa is more than just a teaching-oriented school. Many of the faculty have strong research track records and serve as editors and contributors to national scholarly journals.
- Like many other leading schools, the Iowa Business School has a new building. In the fall of 1993, the business school moved into a new $33 million facility.
- Tuition at Iowa is very low, even for a state-supported school.
- About half of the MBA students come from the state of Iowa. Midwest friendliness is a distinguishing characteristic of the school, and Big Ten sports are an extra benefit.

Limitations:
- Like other business schools in rural locations, Iowa is rather isolated from major urban centers of finance and commerce, which translates into fewer visits from corporate recruiters.
- According to the 1992 *Business Week* Top 20 survey, the quality of teaching, particularly in the core courses, was below that of other leading business schools.

Iowa Admissions Statistics (Graduating Class of 1995)[32]

Class size	92	Median GMAT score	590
Average age	27	Female	30%
Percentage with work experience	76%	Minorities	6%

Annual tuition and fees: $3,396 (resident); $8,708 (non-resident)

Iowa Placement Statistics (Graduating Class of 1993)[33]

Iowa Placements by Concentration

	Mean
Overall annual salary	$38,400
Overall signing bonus	$2,800
Accounting	$38,200
Finance/investment	$38,800
Human resources	$40,500
MBA/JD	$40,200
Management information systems	$34,200
Marketing	$40,000
Production and operations	$35,200

Iowa Placements by Functional Area

	% of Accepted Offers
Finance and investments	26%
Marketing and sales management	19%
Accounting and consulting	14%
General management	13%
Human resources	8%
Operations and engineering management	7%
Management information systems	5%
Law	4%

---

32 Iowa Fall 1993 Entering Class Profile Report.
33 Iowa MBA Graduating Class Placement Profile, 1992-93.

Iowa Placements by Industry

	% of Accepted Offers
Manufacturing	35%
Automotive and mechanical equipment	9%
Petroleum and allied products	5%
Building materials and durable goods	4%
Chemicals, drugs, and allied products	4%
Glass, paper, packaging, and allied products	4%
Electrical machinery and equipment	3%
Electronics, computers, and business machines	3%
Food, beverage, and agricultural processing	3%
Non-Manufacturing	65%
Banking, finance, and insurance	23%
Medical and healthcare services	9%
Accounting, consulting, and research	9%
Government	4%
Merchandising, media, and publishing	4%
Non-profit and educational institutions	4%
Utilities	4%
Other	8%

Iowa Placements by Geographic Area

	% of Accepted Offers
Iowa	36%
Midwest	35%
South	11%
East	8%
West	6%
International	4%

Contact: Academic Programs Office
             121 Phillips Hall
             College of Business Administration
             The University of Iowa
             Iowa City, Iowa 52242
             Telephone: (319) 335-1037

MICHIGAN STATE

The Eli Broad Graduate School of Management at Michigan State University

Accounting	★★★
Finance	★★
Human resources	★★
Marketing	★★★
Operations/logistics	★★★★★

Overview:

The Eli Broad Graduate School of Management at Michigan State University has strong ties to the automotive industry, and the overall focus of the school is on manufacturing and materials management. A recent major gift to the school and an impressive new building have revitalized the MBA program, creating expectations that the school will move up in national prominence.

Strengths:

- The focus at the Eli Broad School is on manufacturing and the whole "value chain" system, from procurement to marketing. In this school, finance takes a back seat to operations management and logistics.

- In keeping with the school's focus on manufacturing, more than one-quarter of graduates take jobs in the automobile industry. Robert Stempel, former chairman of General Motors and Michigan State MBA Class of 1970, is an alum.

- This is a school on the move: In 1991, it received a $20 million gift from Eli Broad, a successful entrepreneur who received his degree in accounting from Michigan State University in 1954. Broad's gift is being invested in upgrading the MBA program with scholarships and chaired professorships. Simultaneously, the school is completing a $22 million new building that will provide state-of-the-art classrooms as well as facilities for study group meetings.

- Broad is truly a regional school—86 percent of the Class of '92 stayed in the Midwest.

Limitations:

- Although it is possible to waive certain core courses based on prior coursework, the curriculum is less flexible than at most other leading schools. In the second year, only four course slots are available for electives and all or most of these are used to fill the concentration requirement.

- Starting salaries have been lower than at many other schools, perhaps reflecting the slow automotive market of the early 1990s.

MSU Admissions Statistics (Graduating Class of 1993)[34]

Class size	277	Mean GMAT score	590
Average age	26	Female	38%
Percentage with work experience	60%	Minorities	11%
		International	12%

Annual tuition and fees: $8,403 (residents); $16,484 (non-residents)

MSU Placement Statistics (Graduating Class of 1992)[35]

MSU Placements by Concentration (Class of 1992)

	% of Accepted Offers	Mean
Overall	100%	$38,428
Finance	31%	$35,853
Marketing	30%	$38,980
Professional accounting	18%	$35,111
Materials and logistics management	13%	
Operations		$40,382
Purchasing		$38,849
Transportation/distribution		$41,851
Personnel/human relations	5%	$37,969
Hotel, restaurant, and institutional mgmt.	2%	NA
Management science	1%	NA

MSU Placements by Industry (Class of 1992)

	% of Accepted Offers
Automotive and mechanical equipment	26%
Accounting	18%
Electronics and instruments	8%
Banking, finance, and insurance	7%
Chemicals, drugs, and related products	6%
Education, college, and university	5%
Government	5%
Graduate school	4%
Merchandising and related services	4%
Medical services	3%
Public utilities	3%
Food and beverage processing	2%
Transportation	2%
Other	7%

---

34 Data from *The Official Guide to MBA Programs, 1992-94*, Graduate Management Admission Council and the Eli Broad Master of Business Administration Catalog, 1993-94.

35 MBA Placement Information 1992, The Eli Broad Graduate School of Management.

MSU Placements by Geographic Area (Class of 1992)

	% of Accepted Offers
Midwest	86%
East	5%
West	3%
South	3%
International	3%

Contact: Jennifer Chizuk
Assistant Director of the MBA Program
The Eli Broad Graduate School of Management
Michigan State University
215 Eppley Center
East Lansing, Michigan 48824-1121
Telephone: (517) 355-7604

MINNESOTA

Carlson School of Management at the University of Minnesota

Accounting	★★
Finance	★★★
Marketing	★★★
Information systems	★★★★★
Operations	★★

Overview:

The Carlson School of Management at the University of Minnesota has a strong research tradition, with national recognition in the field of management information systems. With new leadership in the dean's office and millions of dollars of new funding, the school is making important changes designed to improve its national recognition.

Strengths:

- Carlson is a school in transition: Led by an energetic new dean and fueled by $40 million of new funding, the school has endowed eighteen new faculty chairs, increased student scholarships, expanded faculty research opportunities, and improved student services.[36]

- The Carlson School is building on a tradition of excellence in several academic areas. Its management information systems program, for example, was ranked number 2 in the country in a 1993 poll of deans conducted by *U.S. News & World Report.*[37]

- The school is working hard to increase the multidisciplinary nature of the curriculum. In the first year, the functional core courses in marketing, finance, accounting, etc., are integrated by six faculty who work as a team to tie the functional areas together.

- It's not all theory at Carlson. In the second year, every student participates in a hands-on, two-quarter consulting field project for local companies. Teams of students carry out more than forty projects a year for companies ranging from 3M and Cascade Medical to the Children's Theatre Company. Some project teams even develop business plans for entrepreneurial startups using new technology created at the university.

- For students entering with an undergraduate degree in business, Carlson offers an accelerated one-year program that is initiated in the summer quarter, with graduation the following June.

- The Twin Cities area is a major asset of the school, ranking fifth in the country in the number of headquarters for *Fortune* 500 companies. A recent *Fortune* poll to select the best cities in the country for knowledge workers ranked the Twin Cities as number 10 in the nation.[38]

36 Merrill, A., "Learning to Change," *St. Paul Pioneer Press*, April 19, 1993, pp. F1-F2.
37 "America's Best Graduate Schools," *U.S. News & World Report*, March 22, 1993, p. 59.
38 Labich, K., "The Best Cities for Knowledge Workers," *Fortune*, November 15, 1993, p. 62.

Limitations:

- The Carlson School is currently housed in a dated complex that is not competitive with the new state-of-the-art facilities of many of the other leading schools.

- While students are enthusiastic about the changes at Carlson, they complain that teaching quality—particularly in the core courses—needs improvement. Perhaps the new plan for team teaching in the core courses will solve the problem.

Carlson Admissions Statistics (Graduating Class of 1993)[39]

Class size	178	Mean GMAT score	598
Average age	27	Female	29%
Percent with work experience	85%		

Annual tuition and fees: $8,268 (resident); $12,618 (non-resident)

Carlson Placement Statistics (Graduating Class of 1993)[40]

Carlson Placements by Concentration

	Mean
Overall	$42,011
Accounting	$29,500
Finance	$42,013
Strategic management	$54,725
Information systems	$39,331
Marketing management	$43,653
Operations management	$39,855

Carlson Placements by Major Industry

	% Placement	Mean
Merchandising and services	15%	$36,639
Food and beverage processing	11%	$43,896
Chemicals, drugs, and allied products	8%	$43,864
Research and/or consulting	8%	$35,445
Glass, paper packaging and allied products	7%	$44,795
Utilities/transportation	7%	$36,745
Banking	7%	$39,550
Accounting	6%	$40,234
Computers and business machines	5%	$41,551
Health care and medical services	5%	$36,850

Contact: Donald R. Bell, Assistant Dean and Director
MBA Programs Office, Carlson School of Management, University of Minnesota
295 Humphrey Center, 271 Nineteenth Avenue South
Minneapolis, Minnesota 55455. Telephone: (612) 625-5555

39 Carlson Career Services Center Annual Report, 1992-1993.
40 Ibid.

PURDUE

Krannert Graduate School of Management at Purdue University

Finance	★★
Marketing	★★★
Information systems	★★★★
Operations	★★★★★
Human resources	★★★★

Overview:

The Krannert Graduate School of Management at Purdue University is highly regarded for its program in manufacturing and operations management. The school is particularly attractive to prospective students with engineering or science backgrounds who would enjoy a quantitative teaching approach. A special feature of the school is the eleven-month Master of Science in Industrial Administration (MSIA) program for students with significant prior work experience. Coupled with the low tuition, this accelerated program is definitely a "best buy" for those interested in careers in manufacturing.

Strengths:

- The Krannert School is "quant" school; that is, most of the incoming students have backgrounds in engineering, math, science, or business, and only 15 percent have undergraduate degrees in the social sciences or humanities. The school uses the case method for many of the courses and makes heavy use of spreadsheets and computer modeling for developing case solutions.

- Manufacturing management is the major focus of the Krannert School. The school offers a first-rate program in manufacturing and operations management that was recently ranked number 3 in the country in a survey by *U.S. News & World Report*.[41] The majority of students go to work for very large companies (over $10 billion in sales). Unlike many other business schools where finance dominates career choices, Krannert students choose heavy manufacturing over financial services by a factor of almost five to one (see placement statistics).

- Krannert offers two master's degrees in management—an eleven-month Master of Science in Industrial Administration (MSIA) and a two-year Master of Science in management (MS). The MSIA is for students who have significant work experience, whereas the two-year MS offers the opportunity to develop one or more functional concentrations. The school also offers a special two-year Master of Science in Human Resource Management (MSHR) program that is distinguished by intensive use of the computer in the majority of the human resources courses.

41 "America's Best Graduate Schools," *U.S. News & World Report*, March 22, 1993, p. 59.

- Hands-on experience is valued by Krannert students. More than half of the MS students carry out consulting projects for companies as part of their coursework.

- As a state-supported school, Krannert's tuition is very low, even for those who are not residents of Indiana. The eleven-month MSIA program is a particularly good buy.

- The facilities of the Krannert Building are comparable to many other leading schools, including horseshoe-shaped case rooms to encourage discussion, state-of-the-art projection equipment, and one of the best management libraries in the nation. A special feature of the Krannert Building is the Behavioral Sciences Laboratories complex on the seventh floor, with extensive video and audio recording equipment to study group dynamics and decision making.

- West Lafayette is a handsome college town of 70,000, located between Indianapolis (70 miles) and Chicago (120 miles). Big Ten athletics and many university-sponsored cultural opportunities are popular attractions.

Limitations:

- Krannert is famous for the very heavy workload of its programs, which some students feel is excessive. Coupled with this are complaints about teaching quality, which was rated among the lowest of the thirty-six schools polled in the 1992 *Business Week* Top 20 survey.

- The percentage of students with prior work experience (63 percent) is one of the lowest of any leading school. In recent years, corporate recruiters have shown a distinct preference for students with work experience (see table 13.5 on page 224).

Krannert Admissions Statistics (Graduating Class of 1994)[42]

Class size	153	Median GMAT score	608
Average age	26	Female	30%
Percentage with work experience	63%	Minorities	14%
		International	14%

Annual tuition and fees: eleven-month MSIA program: $3,150 (resident); $10,240 (non-resident); two-year MS program: $2,520 (resident); $8,192 (non-resident)

---

42 Krannert School Report on Admissions and Placement, 1993.

Krannert Placement Statistics (Graduating Class of 1993)[43]

Krannert Placements by Function

	Mean
Finance	$50,064
Marketing	$48,424
Operations	$46,886
Information systems	$44,925
Human resources	$42,209

Krannert Placements by Industry

	% of Accepted Offers
Heavy manufacturing	29%
Computer/electronics	26%
Consumer products manufacturing	16%
Natural resources	10%
Consulting	7%
Financial services/banking	6%
Other	6%

Krannert Placements by Geographic Area

	% of Accepted Offers
Midwest	43%
South/Southwest	21%
West/Mountain	18%
Northeast/Mid-Atlantic	13%
International	5%

Krannert Placements by Company Size

	% of Accepted Offers
Over $10 billion	53%
$5 to $10 billion	18%
$1 to $4.9 billion	15%
$100 to $999 million	6%
Below $100 million	8%

Contact: Associate Director
             Professional Master's Program
             Krannert Graduate School of Management
             1310 Krannert Building
             West Lafayette, Indiana 47907-1310
             Telephone: (317) 494-4365

---

43 Ibid.

THUNDERBIRD

The American Graduate School of International Management

Finance	★★
Marketing	★★★
Operations	★★
International business	★★★★

Overview:

The American Graduate School of International Management is a specialized business school that focuses entirely on educating managers for international business. Long before other business schools 'discovered' global management, Thunderbird was developing managers for this market. For prospective students who have identified international business as their preferred career path, Thunderbird should be given careful consideration.

Strengths:

- The Thunderbird School is as unusual as its name, which was taken from the World War II pilot training airfield that was turned over by the government at the end of the war to house the new school. Most of the traces of the former airfield are gone now, except the old control tower which survives as the student lounge and Tower Café. Although the formal name of the school became the American Graduate School of International Management in 1973, it is still widely known as "Thunderbird."

- From its inception in 1946 as the American Institute for Foreign Trade, Thunderbird has focused on global management. Almost all of the incoming students have had some international experience, and the entire purpose of the current program is to educate managers for international business. The degree is not even called an MBA—it's a Master of International Management (MIM).

- The course requirements for the MIM are at three levels: a group of core courses that may be waived if completed at other institutions, an intermediate level of more advanced business courses such as cost accounting, and a series of high-level seminars on international business. Students must also pass a foreign language requirement, which typically consists of three language courses. Students are encouraged to waive out of as many core courses as possible so they can devote their time at Thunderbird to the specialized international courses. Those who successfully waive several core courses may be able to complete the MIM program in twelve months.

- Another unusual feature of the Thunderbird program is the opportunity to enter the MIM program at any one of four times during the year—January, February, June, or September.

- The Thunderbird campus is located in Glendale, Arizona, a suburb of Phoenix, American's ninth largest city with a metropolitan area population of over 2.4 million. At an elevation of 1,100 feet, Glendale's winters are mild, the sun shines 85 percent of the year, and it seldom rains.

Limitations:

- Unlike other leading business schools, Thunderbird is not associated with a parent university, nor is it currently accredited by the American Assembly of Collegiate Schools of Business (AACSB), although it has applied for accreditation. While some of the faculty engage in scholarly research and almost all have Ph.D.'s, the school's focus is clearly on teaching. Although Thunderbird has been very successful in attracting students to its unique program, the MIM may not earn quite the esteem given degrees from more prestigious institutions.

- The average GMAT score (560) of the incoming students is lower than that of almost all other leading schools.

Thunderbird Admissions Statistics (Graduating Class of 1994)[44]

Class size	1005	Mean GMAT score	560
Average age	26	Female	35%
Average years of work experience	4	Minorities	12%
Percentage with work experience	90%	International	31%

Annual tuition and fees: $15,650

Thunderbird Placement Statistics (Graduating Class of 1992)[45]

Thunderbird Placements by Function (Class of 1992)

	% of Accepted Offers	Mean
Overall	100%	$42,094
Marketing	43%	
Finance	24%	
Production management	10%	
Management development	7%	
Consulting	7%	
Public administration	2%	
Engineering	1%	
Human resources	1%	
Other	7%	

44 Thunderbird 1992-1993 Entering Class Profile Report.
45 The American Graduate School of International Management Catalog, 1993-1994.

Thunderbird Placements by Industry (Class of 1992)

	% of Accepted Offers
Industrial manufacturing	46%
Banking/financial services	16%
Other services	12%
Government/non-profit	9%
Consulting	6%
Consumer product manufacturing	4%
Communications	2%
Accounting	2%
Insurance	2%
Agribusiness	1%

Thunderbird Placements by Geographic Area (Class of 1992)

	% of Accepted Offers
U.S. Southwest	26%
Europe	16%
U.S. Northeast	13%
U.S. Midwest	10%
Japan	10%
U.S. Southeast	7%
Oceania and Oriental Pacific	6%
Latin America	5%
Mexico	3%
U.S. Northwest	1%
Africa	1%
Canada	1%
Middle East	1%

Contact: Judy Johnson
             Associate Dean of Admissions
             The American Graduate School of International Management
             15249 North Fifty-ninth Avenue
             Glendale, Arizona 85306-6000
             Telephone: (602) 978-7210 or toll free (800) 848-9084

USC

Graduate School of Business Administration of the University of Southern California

Accounting	★★★
Consulting	★★★★
Finance	★★★★
General management	★★★
Marketing	★★★
Information systems	★★★
Operations	★★★
Nonprofit	★★★

Overview:

The Graduate School of Business Administration of the University of Southern California emphasizes the soft skills of management along with the technical skills. USC attracts very good students (the average GMAT is 622) and offers high-quality instruction in a number of concentrations, particularly finance and marketing. For those who would enjoy the L.A. lifestyle, USC offers a fine MBA program.

Strengths:

- The USC MBA program is aimed at producing managers with a generalist perspective in the belief that it is no longer sufficient to be just technically proficient. Rigorous training in finance, accounting, and decision theory is necessary, but the qualitative skills of management must be developed as well.

- The emphasis of the program is on cooperation and teambuilding rather than competition between students. Because the MBA program is relatively small (200 in the entering class), it is easier to build a collegial culture between students and with the faculty.

- At the beginning of the first year, each student is given a personal assessment, a process that is continued throughout the program to provide the student with constructive feedback on his or her developing managerial style and skills.

- The first year of the program is taught by a team of faculty who have developed an integrated, sequential core curriculum. The core courses are of different lengths and phase in and out at various times during the first and second semesters. Waivers of the core courses are permitted, allowing more electives to be taken in their place.

- In the second year there's only one required course—the Business Field Study—a projects course in which teams of three to five students take on consulting projects for real companies. Past clients have ranged from entrepreneurial startups and non-profit organizations to *Fortune* 500 companies. Concentrations (four courses in one area) are encouraged, although students are free to design a completely customized set of electives to meet their career objectives.

- The USC campus is located a few minutes from downtown Los Angeles, a world center of business and finance and one of America's gateways to the emerging economies of the Pacific Rim.

Limitations:
- The campus location near the center of Los Angeles will not suit everybody. Traffic, earthquakes, and concerns about crime in Los Angeles in the 1990s may discourage some prospective students.

USC Admissions Statistics (Graduating Class of 1993)[46]

Class size	200	Mean GMAT score	622 [47]
Average age	27	Female	28%
Average years of work experience	4	Minorities	13%
		International	18%

Annual tuition and fees: $16,490

USC Placement Statistics (Graduating Class of 1992)[48]

USC Placements by Function (Class of 1992)

	% of Accepted Offers	Range	Mean
Overall	100%	$30,000–$90,000	$50,322
Investment banking	15%	$44,000–$90,000	$59,012
General management	14%	$34,000–$55,000	$43,675
Marketing	14%	$35,800–$74,000	$48,569
Corporate finance	13%	$30,000–$58,000	$48,500
Consulting	11%	$35,000–$80,000	$52,125
Brand/product management	8%	$45,000–$55,000	$49,030
Operations management	5%	$48,000–$53,000	$50,475
Financial services	5%	$44,000–$65,000	$53,000
Accounting	4%	$38,000–$39,000	$38,670
Information systems	4%	$38,000–$55,000	$46,333
Real Estate	4%	$48,000	$48,000
Commercial banking	3%	$50,000–$60,000	$55,000

---

46 University of Southern California MBA Catalog, 1994-95.
47 For the Class of '94; data from "America's Best Graduate Schools," *U.S. News & World Report*, March 22, 1993, p. 59.
48 University of Southern California MBA Catalog, 1994-95.

USC Placements by Industry (Class of 1992)

	% of Accepted Offers	Range	Mean
Consulting services	17%	$38,000–$80,000	$48,830
Investment banking	15%	$44,000–$90,000	$59,012
Computers/telecommunications	15%	$42,500–$58,000	$51,000
Consumer products	11%	$40,000–$55,000	$47,100
Pharmaceuticals/biotech	6%	$35,800–$50,000	$46,817
Other manufacturing	6%	$30,000–$42,000	$40,000
Financial services	5%	$44,000–$65,000	$52,000
Aerospace	4%	$45,000–$58,000	$54,000
Real estate	4%	$53,000	$53,000
Health services	4%	$38,000–$48,000	$43,000
Entertainment/recreation	4%	$34,000–$42,500	$40,375
Public accounting	4%	$38,000–$39,000	$38,600
Commercial banking	3%	$50,000–$60,000	$55,000
Government/non-profit	2%	$43,000	$43,000

Contact: Admissions Office
             Graduate School of Business Administration
             University of Southern California
             Bridge Hall 101
             University Park
             Los Angeles, California 90089-1421
             Telephone: (213) 740-7846

UNIVERSITY OF WASHINGTON

School of Business Administration at the University of Washington

Accounting	★★
Consulting	★★★
Entrepreneurship	★★★★
Finance	★★★
General management	★★★
Marketing	★★
Operations	★★
Environmental management	★★★★

Overview:

The School of Business Administration at the University of Washington attracts some of the best students of any regional school. The school is in the process of making substantial changes to upgrade its faculty and its educational programs, including innovative new tracks in international management, environmental management, and entrepreneurship. With low state-supported tuition and a beautiful campus location, the University of Washington offers many advantages to prospective students.

Strengths:

- With an average GMAT score of 632, the MBA program at the University of Washington attracts students who are as bright as those accepted in many leading national programs. They also tend to be older and have more work experience than students in other regional programs.

- To integrate international and ethical considerations into the functional courses, a new core course program has been introduced that consists of a single, year-long course taught by a multidisciplinary team of faculty. There are no waivers from the core course.

- In the second year, students are free to pick and choose their electives to fit their particular career goals, or they can select one of three specialized tracks: International Management Fellows (which involves foreign language and overseas coursework), the Environmental Management Program (special environmental management courses plus a yearlong consulting project and a summer internship in an environmental job at a major company), and the Program in Entrepreneurship and Innovation (which includes courses on new venture management plus internships and field studies with startups and small businesses).

- To foster teamwork and cooperation, the traditional grading system was scrapped for "high pass," "pass," "low pass" and "fail." Professors also provide individual performance evaluations to students.

- As with other state-supported schools, the tuition's a bargain.

- The campus setting, with snow-capped, 14,000-foot Mount Rainier in the background, is unusually beautiful, so it's not surprising that more than half of the graduates stay in Washington State.

Limitations:
- The program at the University of Washington is in transition. A new dean has brought in a number of new faculty and is responsible for upgrading the curriculum so that the school can compete with the best national schools. Given the high quality of its students, as the new faculty and programs become established the school should make rapid gains.

University of Washington Admissions Statistics (Graduating Class of 1995)[49]

Class size	160	Mean GMAT score (domestic)	632
Average age	27	Female	33%
Average years of work experience	4	Minorities	13%
Percentage with work experience	96%	International	15%

Annual tuition and fees: $3,978 (resident); $9,963 (non-resident)

University of Washington Placement Statistics (Graduating Class of 1992)

The University of Washington does not publish a placement report with starting salaries. According to *U.S. News & World Report*, the school's median starting salary for 1992 (*without* signing bonuses) was $40,000.[50] *Business Week* reported the school's *1992* median starting pay (*with* signing bonuses) to be $43,000 and the mean starting pay as $43,730.[51]

University of Washington Placements by Function (Class of 1992)[52]

	% of Accepted Offers
General management	19%
Marketing	18%
Consulting	12%
Financial analysis	11%
Accounting/control	6%
Production/operations management	5%
Investment management	4%
Engineering	3%

49 *1994 MBA Bulletin*, University of Washington.
50 "America's Best Graduate Schools," *U.S. News & World Report*, March 22, 1993, p. 59.
51 *Business Week Guide to the Best Business Schools*, 3rd Edition, p. 293.
52 *1994 MBA Bulletin*, University of Washington.

University of Washington Placements by Industry (Class of <u>1992</u>)

	% of Accepted Offers
Computers	13%
Commercial banking	12%
Consulting	11%
Government/non-profit	7%
Computer services/software	6%
Investments	6%
Chemicals/energy	4%
Health care services	3%
Other manufacturing	13%
Other services	6%

University of Washington Placements by Geographic Area (Class of <u>1992</u>)

	% of Accepted Offers
Washington State	51%
California	11%
Other West/Northwest	11%
Other USA	10%
International	17%

Contact: Graduate Program Office
School of Business Administration
University of Washington
Mackenzie Hall, DJ-10
Seattle, Washington 98195
Telephone: (206) 543-4661

Chapter 8

THE MBA ADVANTAGE of Part-Time Programs

In chapter 6 on regional business schools, we introduced the choice of going full-time or part-time. We said that the part-time MBA program makes more financial sense if you currently have a good job you want to keep; that is, you have a high opportunity cost. A full-time program at a regional school is a better choice if you're unemployed or in a marginal job; in this case your opportunity cost is low.

The Advantages of a Part-Time Program

There are five major advantages of a part-time MBA program:

- Since most people who take part-time programs do so at a local business school, there's no need to move. You avoid the cost and disruption of living somewhere else for two years.

- You continue to make a salary while you are in school. The biggest cost of a full-time MBA is not the tuition, it's the salary you give up for the two years you are in school. This is a major cost of getting an MBA that you can avoid. There's no need to take out loans to go to business school.

- There is little risk of being unemployed after you graduate. The new MBA grad from a *full-time* program is thrown on the market and has to scramble for a job. If you plan to change employers after getting a part-time MBA, the job change can take place at the *your* convenience.

- You can start your part-time MBA right after you finish your undergraduate degree, and you'll have your MBA by age twenty-six or twenty-seven, about the age most full-timers are just beginning their programs (because most full-time programs now require three to four years of prior work experience). This means that you can start compounding the advantages of having the MBA degree three to four years earlier.

- For most part-time MBA students, the employer will pick up part or all of the tuition cost. But even if the company doesn't, it's still less costly than a full-time program, because you continue to earn a salary.

As a result, there's no "breakeven" point in a part-time program because there is no investment to recover. Furthermore, you can immediately apply what you are learning in class to your job. You're ahead from day one.

Part-Time Versus Full-Time: A Look at the Numbers

THE MBA ADVANTAGE of a part-time program is shown graphically in figure 8.1 for a typical part-time student whose tuition is paid by his employer and who takes three years to complete the program. (Recall that THE MBA ADVANTAGE is the cumulative difference in annual pay with and without the MBA, through the end of four years of post-MBA employment.)[1]

The annual pay with and without the part-time MBA is shown in figure 8.1 for Bill, the recent engineering graduate we met in chapter 6. Bill is making $35,000 with 5 percent annual raises in Year 1 when he starts his part-time MBA. In Year 4 he is awarded his MBA and gets the promotion he wants to product manager, at $50,000 per year with 10 percent annual raises. By Year 7 he is earning $66,550.

The financial advantage of acquiring the MBA for part-timers like Bill has two components:

- A POST-MBA STEP UP of about $10,000 in Year 4, when the MBA degree is awarded and the graduate assumes a more rewarding job. (For comparison, the POST-MBA STEP UP upon graduation from a full-time program at a Top 20 school is typically $20,000 or more, as shown in table 4.3 on page 37.)

- A POST-MBA FAST TRACK, in which post-MBA pay grows at 10 percent annually, versus 5 percent a year before getting the degree. (Again for comparison, the POST-MBA FAST TRACK growth rate following graduation from a full-time program at a Top 20 school is 15 to 20 percent annually, as illustrated in table 4.4, on page 38.)

Figure 8.1

The financial advantage of a *part-time* program in a typical regional school has two components: an immediate step up in pay following graduation and an increased growth rate in pay raises in the years following graduation.

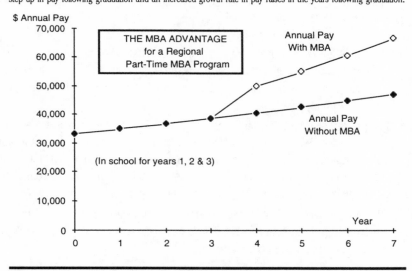

---

1   As noted in chapter 6, four years of post-MBA pay are used when computing THE MBA ADVANTAGE for three-year part-time programs. This is done so that the seven-year span from starting the MBA degree is the same as that used when computing THE MBA ADVANTAGE for full-time programs, allowing the two kinds of program to be compared financially.

Figure 8.2
A typical *full-time* program at a regional school requires two years of foregone salary plus tuition.

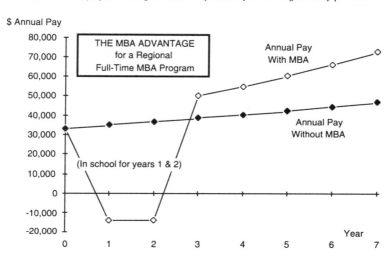

For comparison, in figure 8.2, Bill's annual pay is shown with and without the MBA for a *full-time* MBA program at the same regional school. In this case, Bill quits his job for two years and also pays $14,000 a year in tuition. The advantage of the full-time program is that he graduates a year earlier so that he can start his new, higher paying job in Year 3. The disadvantage is the large cost incurred in Years 1 and 2 in foregone salary plus tuition.

In figure 8.3, the *cumulative* difference in Bill's pay with and without the MBA is shown for both the part-time program and the full-time program through Year 7:

- With a regional *part-time* program, he continues on salary and his employer pays the tuition. By getting the MBA, Bill will be ahead by a cumulative total of $57,417 by the end of Year 7. (If he had to pay his own tuition, he would still be ahead by $29,417 at the end of Year 7.)

- With a *full-time* program at the same regional school, he quits his job, gives up salary of more than $70,000 for two years and pays $28,000 in tuition for the two years. In this case, he will not quite break even on his $100,000 investment by the end of Year 7.

The bottom line: For someone like Bill with a good job and an employer who will pay the tuition, the part-time regional program has a clear financial advantage over the full-time regional program.

In the Short Run, an MBA ADVANTAGE Comparable to a Top 20 MBA
By the end of Year 7, Bill's MBA ADVANTAGE is $57,417. Surprisingly, this compares favorably with an MBA ADVANTAGE of $54,200 in Year 7 for students who go full time to the Darden School at the University of Virginia, a Top 20 school (see table 4.1 on page 30). The reason, of

Figure 8.3

THE MBA ADVANTAGE illustrated here is the *cumulative* difference in pay at the end of each year with and
without the MBA, shown for a regional full-time MBA program and a regional part-time program.

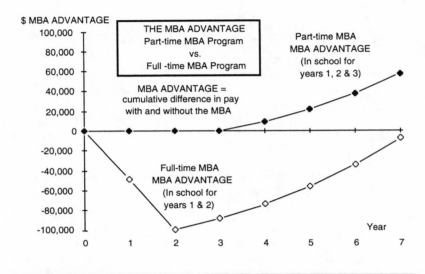

course, is that Bill has avoided $100,000 of front-end costs (two years of tuition and foregone
salary) that the typical full-time Darden student has to incur.

To be fair to Darden, the estimated pay in Year 7 for someone with a Darden degree is
$112,900 (see table 4.6 on page 40) versus $66,550 in Year 7 with Bill's part-time degree from a
regional school. Over a lifetime of post-MBA earnings, the typical Darden student will earn a lot
more than Bill.

Nevertheless, during the early years following graduation, THE MBA ADVANTAGE for part-
time MBA degrees can be comparable to that for full-time degrees from many of the Top 20
schools. And in the comparison of lifetime earnings *with* the part-time degree versus not getting
the MBA at all, the difference will amount to hundreds of thousands of dollars.

What are the Special Concerns Regarding Part-Time MBA Programs?

The list of what to look for when choosing a part-time program is the same as that outlined for
regional schools in chapter 6. As a rule, the choice of school is limited to those in your city, and
perhaps also by those for which your employer is willing to pay the tuition (although the part-
time program is usually a better deal financially even if *you* pay the tuition, as long as you have
a good job that is worth keeping).

There are some special concerns about part-time programs that should be mentioned:

- Look for a school that is accredited by the AACSB. You are going to put a lot of time
  and effort into the degree, and you want an MBA with recognized quality. Part-time

does not necessarily mean mediocre quality. A number of Top 20 schools, including Chicago and Northwestern, offer first-rate part-time programs.

- Recognize that companies frequently are not enthusiastic about having employees get part-time MBA degrees, for several reasons:

  - Tuition is expensive at $20,000–30,000 per MBA, and companies don't get tuition scholarships. They pay the full sticker price.

  - You'll be distracted from your job during the three years or so while you are engrossed in working on your degree. You'll be putting in long hours at night and on weekends, and it may affect your performance on the job.

  - The process of getting your degree will raise your career expectations, so you'll look for a more challenging job when you complete your degree. The company may find it difficult to meet your requirements for an expanded role.

  - The MBA degree will raise your market value. This means that the company will have to pay you more after graduation to keep you.

  - Your boss naturally worries that after investing $20,000–30,000 in your tuition, you'll seek greener pastures after graduation.

- The flip side of the last issue is that you may find it difficult to get your employer to recognize your new capabilities. You may be expected to continue with your old job, and you may find that you *do* have to leave the company to capture the benefits of your new MBA.

- Then there's the question of income taxes: Under certain conditions, the tuition paid by your employer could be construed as taxable income to you. The basic idea is that if the MBA degree is taken to qualify you for a new trade or business—or if it's required to meet the minimum educational requirements for your present employment—the tuition may be considered part of your taxable income. The taxes on $20,000–30,000 of tuition can be substantial. You should get expert advice on this because the tax laws change frequently.

- Recognize that part of the commitment to a full-time MBA means being available twenty-four hours a day if necessary to work with your classmates on cases and team assignments. Part-time students rarely have enough time for this intensity of involvement. Frequently, when part-time and full-time students are on teams together, the full-timers will complain that the part-timers don't carry their share of the workload.

- Finally, don't drag it out. Some part-timers take one course at a time for five or six years. But most part-time programs can be completed in three years if you're willing to carry two courses at a time and go during the summer. The sooner you finish, the sooner that step of post-MBA increased salary will occur. In the example shown in figure 8.1, every year of delay costs Bill about $10,000 in lost salary, plus the delay in getting onto a post-MBA fast track with higher annual raises. A part-time MBA program can be a real grind—it's hard on you and it's hard on your family. So finish it and start enjoying the benefits.

The bottom line: A part-time program at a quality business school is a low-risk way to get an MBA that has most of the benefits of a regular full-time MBA while avoiding the heavy front-end costs of foregone salary for two years. If you can't afford to go full-time to a Top 20 business school or if you have a great job you don't want to leave, a part-time program can be a very acceptable alternative.

Chapter 9

Executive Programs: The Red Carpet MBA

Executive programs are another great way to get an MBA. Instead of preparing people for entry-level jobs, executive programs augment the skills and knowledge of fast-rising young stars. The typical executive student has at least five to ten years of work experience and has been identified as a high-potential person in the organization.

Consider the case of Jodie, who we met in chapter 1. Although only in her late twenties, she is already an associate editor for a major national magazine. While she is very talented as a writer and editor, an increasing part of her work now involves supervising other writers and developing competitive strategies for the magazine's future. An MBA would be helpful not only for her present job, but also as part of her long-term career strategy to run her own publication some day. Her husband, Eric, is partway through medical school and Jodie is not interested in moving to another city to pursue an MBA full time at a Top 20 business school. Recently the publisher of Jodie's magazine spoke with her about the possibility of attending an Executive MBA program at a highly-regarded local business school.

As we shall see in this chapter, the Executive MBA is an excellent choice for Jodie. In fact, the Executive MBA at an accredited business school is an excellent choice for anyone who qualifies.

Executive MBA programs are a recent addition to the academic programs at many business schools. The first Executive MBA program was launched by the Graduate School of Business at the University of Chicago in the 1940s, and until the 1960s it had no competition. Today there are 114 Executive MBA programs in the United States, of which 70 are at schools accredited by the American Assembly of Collegiate Schools of Business (AACSB). Executive education has become an important source of cash flow at many leading business schools, in some cases bringing in more than $10 million in revenue per year.

Two Types of Executive Programs
Executive programs are of two types:

- Executive short courses, usually five days to twelve weeks in length, that grant a certificate of completion but not an MBA.

- Executive MBA programs, that typically meet one day a week for two years, and award an MBA on completion.

Executive Short Courses
Recently, executive short courses have been criticized in the business press. In September

1993, an article in *The Wall Street Journal* charged that these short courses can raise unrealistic expectations on the part of attendees, who return to their companies fired up to make sweeping changes and disrupt corporate culture in the process. The current emphasis on multidisciplinary team building, for example, can be very threatening to the boss who prefers a traditional authoritative hierarchy that affirms his power and status.[1]

Corporations spend nearly $15 billion per year on formal training programs for managers and professionals, according to *Business Week*, and they are demanding that these investments pay off with measurable improvements in on-the-job performance.[2] Off-the-shelf short courses (e.g., "Finance for Non-Financial Managers") are on the decline. Instead, some companies are developing custom programs with leading business schools to attack particular problems, such as how to expand the senior citizen market for their products. Others are hiring well-known faculty on a consulting basis to become deeply familiar with the company's culture and opportunities and then develop specialized training programs to exploit these opportunities. Still other firms are launching in-house schools patterned after Motorola University and General Electric's Crotonville Management Development Institute.

Fortune noted that traditional executive short courses in which professors lecture managers on technical topics, such as queuing theory and the capital asset pricing model, are being replaced by "action learning," Here, teams of managers and faculty take on real projects for sponsoring companies, such as "What is the market for General Electric's financial services business in India?"[3] At the end of the project, the team makes a formal presentation to the senior management of the company. Everybody wins: The managers get the chance to showcase their new skills to senior management, the faculty get some additional real-world experiences to embellish their other courses, and top management gets a significant consulting effort accomplished with supervision by faculty experts.

Although these executive short courses may be valuable to the company for the specific knowledge they impart, they add little permanent market value to the individual. For managers who want to add to their permanent professional credentials, the Executive MBA is the way to go.

The Advantages of the Executive MBA

The Executive MBA may be the best of all worlds in graduate management education. A good Executive MBA program combines the educational challenges and benefits of a full-time MBA program with the cost advantages of a part-time MBA:

- *The best financial deal:* Your employer pays for your tuition much like a part-time program and you continue to earn your salary. You are given time off to attend classes, and you can complete the MBA in two years of less, as in a full-time MBA program but without the front-end cost.

- *Convenient scheduling for you and your company:* Classes usually meet for a full day once a week, on alternating Fridays and Saturdays. A few schools meet once every two

1 Allen, F., "When Things Go Wrong: Executive Education is Sometimes Just a Waste of Money, and Sometimes It's a Lot Worse Than That," *The Wall Street Journal*, September 10, 1993.
2 Bongiorno, L., "Corporate America's New Lesson Plan," *Business Week*, October 25, 1993, p. 102.
3 O'Reilly, B., "How Execs Learn Now," *Fortune*, April 5, 1993, p. 54.

weeks for combined Friday–Saturday sessions. In either case you only miss two days of work a month.

- *The best faculty:* Because Executive MBA students are older and more experienced, they can be a tough audience for the faculty. They're skeptical and they're demanding. Weak faculty don't survive in Executive MBA programs.

- *Outstanding classmates:* Executive MBA programs offer great networking and learning opportunities with other fast trackers. Classmates often have expertise and valuable personal experience to share in class and on team projects. Most Executive MBA programs form study groups that meet informally during the week to do homework assignments and projects. The friendships formed in these study groups often continue for many years after the program is finished. Many alumni of Executive MBA programs rate the opportunity to meet and work with their classmates as the most valuable part of the program.

- *Red carpet treatment:* Executive programs are a major source of cash flow for many business schools, without the heavy discounting in the form of tuition scholarships that is necessary to attract students to regular full-time MBA programs. The sponsoring companies pay premium prices for Executive MBA programs, and the students get a premium product. The price pays for your tuition, your books, your meals on campus, and sometimes a laptop computer loaded with state-of-the-art business software. What's more, 40 percent of the programs now include a trip to Europe or Asia midway through the degree (see chapter 10).

- *Special projects for your company:* Many Executive MBA programs provide academic credit for special projects done by students on behalf of their companies. This could involve running an actual marketing research project on a proposed new product or drawing up the requirements for a new information system for the factory. You get the opportunity to fulfill some of your academic requirements while showing off what you've learned to your boss.

- *Low risk:* Like a part-time program, you keep your job while you're in school and you don't have to job hunt upon graduation, unlike a regular full-time MBA graduate.

The Disadvantages of an Executive MBA

Although the Executive MBA is one of the best ways to earn a graduate degree in management, it is not without a few drawbacks:

- *Late start:* The typical Executive MBA candidate has ten to fifteen years of work experience and is in his or her mid-to-late-thirties. By getting the MBA later in life, you postpone the benefits of getting on the MBA fast track early in your career.

- *No electives:* Most Executive MBA programs have a fixed curriculum developed to enhance the skills of promising middle managers. You can't concentrate in marketing or finance, but executive students are not looking for functional entry-level skills anyway.

- *Competition:* Your classmates will be bright, experienced, and aggressive, and competition for grades and for recognition in classroom discussions can be intimidating at times.

- *Selectivity:* Because of the high cost, companies are very selective about who they send to Executive MBA programs. Even though you want to attend, you may not be chosen.

- *High expectations:* Like the part-time MBA, an Executive MBA will raise your career expectations. It's difficult to go back to the old job after two years of debating the corporate strategies of IBM and General Motors. Moreover, if your MBA is from a recognized accredited program, your market value will be enhanced. Before you graduate, you and your employer should develop a plan for using your new skills for the mutual benefit of your company and your career.

The bottom line: An Executive MBA program is an excellent way to get an MBA. If you are offered the opportunity to attend an accredited Executive MBA program, take it!

Chapter 10

Choosing an Executive MBA Program

Finding a good Executive MBA Program is more restrictive than choosing a full-time MBA program since you need one that's reasonably close by. Although a few Executive MBA programs draw commuters from out-of-state, like Chicago's, for example, students in most Executive MBA programs are from the immediate area. Choosing an Executive MBA program involves finding a good one in your area.

Table 10.1 lists the executive programs from business schools accredited by the American Assembly of Collegiate Schools of Business (AACSB) organized by state for your convenience. Seventy of the 114 Executive MBA programs in the United States are accredited by the AACSB.

Almost all of the programs meet weekly on alternate Fridays and Saturdays or once every two weeks for a combined Friday–Saturday session. In either case students typically miss only two days of work per month. Many of the programs include an overseas trip, which may be optional or required; some schools include the cost of the trip in the tuition while others charge extra. Finally, a number of schools may include a laptop computer with business software in the tuition.

Table 10.1
Executive MBA Programs at ACCSB-Accredited Schools

State	School	City	Special Features
Alabama	University of Alabama	Tuscaloosa	Classes begin in January
Arizona	Arizona State	Tempe	Personal computer provided
California	San Diego State University	San Diego	
	University of California	Irvine	Overseas trip
	University of California	Los Angeles	Ranked #5 by *Business Week*[1]
	University of San Francisco	San Francisco	Ten days overseas in summer
	Univ. of Southern California	Los Angeles	Ranked #8 by *Business Week*
Colorado	Colorado State University	Denver	Meets during weekday evenings
	University of Colorado	Denver	Trips to Europe and Japan
	University of Denver	Denver	
Connecticut	University of Connecticut	Storrs	Trip to Europe
Wash. DC	George Washington Univ.	Washington	International residency required
Florida	Florida Atlantic University	Fort Lauderdale	
	Rollins College	Orlando	Tuition includes computer and trip
	University of Miami	Coral Gables	Classes begin in January
	University of South Florida	Tampa	Optional international trip

---

[1] As ranked in *Business Week's Guide to the Best Executive Education Programs*, edited by John Byrne and Cynthia Green, McGraw-Hill, 1993, p. 187.

Georgia	Emory University	Atlanta	Ranked #15 by *Business Week*
	Georgia Southern University	Statesboro	
	Georgia State University	Atlanta	Ranked #9 by *Business Week*
Hawaii	University of Hawaii-Manoa	Honolulu	Visit four Asian countries
Illinois	Northern Illinois University	DeKalb	Optional international trip
	Northwestern University	Evanston	Ranked #1 by *Business Week*
	The University of Chicago	Chicago	Ranked #2 by *Business Week*
	University of Illinois	Champaign	Ranked #12 by *Business Week*
Indiana	Purdue University	West Lafayette	Ranked #13 by *Business Week*
	University of Notre Dame	South Bend	
Iowa	The University of Iowa	Iowa City	
Louisiana	Tulane University	New Orleans	Ranked #20 by *Business Week*
Maryland	Loyola College	Baltimore	
Massachusetts	Boston University	Tyngsboro	International trip required
	Northeastern University	Boston	Washington and overseas trips
	Suffolk University	Boston	Optional international trip
Michigan	Michigan State University	East Lansing	International trip required
Minnesota	University of Minnesota	Minneapolis	International trip required
Missouri	Washington University	St. Louis	Washington and overseas trips
Nebraska	University of Nebraska	Omaha	International trip
New Jersey	Rutgers University	Newark	Optional international trip
New Mexico	University of New Mexico	Albuquerque	International trip
New York	Baruch College	New York	International trip required
	Columbia University	New York	Ranked #7 by *Business Week*
	New York University	New York	Ranked #11 by *Business Week*
	Rensselaer Polytechnic Inst.	Troy	Laptop computer included
	Syracuse University	Syracuse	
	University of Rochester	Rochester	Washington trip and laptop
North Carolina	Duke University	Durham	Ranked #4 by *Business Week*
	University of North Carolina	Chapel Hill	Optional international trip
	Wake Forest University	Winston-Salem	Ranked #17 by *Business Week*
Ohio	Bowling Green State Univ.	Bowling Green	
	Case Western Reserve Univ.	Cleveland	Ranked #10 by *Business Week*
	Cleveland State University	Cleveland	Notebook computer included
	Kent State university	Kent	International trip required
	Ohio University	Miami	
Oregon	University of Oregon	Beaverton	
Pennsylvania	Temple University	Philadelphia	Must buy laptop computer
	University of Pennsylvania	Philadelphia	Ranked #3 by *Business Week*
	University of Pittsburgh	Pittsburgh	Ranked #14 by *Business Week*
Rhode Island	University of Rhode Island	Kingston	Includes notebook computer
South Carolina	Winthrop College	Rock Hill	
Tennessee	Memphis State University	Memphis	
	University of Tennessee	Chattanooga	International residency required
	Vanderbilt University	Nashville	Ranked #18 by *Business Week*
Texas	Baylor University	Waco	International trip required
	Southern Methodist Univ.	Dallas	Ranked #19 by *Business Week*
	University of Houston	Houston	International summer trip
	University of Texas-Austin	Austin	Ranked #16 by *Business Week*
Utah	Brigham Young University	Provo	
	University of Utah	Salt Lake City	International trip required
Virginia	College of William and Mary	Williamsburg	Tuition includes trip and computer
	George Mason University	Herndon	Two weeks in Europe
	University of Richmond	Richmond	
Washington	University of Washington	Seattle	
Wisconsin	University of Wisconsin	Milwaukee	

For more information on Executive MBA Programs, three books are particularly useful:

- *Directory of Executive MBA Programs*, published annually by the Executive MBA Council and available for $10.00 from the American Assembly of Collegiate Schools of Business, 600 Emerson Road, Suite 300, St. Louis, Missouri 63141-6762. This very useful soft-cover book contains a listing and one-page description of 126 Executive MBA programs (114 in the United States, eight in Canada, two in Australia, one in Austria, and one in the United Kingdom).

- *The Official Guide to MBA Programs*, published by the Graduate Management Admissions Council, P.O. Box 6106, Princeton, New Jersey 08541-6106, and available in many bookstores for $13.95. This 675-page reference book, from the organization that produces the GMAT, provides comprehensive facts and figures on 588 MBA programs (including Executive MBAs) offered throughout the world.

- *Business Week's Guide to the Best Executive Education Programs*, edited by John Byrne and Cynthia Green, and published in 1993 by McGraw-Hill. Based on a 1991 survey of executive program attendees, corporate human resources directors, and business school deans, this helpful book follows the same format as *Business Week's Guide to the Best Business Schools*. The Top 20 Executive MBA programs in the country are profiled, as are the schools that offer the highest rated executive short courses.

Chapter 11

Developing a Personal Strategic Career Plan

Thus far we've looked at a number of options, namely Top 40 schools, regional schools, part-time programs, and executive programs. Now it's time to consider whether getting an MBA makes sense for you. To do that, you need a personal strategic career plan.

The Concept of Strategic Planning

Companies develop plans of all kinds—plans for launching new products, plans for hiring sales personnel, plans for implementing total quality management. One of the most important plans that companies develop is the corporate strategic plan. A strategic plan differs from other kinds of plans in the following ways:

- *It is long range in scope.* Most company plans have a horizon of a year or two. Many are set to be accomplished within the annual budget cycle, such as a plan to launch a new personal computer at the annual trade show in November. In contrast, a strategic plan typically has a three-to-five-year planning horizon.

- *Outside forces are considered.* Most company plans take into account only those things that management can control and can change, such as manufacturing, marketing, or new product development. A strategic plan, on the other hand, considers many things that management cannot change—domestic and international competition, inflation, energy costs, new technologies.

  IBM, one of the greatest corporations in the world, based its long-range strategy on the mainframe computer and then found that personal computers and workstations are taking over much of the mainframe market. Kodak, the world leader in photographic film for 100 years, was first threatened by Fuji Film, a Japanese company with a good product and lower manufacturing costs. Then came a new technology, digital imaging, that also threatens to make obsolete many of the applications of conventional photographic film. What should Kodak's strategy be?

The term "strategy" has a military origin, from the Greek word *strategos*, which means "the art of the general." In the time of Alexander the Great (330 B.C.) it referred to the skill of employing forces to overcome the opposition.[1] In recent times, military commanders continue to learn from the classical strategies of the ancient Macedonians and Greeks. For example, in

---

1   Mintzberg, H. and Quinn, J., *The Strategy Process*, 2nd edition, Prentice Hall, 1991, p. 4.

World War II, the brilliant battle strategies of General Patton (American) and General Rommel (German) were closely patterned after the historical military strategies of Alexander the Great.[2]

In the modern corporation, the battle is not one of armed conflict but rather of economic survival. Even the most powerful corporations, such as IBM, Kodak, and General Motors, have had to develop new strategies to endure. Every company, if it is to survive and prosper in today's competitive environment, must have a sound strategy. Similarly, if *you* are going to survive and prosper in today's competitive environment, you, too, need a sound strategic plan.

A Strategic Planning Outline

You personal strategic plan should contain the same components as a corporate strategic plan. Here's a strategic planning outline adapted from that used by many top corporations. We'll use this outline as the framework to develop a personal strategic plan for you.[3]

1. *Objectives* (What constitutes 'success' for you?)
   Qualitative (What kind of job? In what industry?)
   Quantitative (Your expected pay and rate of growth of pay)

2. *Strengths and weaknesses* (Personal and/or controllable factors—talent, education, motivation, special skills. What are you good at? What do you *like* to do?)

3. *Opportunities and threats* (Uncontrollable external factors, such as the economy, competition, new technology. What changes are likely to occur in your targeted job area? How can you make these changes work for you?)

4. *Development of alternative strategies* (Considering the above points, what are your options?)

5. *Selected option* (with rationale for selection)

6. *Contingency plan* (in case things don't work as planned in number 5)

Objectives

The first step in developing your strategic career plan is to determine your *objectives*. What constitutes success for you? This is a difficult question and most people are not very sure about the answers. Here are some questions that you should ask yourself:[4]

- What would be the "perfect job" for you five years from now? (For the moment, don't worry about how to get there. And don't set your sights too low, just dream a little.) *Why* is this the perfect job? What is it that you really like about this dream job—the freedom, the prestige, the sense of accomplishment, the money?

- How important is making a lot of money? What are you willing to sacrifice in order to

---

2 Ibid., p. 9.

3 For a number of years I taught a course in Corporate Strategy. One of the first assignments was for students to develop a five-year strategic plan for themselves, using this outline. It was hard work, and there were no easy answers. Most students hated the assignment—until they had their first interview with a corporate recruiter who said, "What are your career objectives? What are your most important strengths and weaknesses?" My students were ready with well-thought-out answers.

4 Early in my career I came across a pair of articles on career planning that are among the best I've seen on the subject. Both originally appeared in *MBA Magazine*, April 1968. The first, by Thomas G. Gutteridge, is entitled "The Hardest Job of All: Career Planning." The second, by Alan N. Schoonmaker, is entitled "What Price Career Myopia?" Some of the ideas in the following sections originated in these two articles.

make a lot of money? (The setting of objectives means thinking about tradeoffs since you can't have it all.) How many hours a week are you willing to work? Are you willing to give up a substantial amount of personal freedom in order to make a lot of money? Are you willing to sacrifice your personal life?[5]

- How important is it to become a senior executive? How much do you know about what senior executives do? Are you willing to do the difficult things that senior executives have to do, like laying people off, closing plants, and schmoozing with customers you may not like? Are you willing to drop old friends as you climb the corporate ladder? Is having a fancy title worth the personal freedom you might have to sacrifice?

- Where do you want to live? Where does your spouse want to live?[6]

- How much risk are you willing to take? Would you consider a job that paid straight commission if it allowed you the chance to make a great deal of money?

- What industry do you like? Do you like computers? Do you like home entertainment electronics? What about financial services or health care services? People may change companies, but they tend to stay in the same industry. Much of your career will be spent developing expertise and contacts in a given industry. Pick something you really enjoy because you're going to be involved in it for a long time. The most fulfilling jobs are those in which people are so engrossed that they would love doing it even if they didn't get paid. (Yes, there are such jobs.)

- Finally, recognize that your goals may change over time.[7] Be careful about getting boxed into a situation that you can't get out of.[8]

Strengths and Weaknesses

Strengths and weaknesses are characteristics that you are either born with or you acquire through education and experience. A financial analyst looking at your personal balance sheet would refer to your strengths and weaknesses as your assets and liabilities. An economist would refer to your strengths and weaknesses as your comparative advantage in the marketplace for professional labor. It's what gives you a competitive edge. Some of the key questions are:[9]

---

5 A venture capitalist once told me that the divorce rate among entrepreneurs is very high. The eighty-hour weeks, the pressure, and the heavy travel put enormous strains on a marriage.

6 Years ago when I was a sophomore in electrical engineering at Cornell, I got a summer internship at Kodak. (At that time there were very few women in engineering.) The head of personnel gathered us together in a big conference room and said, "Gentlemen, if you intend to pursue a career at the Eastman Kodak Company, marry a Rochester girl. Sooner or later you will end up living near your wife's parents." I remember being outraged at the time, but he did have a point—your spouse's or your future spouse's preferences must be considered as you formulate your strategic career plan.

7 When I graduated with my engineering degree, all I wanted to do was work as a bench engineer and I accepted a job in the research labs of a large corporation. But after a couple of years I got bored and ended up as a Product Manager in marketing. I decided that I wanted to become a senior manager, and I felt that I needed an MBA, which I got at night. In order to realize the value of the MBA, I found that I had to change companies, and I did—becoming a Vice President of a $30 million health products company while still in my early thirties. But after six years as a VP and later as the company's Executive VP, I found that it wasn't nearly as much fun as I expected. I became a college professor—and I had to go back to school again, this time to get a Ph.D. The point is, your personal goals often change over time.

8 Graduating MBA's are often placed in staff jobs such as financial analyst or marketing analyst. These are appropriate entry-level jobs and the pay is good. But if you stay too long in such a job, your pay may get so high that you cannot afford to transfer to a line job where you actually run something rather than just analyze things. Without line experience, it's hard to get promoted into a senior management position.

9 The best guide I know of for doing a personal strengths and weaknesses analysis is Richard Nelson Bolles' classic, *What Color is Your Parachute* (Ten Speed Press, 1994 Edition), particularly chapters 9, 10, and 11. This manual for career development has been in print

- How many hours a week do you work now? How motivated are you to succeed?
- Are you a leader? Can you demonstrate examples of situations when you provided leadership to your group or organization?
- Who have you worked for and in what positions? What did you accomplish?
- What marketable skills do you have? For example, David has a degree in electrical engineering, but he also has some professional training as a salesman and he really enjoys working with people. He should consider a job in technical marketing or sales where he can leverage his engineering training *and* his proven sales and marketing skills.
- Are you better at running an organization or are you more suited to being an expert resource and consultant to others?
- Last, and certainly of great importance, what are your educational credentials? This is where your MBA degree will pay off, not only because of what you will have learned, but also because it represents a major commitment on your part to the profession of management.

Sometimes what you are interested in (and are currently doing part-time) shows up as a precursor to your next job, as my experience demonstrates:

- While I was an engineering student at Cornell, two other students and I started a retail stereo shop where I gained practical retailing experience along with my degree in electrical engineering. Although my first job after graduation was in a research lab, when a position opened up in the company a few years later for a product manager in marketing, my retailing experience in consumer electronics combined with my engineering background qualified me for the job.
- When I started my MBA at night, I wasn't sure where it would lead, but within two years of graduating I changed employers and leveraged the part-time MBA into a job as a vice president.
- While serving as vice president of my company, I taught part-time in the MBA program at the University of Rochester. This in combination with my practical experiences both as a product manager and as a vice president led to a full-time appointment as a faculty member in the business school.
- Now I'm a professor and I'm writing this book part time, based on all of my experiences to date. Who knows what this will lead to!

In all cases, my part-time activity was a precursor for the next phase of my career, and in each change the new job built on everything I had done in all the previous jobs. So as you think about your strengths and weaknesses, look at what you are doing now on a part-time basis to help you decide what you want to do next.

---

since 1970 and is now in its twenty-second edition. This book takes the reader through a highly-structured method for determining his or her special skills and interests, and it is full of practical and inspirational advice for the job seeker. According to the publisher, 25,000 people a month buy this book.

Opportunities and Threats

Opportunities and threats are external factors that affect you but that you cannot control. If you are working for an aerospace company and your project gets canceled, this is clearly a threat, but maybe it can be turned into an opportunity. According to Richard Nelson Bolles, author of the best-selling book *What Color Is Your Parachute?*, a person goes job hunting typically about eight times during his or her career.[10] And each time you will encounter opportunities and threats.

To better understand the opportunities and threats that may influence your career plan, ask yourself:

- How well is your industry doing? If your company makes all its money on mainframes and the industry is moving to personal computers, this is a threat.

- How well is your company doing within its industry? Is your company bringing out new products and expanding its market share or is it losing ground to the competition?

- How well is your division doing? Is it in the mainstream of the company's business, or is it a peripheral business that can be sold or liquidated if necessary to protect the company's core business?

- How is your boss doing? Is he or she promotable?[11]

- And how are *you* doing? When was the last time you had a real promotion? Are you making as much as others in your field with the same education and experience? If not, why not?

- What about your skills—are they vulnerable to technological obsolescence? If you're an engineer or scientist, are you keeping up with the latest technology in your field? If you're a middle manager, do you know how to use the latest computer graphics technology to knock 'em dead with your next presentation?

- And finally, as you review your personal objectives, is your present career path going to get you there?

Maybe you think that you don't have to worry about these opportunities and threats; you feel that if you do a good job, your boss (or your company) will take care of you. Well, think again. In today's environment, your boss worries about *his* career, not yours. Your boss is not opposed to your getting ahead, he just doesn't spend very much time thinking about it.[12] Your success is your responsibility, not his.

As for the company taking care of you, don't plan on it. Even though the management of your company may have the best of intentions, intense economic pressures are forcing large firms to lay off tens of thousands of highly-qualified professionals. This trend may continue through the decade of the '90s.

---

10 Ibid., p. 18.
11 When I was a young engineer working in research, I had lunch one day with one of our senior physicists, by the name of Jim. A Group Vice President from our division who had been fired for gross incompetence had just been hired by another firm for a senior position. I asked Jim how this could be. His response: "When you get to that level, it doesn't matter whether you succeed big or fail big—the sign doesn't matter, only the magnitude counts." Perhaps this was true at the Group Vice President level 20 or 30 years ago, but I don't think it's true in today's competitive market.
12 If you are really outstanding in your job, your boss may decide that you are too valuable in your present job to promote, particularly if your company has a hiring freeze. In this case, your boss *may* be opposed to your getting ahead—because he's worried about *his* career.

It will be worth your while to think about what is happening in your industry, in your company, and in your profession. Are you keeping ahead of the changes?

Better yet, have you figured out how to make these changes work *for* you? When OPEC raised the price of oil in the early '70s, most automobile companies viewed this as a massive threat. But companies like Toyota and Honda built fuel-efficient cars and their sales curves went right off the top of the chart. So did companies that made fiberglass insulation for houses and energy-efficient electric motors for industry. This is because *whenever there is a major threat, inevitably there are major opportunities awaiting those who are alert enough to seize them.* Changes, even in the form of threats, create opportunities.

Development of Alternative Strategies

Now that you've thought about your objectives, your personal strengths and weaknesses, and the opportunities and threats in your situation, what are your options?

1. One option is to continue doing what you are doing now. The critical question is whether this path is likely to lead to the achievement of your objectives.

2. Another option is to quit what you are doing and invest in more education, such as an MBA. Since you are reading this book, this must be an option you are considering. As you know by now, I'm firmly convinced that graduate professional education is one of the best investments you can make, because it can pay off not only in dollars (as per our calculations of THE MBA ADVANTAGE) but also in greater personal freedom to pursue what you really want to do.

3. A third option is to continue in your present job and start on a part-time MBA program. If your current job is going well, this may be the best alternative (see chapter 8 for a full discussion of this alternative).

4. A fourth option is to continue doing what you are doing now but set some date in the future when you will make a decision ("If I don't get that promotion in the next eighteen months, I'm going to quit and go back to school."). This is a conditional decision.

These are just a few of the options that may be relevant to your situation, and as time passes new career options may develop. The underlying question you should ask when this happens is, "Will this new opportunity contribute to the fulfillment of my personal objectives?" That's the advantage of having a personal career strategy—you have a rational benchmark for evaluating new alternatives and opportunities.

Selecting an Option

If you do decide to go to business school, you'll learn how to evaluate this kind of choice using what is called a decision tree. The basic idea is to estimate the dollar value of each option and then multiply each of these dollar values by the probability of the option's occurrence. This gives the "expected value" of each option. Then, if you are comfortable with the assumptions behind the analysis, you choose the option with the highest expected value.

For example, let's assume that Option 1, to continue what you are currently doing, is your "base case" and the other options will be compared to this one. Assume that Option 2, to quit and pursue an MBA, has a dollar value of $50,000 more than Option 1 (based on THE MBA ADVANTAGE of your school choice, as listed in the table in chapter 4). You believe that you have a 50 percent chance of being admitted and getting a job following graduation that is as good as the average post-MBA jobs obtained by the graduates of that school. Then your expected value of Option 2 is $25,000 (i.e., 50 percent of $50,000) more than the value of your base case of continuing what you are currently doing.

You can do the same kind of expected value analysis for your other options. But a word of caution: Expected value is an analytical tool to help you evaluate alternatives. Experienced managers use decision trees and expected value as just one input in the decision process. Before you make an important decision like this, sleep on it, think about it, talk to other people about it, and proceed only when you are comfortable with it.

A Contingency Plan

What will you do if you pick an option and it doesn't work out? For example, you might decide to keep your present job and start working on your MBA at night but find that your travel schedule interferes with class. What now?

Every good strategic plan includes a "Plan B," which is what you'll do if Plan A doesn't work out. One possibility is to change your objectives. In the light of these problems with your part-time program, do you still want to get an MBA?

If the answer is still "yes," then what are your choices? You could quit and go to school full time. Or you could change to a different job with a less demanding travel schedule. Another option is to choose another part-time program where the instructors are more willing to work around the travel schedules of their part-time students. It's wise to think about these backup options when you select the strategic career option you are going to pursue.

Climbing the Corporate Ladder

Let's assume that you have decided to pursue an MBA with the objective of working toward a senior management position in a large corporation. It used to be that if you stayed in one functional area—say, finance—and you did an outstanding job, you would eventually become a top manager. It also helped to have a mentor, a senior person in your functional area who would advise you and open a few doors in the process.

In today's fast track career paths, there are some new essentials:

- *Cross-functional training*: It isn't enough to just be an expert in one field. Now you need some hands-on experience in marketing and production as well as finance. In today's flat organizations, this may involve some horizontal moves to get experience, as well as vertical moves up the corporate ladder.

- *Overseas experience*: In the past, an overseas assignment was often a dead-end position for someone who wasn't going to make it to the top. But with many global companies earning more than half their profits from overseas operations, firsthand international experience is vital. According to The *Wall Street Journal*, General Electric recently "began sending its brightest stars abroad rather than the run-of-the-mill managers it once picked for foreign posts."[13]

- *The ability to operate in situations with high ambiguity:* The high rate of change in today's markets means that situations arise for which the standard operating procedures of the company have not been written. Managers may have to make up the rules as they go along:

  > "As part of its management-development process, Dow Chemical Co. three years ago asked 300 senior managers what skills their successors should have. Among the most common answers: an ability to lead effectively in 'ambiguous, complicated and dynamic situations.' 'The key work there is ambiguous,' says Larry Ward, manager of executive development at Dow Chemical. 'We are looking at constant change, and the only constant is change.'"[14]

Climbing the Entrepreneurial Ladder

Suppose you decide that instead of climbing the corporate ladder you want to start your own company someday. The best book I know of on the subject of entrepreneurship is *Startup: An Entrepreneur's Guide to Launching and Managing a New Venture*, by Bill Stolze.[15] Bill is a very successful entrepreneur himself. He started a company in 1961 that now has annual sales in excess of $150 million, so he understands what he is writing about because he's been through it. He is also the founder of the Rochester Venture Capital Club, a group of successful men and women who are now looking for opportunities to invest in the success of new enterprises. To learn how to cope with the opportunities and the uncertainties faced by an entrepreneur, you should obtain a copy of Bill's book.

Another excellent book for would-be entrepreneurs is *Business Plans that Win $$$: Lessons from the MIT Enterprise Forum*, by Stanley Rich and David Gumpert.[16] This book was developed by a panel of MIT alumni who volunteered to counsel prospective entrepreneurs on the development of their business plans.

Will getting an MBA raise the likelihood that you will be successful as an entrepreneur? Frankly, the evidence is mixed. Henry Kravis, founding partner of Kohlberg Kravis Roberts & Company, has an MBA (Columbia Business School Class of 1969). His Wall Street firm arranged the largest leveraged buyout in history, of RJR Nabisco. The CEO of Sun Microsystems, Scott McNealy, also has an MBA (Stanford Class of 1980). Sun went from a startup to over $3 billion in sales in less than ten years.

But there are many successful entrepreneurs who never finished college, let alone an MBA program, including Bill Gates of Microsoft, Steve Jobs and Steve Wozniak of Apple Computer, and Michael Dell of Dell Computer, to name some of the most successful. Some people feel that getting an MBA makes potential entrepreneurs too cautious.

Chances are that if you are determined to start your own company, you will probably do

13 Bennett, A., "General Electric Company Rearranges the Rungs of its Corporate Ladder," The *Wall Street Journal*, March 15, 1993.
14 Bennett, A., "Path to Top Job Now Twists and Turns," The *Wall Street Journal*, March 15, 1993.
15 Stolze, William J., *Startup: An Entrepreneur's Guide to Launching and Managing a New Venture*, 2nd Edition, Rock Beach Press, 1255 University Avenue, Rochester, NY 14607, 1992, $14.95. The book can be ordered from Career Press, Inc., 180 Fifth Avenue, P.O. Box 34, Hawthorne, NJ 07507, or by calling toll-free 1-800-CAREER-1.
16 Rich, S. and Gumpert, D., *Business Plans that Win $$$: Lessons from the MIT Enterprise Forum*, Harper & Row, 1985.

so whether or not you have an MBA. The determination of who becomes a successful entrepreneur may be as much in the genes as it is in the intellect and the education. But what you learn and the contacts you make in business school may help, as they helped Henry Kravis and Scott McNealy.

Politics and Promotions

My students often say to me that they didn't like their former job "because of the politics." But whenever there are more than two people in an organization, there are "politics." Alan Schoonmaker explains why every company has politics:[17]

> "The term (politics) refers to the distribution of power. If we use the term in this sense it becomes obvious that politics is unavoidable. Since power exists in every group or organization, politics must necessarily exist in every firm. You can therefore get away from politics only by becoming a hermit. As long as you live and work in groups and organizations, politics will influence you career—whether you like it or not!"

Schoonmaker then goes on to explain why MBAs are particularly vulnerable to politics:

> "Politics is particularly important for an MBA, because you work at jobs which are very hard to evaluate objectively. A (production line) worker's performance can usually be measured by fairly objective criteria such as number of units produced or amount of scrap. Your performance can rarely be measured accurately and objectively, and the standard 'measurement' is usually some form of performance rating (i.e., an opinion). Since ratings are notoriously subject to bias, your performance record depends on politics . . . whether you like it or not, your career is very dependent on politics.
>
> "The question is not, then, whether you should play politics, but what kind of politics you should play. And to answer this question you must learn who has the power in your firm and how he (or she) uses it. You should do three things: 1) Understand the rules of the political game in your firm; 2) Decide which game you want to play, (and) whether you want to play the games in your firm at all . . . (or) go someplace where the game is more to your liking; and 3) Play the game you select more efficiently."

It is unrealistic to hope that getting an MBA will lead to a job without politics. But having an MBA from a good school gives you more bargaining chips. It raises your market value as a result of the skills you obtain and the additional academic credentials on your resume. Sooner or later, you may be faced with the choice of staying or leaving. The MBA will give you more bargaining power to get what you want if you stay, and it will give you more employment options if you decide to leave.

Let me close with my belief about the value of the MBA degree for one's career:

> *The bottom line:* I believe that for most people, the MBA degree from a good school is a superb investment in one's professional capital. Jobs and promotions may come and go, but the knowledge and the credentials from a graduate degree in business are permanent assets.
>
> Business has become too complex and too competitive to wing it. If one is se-

---

17 Schoonmaker, A., "What Price Career Myopia," *MBA Magazine*, April 1968, pp. 15–20.

rious about a career in management, the education and the credentials of the MBA are indispensable.

The world of business is changing. It's fashionable these days to talk about "the learning organization." But organizations don't learn, people do. And lifelong learning will be greatly enhanced by a thorough grounding in the fundamentals, which is best acquired through the formal process of education. To paraphrase Louis Pasteur, "Change favors the prepared mind."

Chapter 12

What Prospective Students Are Looking for in an MBA Program

The atmosphere around the fifteen-foot conference table in Dewey 219 was intense. Jackets and bookbags were piled along one wall. The conference table was littered with Diet Coke cans and piles of colorful business school catalogs from all over the country.

Nine MBA students, a marketing professor, and a recent alum working as a marketing consultant were staring at the blackboard at one end of the room where a tenth student was listing business school attributes as they were called out by the others. "Tuition. Starting salaries. Prestige of the university. Quality of the student body. Courses in brand management. Teaching quality. . . . " At the end of the two-hour brainstorming session there were fifty-four attributes listed on the board that might influence how prospective students choose a business school. Which ones are most important in choosing a business school?

Welcome to *MKT 441: Product Leadership Laboratory*, a course I have taught for the past twelve years. In this course, teams of second-year MBA students carry out comprehensive marketing studies for real companies and non-profit organizations. The objective of the course is to give students extensive practical experience in applying state-of-the-art marketing methods to the development of comprehensive marketing strategies. (This is the kind of course you can expect to find in a first-rate MBA program. Not all MBA programs offer projects courses since they are much more difficult to teach than lecture or case courses. My purpose in telling you about this is not only to give you some understanding of how prospective students choose their business school, but also to give you an insider's look at how a second-year MBA projects course is organized.)

Every year, dozens of requests cross my desk from companies and organizations seeking help with business planning and analysis. In more than sixty projects carried out over the past twelve years, my students have studied a wide range of product markets—test marketing new bakery products (for a large super market chain), focus groups on consumer attitudes regarding laser sculpturing of the corneas (for a maker of prescription eyeglasses), industrial packaging materials (for an international oil company), consumer financial services (for a local bank), and more. Client organizations have ranged from entrepreneurial startups to *Fortune* 500 companies, from a $2 million high tech company run by an alumnus to the fund-raising organization of a world-class children's hospital.

Most of our work is for alumni who are CEOs or senior managers of the client companies. But this client was different. In the spring quarter of 1990, with competition beginning to heat up among the top business schools, we decided to run a marketing study for the Simon School. The client was the admissions office. The questions were:

- What are potential MBA students looking for in an MBA program? How do they choose one program over another?

- What attributes of the program are most important to them?

- What sources of information do they use? How important are published rankings like the *Business Week* Top 20 and the *U.S. News & World Report* Top 25?

- What is the image of the Simon School relative to its competitors? How are we perceived by potential customers?

- Finally, what could the Simon School do to improve its educational product and how could these improvements be communicated most effectively to prospective students?

How the Course Works
I run the MKT 441 course like a professional consulting firm:

1. Before the course starts, I go through many requests in search of five or six projects with the best potential educational value for the students—and projects that can be done from start to finish within the ten-week quarter. (Because of the time constraint, we have to move faster on these projects than most real consulting firms.)

2. At the beginning of the course, the student teams hold informal discussions with the clients' management to clearly *define the problem*.

3. Each team prepares a *written project proposal* which must be signed by the client's management and by members of the project team before work can begin (negotiation of the proposal is an important part of the learning experience). The proposal includes a statement of the problem, the overall approach to be taken, a Gantt chart showing what tasks are to be accomplished and by when, a specification of the deliverables, and a line item budget.[1] A confidentiality clause may be included if requested by the client. The signed proposal provides protection for both the client and the project team in terms of what is expected.

4. *Secondary research* on the problem is carried out. This may involve a review of the academic literature to determine the most appropriate way to model the problem, a literature search to see how others have approached this kind of problem and what they learned, a competitive analysis, computer database searches, and so on.

5. Next comes *exploratory research* with focus groups representing potential customers. Students draw up an interviewing guide and train themselves to lead the focus group discussions without biasing the results. The purpose of the focus groups is to gain more insight into the problem and to formulate a list of attributes to be tested later in the full-scale survey. Focus groups are often conducted by our students in a rented professional interviewing suite complete with one-way glass and full audio-visual recording equipment.

6. From what has been learned so far, it is now possible to draft a *formal marketing*

---

1 Clients agree to reimburse the students for any out-of-pocket costs incurred, such as postage and printing for mail surveys, mileage, etc.

research questionnaire, which may be designed to be administered by phone, mail, or by personal interview. The questionnaire is thoroughly pretested by administering it to respondents who are representative of the target audience.

7. Concurrently, a *sampling plan* is developed to ensure that the right potential customers will be reached, and that a sufficient number will respond to permit a meaningful statistical analysis of the completed questionnaires. At this point the client is given a chance to review the sampling plan and the draft questionnaire.

8. The team supervises the *administration of the questionnaires*. This involves envelope-stuffing parties (with pizza) for mail surveys, phone banks where teams hire fellow students at $4 per completed phone survey, or one-on-one mall intercepts at a rented marketing research facility in a nearby mall.

9. As the data comes in, it is entered into computerized spreadsheets for *analysis*. This process invariably leads to late nights in the Computer Center, and this is where students really learn about statistics.

10. As the significant findings miraculously emerge from the statistical swamp, the team is faced with the most important part of the study—what does it all mean? In particular, what *strategic recommendations* can be made to the client on the basis of these findings?

11. The findings and the first draft of the managerial recommendations are reviewed informally with the client. An *oral presentation* with professional-quality computerized graphics is created and shown to the client. Frequently this leads to a second presentation for the client's top management. Simultaneously a *comprehensive written report* is prepared, printed, bound, and delivered to the client.

12. Finally, when the last computerized graphic has been shown, the computers have been turned off and all the copies of the report have been delivered, it's time for the traditional *post-project party*!

It's a lot of work for three credit hours. Somehow it all gets done in ten weeks. Casual acquaintances become welded into effective high-output teams. There's a tremendous feeling of accomplishment when it's all over; in fact, the course receives the highest student ratings in the school.

THE MBA MARKETING PROJECT

In March 1990, we initiated the Simon School MBA Marketing Project. The specific objective was to develop a database of relevant information and a set of recommendations to improve future MBA course offerings and catalogs at the Simon School.[2]

Once the project team was assembled, a proposal was written and approved by the Dean's Office. The basic approach was to be a large-scale national survey of recent GMAT-takers. To avoid bias, the Simon School would not be identified as the sponsor of the project.

---

2 "What Potential Students are Looking For in an MBA Program," William E. Simon Graduate School of Business Administration, June, 1990. This study was developed and carried out by the following team from the Simon School MBA Class of 1990: Ron Bingham, Maureen Blitzer, Chris Carosa, Ted Fagenson, Susan Hermenet, Laurel Izuno, Carolyn Keegan, Abu Moosa, Marianne Quercia, and Jean Tunnell. Special thanks also to Kris Lemke, Simon MBA '88, for her assistance with this project.

The team began by performing an analysis of competitive business schools. All the top forty business school catalogs, as rated by the 1988 *Business Week* survey, were obtained, thoroughly read, and compared. Using secondary data from the Admissions Office on co-admitted prospective students, nine schools were chosen to be included in the survey based on their level of competitiveness with the Simon School. The ten schools—Simon and its nine competitors—were listed in the survey in alphabetical order.[3]

A mail survey was employed for a number of reasons. A mail survey minimizes the effects of interviewer bias and generally allows the collection of much more information for a given cost. Mail is slower than other methods, but the majority of responses typically are received within two weeks. Based on the evaluation of these trade-offs, the team selected the mail survey as the most effective method for our research objectives.

The consumer behavior model selected for the study was the linear compensatory expectancy value model. This simply means that products can be considered as bundles of attributes, and people make choices about important purchases by selecting the product, in this case a business school education, that offers the highest weighted average of the attributes they consider important. The power of the model is that you can study products by breaking them down into their attributes, and evaluating their attributes one at a time.

A mail questionnaire was constructed to identify and weight the attributes prospective students consider when selecting a business school. Using a survey format I have developed over the years, it is possible to collect comprehensive information on customer *ideal points* (for example, preference for small schools versus large schools), *attribute importance weights*, and *customer ratings of ten or more competitive products* on a variety of attributes. It all fits, including the cover letter, on a single 11 x 17-inch sheet of paper folded in half to make a very compact four-page printed questionnaire. (Constructing a good marketing research questionnaire is much like constructing a good midterm exam—you get better with practice.)

Choosing the Attributes

The selection of the attributes to be included in the questionnaire was an arduous task. After several brainstorming sessions, the team formulated a list of fifty-four possible factors that could go into the decision of choosing an MBA program. In addition to finding qualities important in deciding which MBA program to attend, it was hoped that these attributes would also be useful in differentiating one school from another. An informal survey of current Simon School students reduced the team's original list to forty attributes. After pretesting various drafts of the questionnaire on fellow students, it was further condensed.

Finally, the draft questionnaire was pretested on a class of current University of Rochester undergraduate marketing students. The pretest showed which attributes would likely be important to them in choosing a business school. This exercise also clearly indicated that, for reasons of space constraint on the survey form and time constraints on the respondents' part, the number of attributes chosen should not exceed ten.

Based on this exploratory research, the final attributes chosen were the following:

---

3   To maintain confidentiality of the competitive analysis, the identities of the nine competitive schools will not be disclosed, nor will their individual ratings on the various attributes.

1. tuition for MBA degree

2. availability of financial aid

3. prestige of MBA degree

4. starting salaries of graduating MBAs

5. size of MBA program (number of full-time students)

6. offers courses I would like to take

7. faculty orientation (research versus teaching)

8. reputation for quality of teaching

9. emphasis of the curriculum (quantitative versus case)

10. student life (social and recreational)

Constructing the Questionnaire

The questionnaire was constructed with the following overall format:

- Page 1 was a cover letter to the respondent describing the basic purpose of the questionnaire ("to determine how various business schools are perceived by potential applicants like you"), noting the importance of their response to the study, and setting a deadline by which the completed questionnaire had to be received in order to be included in the study. Every cover letter was individually signed by a member of the team.

- Page 2 opened with a section for basic demographic information (gender, undergraduate major, intended area of concentration in business school, years of work experience, and whether the respondent intended to pursue a full-time or a part-time MBA program.) This was followed by a series of questions designed to determine the respondent's "ideal point" on a number of the attributes.

- Pages 3 and 4 contained the questions that allowed the respondent to evaluate the ten business schools in the study on the ten attributes listed above, using a five-point scale. There was also a "don't know" column for schools the respondent was not familiar with to measure *awareness*. Page 4 also contained a constant sum question for determining the relative importance of the attributes in making a choice about business schools, and another constant sum question for indicating the relative importance of various sources of information, such as catalogs, *Business Week*, and MBA forums, in making the decision about which school to attend. The last question on page 4 was a *preference for attending* question that asked the respondents to rank the ten schools in the survey in the order they would most like to attend, assuming they were admitted to all of them.

Ideal Point Attributes

Several of the attributes used in this study had "ideal points" that are not readily apparent. For instance, it is obvious that respondents would prefer a school with more *prestige* over a school with less *prestige*, but respondents' ideal point for *size* is not as obvious. Do prospective students prefer large schools or small schools? To determine these less obvious ideal points, respondents were asked to indicate their preference on seven of the attributes using a five-point scale. These attributes and their endpoints were:

1. size of school (number of full time students—large/small)

2. teaching methodology (case courses/lecture courses)

3. curriculum emphasis (quantitative/qualitative)

4. environment (competitive/cooperative)

5. faculty orientation (research/teaching)

6. location (rural/urban)

7. workload (light/heavy)

The question gave respondents an opportunity to check one of five boxes along a continuum between two stated extremes or endpoints. Also, a "no preference" box was available; in this way, checking the box midway between the extremes indicated a middle-of-the-road response, not a position of indifference.

Results of the Survey

The survey was mailed to a nationwide random sample of 1,680 potential MBA students who took the GMAT in January 1990, and whose scores met the Simon School's admissions criteria. Each potential respondent received a cover letter describing the research project, a survey color-coded according to that respondent's GMAT score, a self-addressed, stamped envelope, and a $1 bill as an incentive.[4] All 1,680 cover letters were signed by a member of the research team. In order to disguise the identity of the Simon School as the sponsor of the study, the completed surveys were returned to an address in Middlesex, New York. To further prevent connection with the Simon School or the University of Rochester, the surveys were mailed out from Framingham, Massachusetts.[5]

The overall response rate was 45 percent. Of the 1,680 surveys mailed, 750 were returned by the cutoff date and were used in the analysis. The computerized spreadsheet for capturing all of this data was huge, 750 rows by 177 columns.

As a whole, the sample of 750 respondents preferred:

1. a small-to-medium size program

2. a teaching methodology that uses somewhat more cases than lectures

3. a curriculum emphasis that has an equal mix of quantitative and qualitative material

4. an environment that is more cooperative than competitive

5. a faculty that is more teaching-oriented than research-oriented[6]

---

4   In a number of controlled studies, I found that including a $1 bill doubles the response rate of a mail survey, typically from 22 percent to 45 percent. See Yeaple, R. N., "Using Financial Incentives to Increase the Response Rate of Mail Surveys," *Simon Research Review*, fall 1989.

5   Concealing the identity of the sponsor of this kind of marketing research study is not done to mislead the respondents. It has been found that if the identity of the sponsor is disclosed, the results may be biased by respondents who use the questionnaire to "send the sponsor a message."

6   This was the strongest preference shown for any of the "ideal point" attributes. As noted in chapter 14, there appears to be a strong

   6. an urban location rather than a rural location

   7. a fairly heavy workload

When each of the demographic segments was separated out and compared to the aggregate, the following preference differences were found:

- Women showed a strong preference for a more cooperative environment.

- Respondents intending to concentrate in finance or accounting showed a preference for a more quantitative curriculum.

- Respondents intending to concentrate in marketing showed preferences for a more cooperative environment and a more qualitative curriculum.

Relative Importance of Attributes and Ratings of Individual Schools

Respondents were asked to divide up one hundred points among the ten attributes to indicate the relative importance of each attribute when choosing a business school.[7] At the end of the survey, they were also asked to rank the ten schools in the survey in the order they would most like to attend, assuming they were admitted to all of them.

- *Prestige of the MBA degree* dominated all other attributes. It was weighted as almost twice as important as the next most important attribute. The prestige ratings of the individual schools in the survey closely followed the 1988 *Business Week* Top 20 ranking. Schools that were rated highly by *Business Week* were also rated highly by our respondents.[8]

- *Starting salaries, reputation for quality of teaching* and *net cost* were statistically tied for second most important. These attributes were significantly more important than the remaining attributes, but not as important as *prestige of the MBA degree.*

   Starting salaries for the individual schools were rated in about the same rank order as *prestige.* Respondents believed that the most prestigious schools also provided the highest starting salaries.[9]

   Respondents perceptions of *teaching quality* for the individual schools followed exactly the same rank order as the *preference for attending* ranking from the question at the end of the survey. This underscores the importance of *teaching quality* as a major determinant of school choice. (The *preference for attending* ranking was similar but not identical to the 1988 *Business Week* Top 20 ranking.)

   Net cost had two components: *tuition* (for which students had a very accurate school-by-school perception) and *financial aid* (for which students saw no significant differences across the ten schools).[10]

---

positive relationship between faculty research intensity and the value of THE MBA ADVANTAGE–there is evidence that a research-oriented faculty enhances the value of the MBA program. But prospective students apparently don't believe this, which raises a question about the wisdom of stressing faculty research in MBA catalogs.

7   The relative importance of the ten attributes was also calculated using a preference regression based on a ranking of the schools the respondents indicated they would most like to attend. The importance weights determined by the two methods were almost identical.

8   It is possible that some of the respondents looked up the schools' rankings in the First Edition of *The Business Week Guide to the Best Business Schools,* which was on the market a year before this survey was carried out.

9   They could have also looked up the starting salaries in the *Business Week Guide.*

10 As we will see later in this chapter, *Net cost* becomes very important in the final stages of the choice process.

- *Location, proximity to home, quality of student life, faculty orientation (teaching versus research)*, and *teaching approach (case versus quantitative)* were less important and were all weighted about the same.

  Perceived *quality of student life* varied significantly across schools, although universities associated with nationally-known sports activities had a decided advantage.

  Research-oriented faculties tended to be associated with the schools ranked highly on *Prestige*, but there was no correlation between the schools' *teaching approach (case versus quantitative)* and *prestige*.

- *Size* of the school was the least important attribute in choosing a school. *Size* was uncorrelated with either p*restige* or with the p*reference for attending* ranking. Although respondents tended to prefer a small-to-medium size school, apparently it is not a major factor in school choice for most prospective students.[11]

Relative Importance of Information Sources

The purpose of this question was to determine the relative weighted importance of eight commonly used sources of information on MBA programs: *Barron's, Business Week, U.S. News and World Report*, MBA forums, direct mailings from the school, personal contact with the school, personal recommendation, and other. Again, the constant sum methodology was used to ascertain not only the rank, but also the weighted importance.

Personal recommendation was the most important source of information about business schools,[12] followed closely by *personal contact with the school*, both of which were significantly ahead of all other sources. The next most important sources were *Business Week* and *direct mailings from the school*. Significantly less important were *Barron's* and *U.S. News and World Report*. Finally, *MBA forums* and the *other* category ranked last, indicating the relative unimportance of these sources.

"Awareness" and Perceived Excellence

One of the most interested and unexpected findings from this study was the very high correlation between *awareness* of a school and its perceived *prestige*. Marketing theorists know that before a consumer will consider buying a product, he or she must first be aware that such a product exists and must know something about it.

Every question on the survey about individual school ratings included a "don't know" column. For example, if respondents didn't know whether a particular school had a *quantitative* or *qualitative* teaching approach, they could check "don't know." A school with high a*wareness* was defined as having very few "don't know" responses. In our survey, the nationally known Top 20 schools had awareness levels in the 90 percent range (i.e., 700 of the 750 respondents were willing to rate the top schools), whereas the regional schools on our questionnaire had awareness levels in 70 to 80 percent range.

What was most striking was the almost perfect correlation ($R^2 = 0.965$) between *awareness* and *prestige*, the most important attribute in choosing a school. The highest rated

---

11 The finding that *size* is not an important choice factor for the average prospective student does not mean that it is unimportant to a subset of students. *Size* may be very important to some students. In this sense, averages from these studies can be misleading.

12 This confirms the well-known marketing belief that word-of-mouth of satisfied customers is the most effective form of product promotion.

school on the survey had an awareness level of 95 percent and a *prestige* rating of 4.9 on a five-point scale. The lowest rated school had an awareness of 73 percent and a *prestige* rating of 2.3. The other eight schools were arrayed along a straight line joining these two points.

The same association held for two other important attributes. *Awareness* and *reputation for teaching quality* were very highly correlated (R-squared = 0.988), as were *awareness* and *starting salary* (R-squared = 0.971).

The implication is that the better known a school is, the more highly its program is regarded. Business schools associated with major universities have an advantage in perceived quality. It is noteworthy that Harvard, the school with the highest MBA ADVANTAGE (see chapter 4), benefits from a powerful "awareness" campaign through its publications. According to the dean of the Harvard Business School, the school's MBA and executive programs generate about $50 million in revenue per year, while revenues from its publishing unit—books, videos, case studies, and the *Harvard Business Review*, all of which carry the Harvard Business School logo—were expected to reach about $70 million in 1993.[13]

THE DECISION PROCESS EXPLORATORY STUDY

A follow-up exploratory study done during the summer of 1990 by a team of Simon School alumni gave us additional insight into some of the issues raised in the MBA Marketing Study.[14] Two areas were of particular interest:

- What is the sequence of events that occurs between the time someone first begins thinking about getting an MBA and the time that person enrolls in an MBA program? What decision process do prospective MBA students follow?

- What does the most important attribute, "Prestige," really consist of? How is it measured? How is it communicated to prospective students?

The subjects for this study were thirty-one MBA summer interns working at Xerox Corporation, representing eleven different business schools. These students were interviewed by telephone and were asked to recall details about the process that led up to their decision to enroll in an MBA program.[15] As with most exploratory research, the questions were open-ended, encouraging the respondents to develop their answers with a minimum of interference by the interviewers. Although the sample size was small and the composition was not representative of the population of MBA students, some interesting insights were developed.

The following is reproduced directly from the final report of this study with only minor editorial modifications:[16]

---

13 Fuchsberg, G., "Harvard Weighs One-Year Version of MBA Program," The *Wall Street Journal*, October 29, 1993.
14 "The Decision Process of Choosing an MBA Program," by Ron Bingham, Simon MBA '90; Suzanne Gray, Simon MBA '91; and Kris Lemke, Simon MBA '88; William E. Simon Graduate School of Business Administration, September 1990.
15 Retrospective studies of this kind can be unreliable. The objective of this exploratory study was to gain insight, however, not to make detailed quantitative statements.
16 "The Decision Process of Choosing an MBA Program," by Ron Bingham, Simon MBA '90; Suzanne Gray, Simon MBA '91; and Kris Lemke, Simon MBA '88; William E. Simon Graduate School of Business Administration, September 1990.

Results

1. Deciding to Attend Business School

The majority of students (77 percent) had some work experience; only 23 percent went straight to an MBA program after undergraduate school. Table 12.1 shows the responses received when they were asked what caused them to think about going to business school (multiple responses caused the sum to exceed 100 percent):

Table 12.1

Reasons for deciding to go to business school (N = 31)

	Number of Responses	%
Worked for experience, had reached logical point in career	24	77
Wanted to develop professional/management skills	10	32
Career advancement	10	32
Had planned throughout undergraduate school	9	29
Dissatisfied with job, wanted to increase opportunities	9	29
Went straight to business school after undergrad, no work experience	7	23
Didn't want available positions (jobs) after undergrad	5	16
Career change	5	16
Requisite for desired field	5	16
Went to night school, decided to go full-time	2	7

2. Choosing Where to Apply
A. The process

After deciding to pursue an MBA degree, the students undertook a similar progression of actions to investigate schools and gather information before deciding to which programs to apply. The typical progression included the following steps (which do not necessarily occur in this order):

- register, study for, and take the GMAT exam
- research schools through library, books, and articles
- contact schools to request catalogs and additional literature
- seek recommendations from managers, peers, role models, family, and friends (word-of-mouth)
- choose schools to apply to based on the *reputation of the business school*

B. Sending GMAT Scores

At the time they took the GMAT, most students did *not* have a clear idea of which schools they were definitely interested in; they were still gathering information and forming perceptions. The three largest influences in deciding where to send their GMAT scores were *reputation, location,* and *familiarity with the school.*

C. Contacting Schools for Information

On average, students called 7.23 (standard deviation = 5.7) schools for information.

D. Information Sources

The three most important sources in gathering information before deciding to which schools to apply were *catalogs, personal recommendations,* and the *Business Week survey.* The information sources which students used and which influenced them the most are listed in table 12.2:

Table 12.2
Information sources used when applying to business school

	% Used	% Influenced
Catalogs	90	52
Recommendations (friends, managers, role models)	87	61
Business Week article	77	45
Personal contact with someone at the school	61	42
Barron's Guide	61	19
Alumni contact	48	29

As in the previous study, the most influential source of information about a business school was *personal recommendations from friends and others.*

When asked for the most influential consideration in deciding where to apply (see table 12.3), students most often responded with *reputation (quality of program), personal recommendations (word of mouth),* and the *Business Week survey.*

Table 12.3
Influential factors for choosing where to apply to business school

	Number of responses (N=31)		%
Reputation (quality of program)	llllll	6	19.4
Personal recommendation/word of mouth	llllll	6	19.4
Business Week ranking	lllll	5	16.1
Location	llll	4	12.9
Cost/financial aid	lll	3	9.7
Catalog	lll	3	9.7
Curriculum/emphasis	ll	2	6.5
Application waiver	ll	2	6.5
3-2 program	ll	2	6.5
Contacts at the school	ll	2	6.5
Personal reasons	ll	2	6.5
MBA forums	l	1	3.2
Atmosphere	l	1	3.2

E. Application

The respondents listed the schools they applied to, visited, and were accepted at, in the order of preference at the time they applied. This sample of students applied to an average of 3.2 schools (SD 1.7). Twenty three percent applied to only one school. Fifty five percent got into their first choice, and 94 percent went to the highest-preferred school (on their list) that accepted them. Less than half of the sample (nine out of thirty-one) claimed they applied to a "safety school."

3. Choosing Where to Attend

In deciding where to attend, the importance of several decision factors increased. After being accepted to various MBA programs, *location, cost/financial aid,* and *curriculum/emphasis* were the main decision factors in deciding where to attend (see table 12.4):

Table 12.4

Final decision factors in deciding where to attend a business school

	Number of responses (N=31)		%
Location	111111111	9	29
Cost/financial aid	111111111	9	29
Curriculum/emphasis	1111111	7	22.6
Default (not accepted anywhere else)	1111111	7	22.6
Reputation, quality of program	1111111	7	22.6
Got into number 1 choice	11111	5	16.1
3-2 program	11	2	6.5
Atmosphere	11	2	6.5
Campus visit	11	2	6.5
Contacts at the school—follow-up	1	1	3.2
Size	1	1	3.2
Personal recommendation/word-of-mouth	1	1	3.2

All the factors above were considered, but when asked for the most important factor, *cost/financial aid* increased to the same importance level as *reputation* (as shown in table 12.5):

Table 12.5

The most important factor in deciding where to attend a business school

	Number of responses (N=31)		%
Cost/financial aid	1111111	7	22.6
Reputation, quality of program	1111111	7	22.6
Default (not accepted anywhere else)	111111	6	19.4
Location	11111	5	16.1
Got into number 1 choice	1111	4	12.9
Curriculum/emphasis	111	3	9.7
3-2 program	11	2	6.5
Atmosphere	11	2	6.5
Campus visit	11	2	6.5
Contacts at the school—follow-up	11	2	6.5
Personal recommendation	1	1	3.2

Cost and financial aid were the most important considerations for 22.6 percent of respondents, who we will refer to as the "cost-sensitive segment:"

"After four years of private undergraduate schools that were expensive, Chicago and Simon were too expensive—I didn't want to come out $80,000 in debt."

Reputation and quality of program were still the main influences for 22.6 percent of respondents, referred to as the "reputation-sensitive segment:"

"Cost was irrelevant—all seemed somewhat comparable. Starting salaries were part of the ranking process, but not an important factor—I was already earning more than the average. If someone gets into Harvard, Wharton, or Stanford, they should just GO . . . otherwise, go somewhere that you feel comfortable."

Location was also an important factor in the final decision for 16.1 percent of the respondents in the "location-sensitive segment." These people tended to live in the area *before* graduate school or intended to locate in the area *after* graduation:

"Something else that influenced my decision was the number of Simon School grads that get hired each year in upstate New York."

4. Decision Model

From the respondents in this survey, it appears that applicants typically apply to MBA programs with *reputations* above a certain cutoff level that is unique to each individual. Each applicant has a minimum level of reputation in mind when applying to programs that he or she prefers to attend. This "reputation level" is commonly derived from rankings such as *Business Week* or *U.S. News & World Report* Top 20 lists. Concurrently, students evaluate their own credentials and typically screen out the most prestigious schools as being unattainable (e.g. among the thirty-one students in the study, Chicago, Harvard, and Stanford were listed only once as first choices).

This set of schools is then narrowed down by other factors (such as curriculum, location, and cost), whose importance differs with each individual. The *number of schools applied to* is a function of the *size of the intersection set of relevant factors* (reputation, cost, curriculum, location, etc.), the *confidence in being admitted to the programs*, and the *application fees*.

When the applicant is admitted to schools and knows the true cost (after receiving financial aid packages), he or she typically chooses the school with:

a) the highest *reputation/cost ratio* or

b) the school with the highest reputation which doesn't exceed his or her financial constraints, again considering the peripheral factors of curriculum, location, etc. Thus, the majority of applicants select their school based on reputation, and a portion of those take the decision one step further to include a cost constraint. A few unique individuals select a school on a specific attribute which has overwhelming importance to them: location, curriculum, 3-2 program, etc.

5. Other Factors Influencing the Final Decision
A. Importance of University versus Business School

The majority of respondents identified the *business school* name and reputation as more important in choosing an MBA program than the *university* name and reputation. Table 12.6 shows the responses received when asked which was more important in deciding on an MBA program:

Table 12.6
Importance of name and reputation in choosing an MBA program

Business school	University	Both
23	6	2

The main reasons for considering the name and reputation of the business school are:

- "Recruiting—*corporate recruiters know the names of B-schools.*"
- "*Since I'm entering the business community, a quality* business education *is my primary concern.*"
- "*The* B-school name is recognized *in the business community, and is separate from the university name.*"

  One student expressed the importance of the length of time a business school has been recognized:

  "*My decision to go to North Carolina was tough when Georgetown gave me a scholarship, but* [Georgetown] *was new. It would be lots of work to explain the program to recruiters . . . there is a lack of reputation.*"

The majority of respondents also identified the *alumni network of the B-school* as more important than that of the *university*, stressing the loyalty, bonding, and enthusiasm they have encountered in discussions with alumni. When asked to identify the most important alumni network when considering MBA programs, the sample responded as shown in table 12.7:

Table 12.7
Importance of alumni network in choosing an MBA program

Business school	University	Both
24	4	3

The following reasons were most common:

"*The* job search *is the most important consideration; these people are in the positions that you want.*"

"*The alumni of the B-school will* know the program.*"

"*Job potential—in entering the business community, B-school contacts are more* relevant.*"

"B-school alumni have a concentrated network, and are willing to help those who went through the same program."

There is a small segment who *did* identify the *university* as more important or equally important than the B-school in the two areas mentioned (name/reputation and alumni network). They described the *"Halo Effect—the characteristics of a well-known university imply a certain standard, so the B-school is also associated with that standard."* Also, three students mentioned the benefit of being able to take classes throughout the university.

Several respondents also emphasized the importance of the halo effect for a *new* business school:

"If the school is new, then the halo effect is important."

"Because U of R is only a twenty-year-old business school, maybe the university alumni are more important."

B. Components of *Prestige*

The *prestige* attribute has been identified as a major force in attracting students to a business school, both in the MBA Marketing Study (using the nationwide GMAT test sample) and in this study. To understand the implications of the "prestige effect," the students in this sample were asked what determines the prestige of a business school, as shown in table 12.8.

Table 12.8
Elements of *prestige*

	Number of Responses (N=25)		%
Alumni achievements	11111111111	11	44
Reputation	111111	6	24
Well-known faculty (publications, committees, etc.)	11111	5	20
Name recognition	11111	5	20
Dean	1111	4	16
Quality of research	1111	4	16
Quality of teaching	111	3	12
Academic reputation	111	3	12
Placement	111	3	12
Strong alumni base	11	2	8
Alumni satisfaction and loyalty: value of education	11	2	8
Ranking	11	2	8
Starting salary	11	2	8
Professors' real-world experience	1	1	4
Length of time well-known	1	1	4
Facilities	1	1	4
Exposure/well-known in business world	1	1	4
Ability to adapt to changes in market	1	1	4
Practical base of tools to use in business	1	1	4
Cost	1	1	4
Quality of program	1	1	4

As seen above, *alumni achievements* are extremely important in assessing the prestige of a given school, along with *well-known faculty*. This finding has important implications for the catalog, school literature, and public relations in general. Several direct quotations defining *prestige* emphasize the achievements of the alumni:

> *"what alumni have done and where they've been show what you* [as a graduate of the program] *are capable of, as judged by recruiters"*

> *"how the business school name is held in the market . . . success of the graduates"*

> *"what happens after you get out of school . . . what alumni are doing, running today's companies"*

> *"MBA satisfaction—alumni in the business community, and how they view the value of their education"*

> *"exposure—being well-known in the business world"*

> *"performance and careers of alumni"*

Conclusions about How Prospective Students Choose an MBA Program

The results of these two studies are interesting and provocative. The large-scale MBA Marketing Project was based on a national survey of 750 GMAT-takers, and should be fairly representative of how the typical prospective MBA student evaluates business schools. It should be borne in mind, however, that the second study—the exploratory project on the decision process of prospective students—was based on a very small sample (thirty-one summer interns) that was not necessarily representative of the national population of MBA students; it was done only to provide insights into the choice process. Nevertheless, the findings of the two studies are consistent.

We learned that prospective MBAs prefer:

- small-to-medium size schools over large schools
- an urban campus over a rural campus
- a faculty that is oriented more toward teaching than research
- a school where teamwork and cooperation among students are stressed over competition
- a school that requires them to work fairly hard, not a "country club"

In choosing a business school, prospective students said that the most important attributes are:

- prestige of the school (twice as important as any other attribute)
- quality of teaching
- starting salaries, and
- net cost, defined as tuition less financial aid

Prospective students are most heavily influenced about school choice from *word-of-mouth recommendations* and from *personal contact with the school*, both of which were twice as important as the *business school rankings* published by *Business Week* and *U.S. News & World Report*.

A very strong correlation was found between *awareness*—the percent of respondents willing to rate a school on the survey—and *prestige*, the most important attribute. This suggests that it pays the dean's office to aggressively publicize the name of the school.

In the follow-up exploratory study, we learned that the decision process to get an MBA follows these steps:

1. The decision to go to business school is most frequently triggered by an awareness that the time has come in one's career to develop managerial skills.

2. The next step is to gather published information about various programs, to take the GMAT, and to seek recommendations about schools from friends and associates.

3. When deciding which schools to apply to, the most important factors are the *reputations* of the various programs and word-of-mouth *recommendations* about the programs.

4. When deciding which school to attend, the most important factors are *net cost* and *reputation*, followed by *location*.

We also asked MBA students from a number of schools to help us better understand how the prestige of a school is determined.[17] The answer: *Achievements of the alumni*—cited twice as frequently as *well-known faculty* and *name recognition of the school*. Given the concerns that prospective students have about faculty research crowding out good teaching, the producers of business school catalogs are wise to devote more space to the accomplishments of their alumni than to the research agendas of their faculty.

The bottom line: Prospective MBA students know what they are looking for: a small, urban business school that values teamwork and high quality teaching, with a prestigious name that reflects the achievements of the school's alumni.

---

17 The research team found that prospective students considered the terms "prestige" and "reputation" synonymous.

Chapter 13

What Corporate Recruiters Are Looking for in an MBA Program

Prospective students constitute only one set of business school customers. An equally important group are the corporate recruiters who ultimately determine the demand and the prices for our products by deciding how many of our graduates they are willing to hire and how much they are willing to pay them.

How do corporate recruiters decide at which business schools to recruit? In the spring quarter of 1991, one of our second-year MBA student teams in my MKT 441 projects course carried out a national mail survey of 136 corporate recruiters to find out what factors are most important to them in choosing schools at which to recruit MBAs.[1] For this study, the client was the Simon School's Placement Office.

Although a few of the topics in the study related only to the Simon School, most of what was learned applies to any top business school. By understanding how corporate recruiters choose the schools at which they recruit, you as a prospective MBA student will gain insight about an important process that may influence your choice of business school.

Here, in the MBA team's own words (with minor editing for brevity), is what they did and what they learned.

THE CORPORATE RECRUITING PROJECT

In the spring of 1991, the placement office staff at the Simon School was interested in future hiring trends among corporate recruiters. Many questions had been raised: What characteristics are corporate recruiters looking for when screening candidates? Are recruiting trends decreasing due to the recent economic situation? How is the Simon School perceived? How can the placement office attract more recruiters to come to the campus?

In order to address these concerns, we developed a market research study to identify the factors that are important to recruiters when making recruiting decisions and to find out how the Simon School is perceived by recruiters relative to its competitors. The objectives of this study were:

1. To identify and weight the factors that are important to recruiters in selecting schools at which to actively recruit;

---

1 "An Analysis of Recruiters' Perceptions," by Scott Beaudry, Marcy Eisenstadt, Sue Koerner, and Karen Vignare from the Simon MBA Class of 1991; William E. Simon Graduate School of Business Administration, May 1991.

2. to identify the perceptions of corporate recruiters about the Simon School and its competitors;

3. to determine the most important placement office services;

4. to determine the most important information sources for recruiters; and

5. to determine hiring trends, minimum class size, and the time of the year when corporate recruiters decide at which schools they will recruit.

In addition, a number of questions were raised by the placement office about the perceptions and requirements of different segments of the recruiter market:

- *Size of the company:* Do small companies have different perceptions or needs than large companies? Small organizations may seek different attributes in students, or be less knowledgeable about particular schools. (Small organizations were defined as having one-to-five hundred employees.)

- *Position of the recruiter:* Do human resources (HR) recruiters from companies differ in their perceptions or needs from manager (MGR) recruiters (line managers who are asked to help out with the recruiting process)? The HR respondent is responsible for interviewing and hiring whereas the MGR will supervise the prospective employees.

The following is a discussion of the development of the survey instrument and the sampling plan. Next, the respondent profile and response rates are described, followed by the results section which answers the five objectives of the study.

Exploratory Research

We began our exploratory research with a preliminary telephone survey of recruiters in order to establish relevant areas of concern. We learned which schools were most frequently visited, sources of recruiting decisions, and factors influencing these decisions. The information from this preliminary telephone survey was used to develop the final mail questionnaire.

In the exploratory telephone survey, we contacted a number of recruiters who had established a good rapport with the Simon School. The following five questions were posed:

Question 1:

From which schools do you recruit? We began with this question in order to generate a relevant list of schools to include in the survey. After tabulating the responses, we developed a potential list of schools to include in the final survey.

Question 2:

Who within your organization makes the decision where to recruit? This question was posed so that we would know whom to target with the mail survey. We found wide variation between firms. Some firms use only human resources staff, while at other firms the recruiting decisions are made at the senior management level. Because of the variation, we decided to target our survey to all recruiters, HRs and MGRs.

Question 3:

How often do you add or delete schools? We were trying to determine if firms were "brand-loyal" to the schools currently on their recruiting schedules. The results indicated that the schools chosen depend on economic conditions and proximity of the school to the firm.

Question 4:

What factors most affect the decision to recruit at a particular school? This question was aimed at developing a list of attributes to include in the mail survey questionnaire. Those surveyed responded with the following attributes: *diversity of student body, success of graduates, quality of admissions, geographic preference, reputation of the school,* and *alumni network.*

Question 5:

What information sources do you currently *use to make recruiting decisions?* We were interested in finding out what information sources the recruiters considered most important. They responded that their *relationship with the placement office* was most important. The list also included their *informal recruiter network, publications* (e.g., Business Week), and *the success rate of graduates.*

Sampling Plan

To conduct a survey of this type, a list of appropriate recruiters had to be compiled. The Simon School Placement Office keeps a database of 2,200 employers that include human resource personnel as well as line managers. Concern whether this list might be biased led us to examine other schools' placement reports and then compile a list of companies currently recruiting at the other top business schools.

To assure that the sample was representative of the population of MBA recruiters, this list was cross-referenced to Simon's database, and the matching company entries were included in the sample. All companies that either currently or formerly recruited at Simon were also included in the sample. Color-coded surveys were used to identify the recruiters as being either current, former, or potential Simon recruiters. Where companies had more than one name listed in the same office, duplicates were eliminated. The resulting list contained 1,634 names. The geographic and industry distributions of the sampling plan are shown in tables 13.1 and 13.2.

Table 13.1
Sampling plan geographic distribution

Region	Surveys Sent
Northeast	710
Mid-Atlantic	276
Midwest	348
Southeast	107
Southwest	54
West	139
Total	1,634

Table 13.2
Sampling plan industry distribution

Industry	Surveys Sent	Industry	Surveys Sent
Banking–commercial	168	Manufacturing–consumer	244
Banking–investment	50	Manufacturing–industrial	189
Communications	130	Pharmaceuticals	49
Consulting	139	Public Accounting	29
Financial Services	163	Real Estate	32
High Technology	81	Other	360

Designing the Mail Survey

During the exploratory survey it became apparent that recruiters were very difficult to reach by phone. They were frequently away from their desk, and many had secretaries who screened their calls. Consequently, a mail survey was chosen for the main part of the project to allow us to bypass the secretaries and reach the recruiters at their desk. A mail survey would also insure that the respondents would remain anonymous, which might result in more candid responses. Moreover, the questionnaire was considered too lengthy to complete over the phone.

The questions posed on the mail survey were grouped in three sections. The first section included self-reporting demographics, the second was composed of preference and attribute data on competitive schools, and the third section included questions related to hiring trends and and recruiting calendars.

We focused our survey on nine schools that compete with the Simon School across four dimensions: *geographic region*, *program emphasis*, *national rank*, and *placement services reputation*. The ten schools–Simon plus the other nine–were listed in the questionnaire in alphabetical order.[2]

Selection of Attributes

A comprehensive list of attributes was needed in order to test the respondents on their perceptions of the various schools. After initial meetings with the placement office staff, the team brainstormed ideas regarding the appropriate attributes to include in the survey. Additionally, ideas from the preliminary telephone survey were included on the list. We started with a list of fifteen attributes, and with advice from the placement office, reduced the list to the following attributes on which respondents would compare the ten schools:

1. Familiarity with the school (how often do you hear or read about the school);

2. analytical skills of the school's MBA graduates;

3. ability to apply MBA education in a practical work setting;

4. potential to reach top management position;

5. communication skills of MBA graduates;

6. interviewing skills of graduates;

2 To maintain confidentiality, the identities and ratings of the competitive schools will not be disclosed.

7. admission standards of schools;

8. alumni influence over the decision to recruit MBAs from their respective schools;

9. overall reputation of MBA program; and

10. salary levels necessary to hire MBA graduates.

Formatting the Questionnaire

Once we established the competitive schools and the attributes to be included in the survey, we designed a four-page mail questionnaire with the following format.

Part I: Demographics (page 1)

The survey began with a demographics section that included:

- Location of the company's facility (first three digits of zip code);
- size of company (number of employees);
- respondent's position (human resources or manager);
- industry classification (banking, pharmaceuticals, etc.); and
- functional area(s) typically recruited for (finance, marketing, etc.).

Part II: Hiring Trends (page 1)

The next set of questions asked the recruiters about their division's approximate hiring levels for the current year, last year, and two years ago.

Part III: Hiring Preference by School (page 1)

Respondents were asked to assign points to each of the ten schools on a scale of 0 to 100 (with 100 being the best) based on their hiring preference for graduates of that school, regardless of whether they recruit there. (The schools listed were the same ten schools used throughout the survey.)

Part IV: Rating of Individual Schools (pages 2 and 3)

The next section asked the respondents to rate each of the ten schools on the ten attributes using a five-point scale. We asked the recruiters to rate these characteristics based on their perceptions, regardless of whether they recruited at the schools.

Part V: Miscellaneous Market Information (page 4)

The remaining questions inquired about the importance of various placement office services and about information sources. We asked recruiters to predict future hiring trends, namely whether MBA hiring would decrease, remain the same, or increase. Two questions addressed the following areas of special interest to the Placement Office:

- The optimal number of years of prior work experience before getting an MBA and
- the minimum class size of graduating MBA students at a school to justify on-campus recruiting.

Finally, additional questions pertained to the time of the year when recruiters set their recruiting schedules for the year, when they actually appear on campus for active recruiting, and when they make offers.

When the first draft of the survey was completed, we pre-tested the questionnaire on a number of people, mainly recruiters visiting the Simon School, and made numerous corrections for clarity and accuracy before printing the final version.

To avoid bias, the Simon School was not identified as the sponsor of the survey. The surveys were mailed from three non-Rochester locations: Detroit, Michigan; White Plains, New York; and Baltimore, Maryland. All of the surveys were received at a Baltimore, Maryland post office box.[3]

Results of the Survey

A total of 136 useable responses were received, resulting in a response rate of 8.3 percent. (It was decided not to enclose a financial incentive, such as a $1 bill, for this study.) This response was substantially below the anticipated rate of 20 percent. The low response raised concern about non-response bias (the possibility that those who didn't respond were systematically different from those who did). A careful analysis of the distribution of respondents along the two sampling parameters, geography and industry, showed that the responses were in about the same proportions as in the sampling plan, and therefore increased our confidence that the responses were representative of the original sampling plan.

With regard to the specific objectives of the survey, the following was learned:

Objective Number 1:
Identify the attributes that most influence recruiters' opinions of a school.

Through the use of a preference regression, we were able to determine the attribute importance weights from the recruiters' ratings of the individual schools and their overall stated preference for these schools. The results indicate that three attributes best explain recruiters' preferences for recruiting at certain schools. Table 13.3 lists these attributes, along with their associated importance weights.

Table 13.3
The attributes most important to corporate recruiters

Attribute	Importance Weight
Ability to apply MBA education in a practical work setting	9.55
Familiarity (how often the school is heard of or read about)	5.27
Admissions standards of the school	3.35

It is important to note that these weights are relative magnitudes. *Ability to apply the MBA education* is twice as important as *familiarity*, and nearly three times as important as *admissions*

---

3 As with the survey of prospective MBA students described in chapter 12, it was decided to conceal the identity of the sponsor in order to avoid bias. If recruiters knew who was sponsoring the survey, they might not be as candid. To protect the confidentiality of the responding recruiters, all returned questionnaires were completely anonymous, and no attempt was made to identify them individually.

standards. When choosing where to recruit, the ability of the school's graduates to apply their MBA education takes precedence over both familiarity with the school and the school's admissions standards. The importance weights of all of the attributes tested are shown in table 13.4.

Table 13.4
The relative importance weights of all ten attributes

Attribute	Importance Weight
1. Familiarity (how often the school is heard of or read about)	5.27
2. Analytical skills of the school's MBA graduates	Not significant
3. Ability to apply MBA education in a practical work setting	9.55
4. Potential to reach top management position	Important only for small firms
5. Communication skills of MBA graduates	Not significant
6. Interviewing skills of graduates	Important only for small firms
7. Admission standards of schools	3.35
8. Alumni influence over where to recruit	Not significant
9. Overall reputation of MBA program	Not significant
10. Salary levels necessary to hire MBA graduates	Not significant

The results in table 13.4 were surprising. After years of hearing about the poor communications skills of graduating MBAs, how could this attribute be "not significant"? And what about analytical skills? Are they also unimportant?

Our interpretation is that the top schools have worked hard on improving the communications skills and the analytical skills of their graduating MBAs, perhaps to the point that all the best schools are judged by recruiters to be about equal. These attributes *are* important, but if all the schools are perceived as equally good, these attributes are no longer the basis by which recruiters choose one school over another. They *expect* the graduates of all of these top schools to have excellent analytical and communications skills. Instead, they make their decisions about where to recruit based on the three attributes in table 13.4 where they *do* perceive significant differences across the best schools.

Ability to Apply the MBA: the Number One Attribute

It appears that the top schools have reached parity on analytical and communications skills. If this interpretation is correct, then the competition among business schools may be shifting in a new direction—toward the ability to apply the MBA education in the workplace. This implies that in the future, schools may be competing more aggressively on the basis of internships and projects courses such as the one that produced this survey.

The relative importance of *familiarity with the school* matches the finding described in chapter 12 about the strong association in the minds of prospective students between *awareness* and excellence of the MBA program. Whether we're talking about influencing corporate recruiters or prospective students, it pays to continuously publicize the school.

A school's *admissions standards* determine the quality of incoming students. The finding that corporate recruiters give this attribute significant weight is consistent with the finding in appendix B that the quality of the incoming students is the most important determinant of a school's

MBA ADVANTAGE. Recruiters seem to be aware that the success of most MBA programs is largely determined in the admissions office.

The finding that small companies choose schools at which to recruit based in part on the *top management potential* of the graduates was also interesting. Large firms apparently are more focused on filling entry-level openings in finance and marketing, whereas small firms may be looking for an MBA to be groomed as backup for the CEO. Small firms use two attributes, *the potential to reach top management positions* and *interviewing skills*, much more than large organizations in evaluating an MBA program.

There were no significant differences in attribute importance weights whether they were assigned by human resources (HR) personnel or by other recruiters. We tested for differences in attribute weights assigned by HR and by MGR (managerial) recruiters; no statistically significant differences were found.

> *Objective Number 2:*
> *Identify the perceptions of corporate recruiters of the Simon School and its competitors.*

A number of significant observations were reported regarding the Simon School's competitive position relative to the other nine schools covered in the survey.[4]

> *Objective Number 3:*
> *Determine the most important placement office services.*

Several schools across the country have renowned placement office personnel. It was suggested that this characteristic may influence a corporate recruiters' school choice decision. Respondents were asked to indicate the importance of various placement office services on a five-point scale ranging from "not important" (1) to "very important" (5). Responses were clustered into three groups based on relative importance. The numbers in parentheses indicate the mean score on the five-point scale.

The most important functions and services of placement offices were:

- On-campus recruiting (4.41),
- contact with placement office staff (4.15),
- placement office staff knowledge of individual students (3.93), and
- resume books (3.79).

The second most important group of placement office services included:

- Internship programs (3.36),
- published placement reports (3.33),
- job listings (3.06),
- job fairs (2.87), and
- lunches with faculty members (2.76).

---

4   As mentioned previously, competitive information about various schools will not be disclosed.

The least important group contained only one factor, that of *tickets for special events*. Our hope was to determine the importance of recruiting perks, such as tickets to a Top 10 basketball game or Broadway theater tickets. This question received a very low importance rating (2.09), indicating that it is either of little importance or that recruiters would not consciously admit to its importance. Large organizations rated this factor slightly higher than did small organizations.

When the various segments of the respondents (*large firms* versus *small firms; HR recruiters* versus *MGR recruiters*) were analyzed individually, a number of interesting findings were obtained (all differences listed below were significant at the 90 percent level).

- *On-campus recruiting* was rated higher in importance by *large firms* than by *small firms*. Large firms may be more likely to recruit at schools away from their home cities, making on-campus interviews more attractive.

- *Resume books* were rated higher in importance by *MGR recruiters*. The MGR respondents (line managers) may dislike the initial screening of applicants traditionally done by the HR department and perhaps enjoy looking through resume books as a way to circumvent this screening process.

- *Lunches with faculty* were rated more highly by *large firms*. Since smaller firm employees are apt to "wear many hats," they may be too busy to have lunch with faculty members. Large firm recruiters are more likely to be HR personnel and may feel it is part of their job to meet the faculty and find out what is happening on the various campuses.

- *Large firms* rated *internship programs* more highly, probably because they are more likely to be able to offer summer internships.

- *Job fairs* were also rated higher by *large firms*, and are also rated more highly by *HR recruiters*. Job fairs may be less attractive to small firms because the timing of fairs may not necessarily coincide with the timing of their hiring needs. (Large firms may have the option of "stocking up" on managerial talent.) The fairs are usually held in large cities requiring representatives of the firms to travel. Small firms may not be able to justify the time and expense needed to participate in job fairs, particularly if they are in the market for just one or two graduates. The HR preference for job fairs may also reflect their desire to use these occasions to network with other recruiters.

Objective Number 4:
Determine the most important information sources used by recruiters.

Respondents were asked to rate how frequently they used the following sources of information about schools and graduates on a *four*-point scale, from "never" (1) to "consistently" (4). The average ratings on this four-point scale are shown in parentheses.

- *Business Week* rankings (2.24)
- Published faculty research (1.96)
- Networking with other recruiters (2.51)
- Student newspapers (1.68)

- *U.S. News & World Report* rankings (1.99)
- Discussions with faculty (2.49)
- Other: please specify _____ (3.75)

Surprisingly, the highest rated choice was "other," with a mean rating of 3.75 on the four-point scale, significantly higher than any other choice. When the write-in comments were tabulated, they were dominated by comments related to *success of previous graduates*. Of the forty-eight who specified "other" responses, thirty-three (69 percent) wrote comments related to *success of previous graduates*. The mean value of the thirty-three *success of previous graduates* responses was 3.95 on the four-point scale. Given that this was a write-in response, this extremely high rating confirms the intuition that *performance of alumni* has great influence on a recruiter's school choice decision.[5]

Next in importance was the recruiters' *network* (mean of 2.51) and their *discussions with faculty* (mean of 2.49). The *Business Week* Rank and *U.S. News & World Report* Rank followed with mean values of 2.24 and 1.99 respectively. *Faculty research* was rated next to lowest at 1.96, suggesting that recruiters were not interested in talking with faculty about their research. Rather, they may view faculty as a good source of information about individual students' capabilities. *Student publications* were ranked significantly lower than all of the other sources, at 1.68.

Objective Number 5:
Evaluate hiring trends and other miscellaneous market information.

The following questions were asked regarding overall market conditions and preferences:

- *What is your prediction for the future regarding MBA hiring trends?* Eleven-point-five percent of the respondents said that MBA hiring would increase, 62.3 percent felt hiring would stay the same, and 26.2 percent said it would decrease.
- *What is the optimal number of years of work experience before students return to school for their MBA?* The majority of respondents (70 percent) indicated that two to four years is optimal. Recruiters were strongly opposed to hiring MBAs with no prior work experience; only one recruiter in the 136 respondents replied that zero work experience is optimal. The responses by range of optimal work experience are shown in table 13.5:

Table 13.5
Optimal pre-MBA work experience

Years of work experience	Responses
No work experience	1%
1–2 years	14%
2–4 years	70%
4–6 years	15%
More than 6 years	0%

5 It is interesting to note that in chapter 12, prospective students reported that *alumni achievements* are the best measure of a business school's *prestige*, and *prestige* is the most important attribute in choosing a business school.

- *Is there a minimum number of MBA students per graduating class necessary to make it worthwhile to recruit at a school?* The most frequent response (73 percent) was "no minimum." Of the rest, 7 percent replied "greater than 100" and 6 percent said "greater than 200." The remaining 14 percent responded with "don't know."

- *What reasons would you have for* adding *a school to your recruiting schedule?* Answers to this open-ended question included *geographic area, diversity of students, alumni influence,* and *strength of a school's functional areas.*

- *What reasons would you have for* dropping *a school from your recruiting schedule?* Answers included *poor quality of students, downward trends in hiring, lack of success at certain schools,* and *budget constraints.*

- *When do you decide at what schools you will recruit?* These decisions are typically made in the summer, between May and September.

- *When do you conduct on-campus recruiting?* There is a peak in October, and another peak in January, February, and March.

- *When do most of the students visit the company for on-site interviews?* These interviews begin in January and are completed by the end of April.

- *When do you extend job offers?* As early as January and February with a peak in March and April. A few offers are made as late as June.

- *When do you make offers for summer internships?* Typically in March, April, and May.

WHAT BUSINESS MANAGERS WANT FROM BUSINESS SCHOOLS

In the spring of 1993, a team of four students in my Marketing Research class carried out a related study to explore what *business managers* (not just recruiters) are looking for from business schools.[6] Analysis of the data was continued by Howard Mulcahey during the summer of '93. The following is a synopsis of this study.

Exploratory Research

The exploratory research for this study was carried out by Professor Larry Matteson and I during the winter quarter of 1993 in a series of lunches and meetings with twenty-five senior managers, Simon School alumni, and corporate recruiters. The fundamental question we asked was "How can we improve the MBA graduates we are turning out so as to make them more valuable to your company?"

Simultaneously, a mail survey of over 200 Simon School alumni who had graduated with a major in marketing was carried out to gather information on proposed course modifications and improvements in the marketing curriculum.

On the basis of insights from these two activities we compiled the following list of MBA curriculum topics of current interest to alumni, recruiters, and managers:

- Creativity and innovativeness,

---

6 "What Businesses Want from Business Schools," by Larry Kleehammer, Juan Lugo, Howard Mulcahey and Keith Sawyer, all from the Simon MBA Class of 1994; William E. Simon Graduate School of Business Administration, May 1993.

- teamwork,

- demonstrations of leadership,

- ability to work across functional boundaries,

- application of the traditional MBA quantitative and analytical skills to real business problems, and

- ability to apply MBA training immediately upon graduation (i.e., the ability to "hit the ground running").

The Research Questions

Based on insights from our exploratory research, the student team formulated the following research questions:

1. Is there a significant *change in organizations* away from the traditional hierarchy?

2. When hiring MBAs, what is the relative preference of managers for *functional specialists* versus *cross-functional generalists*?

3. What is the relative importance of *teamwork*, *leadership*, and other "soft skills" compared to the business skills traditionally taught in MBA programs?

4. What is the relative importance of *personal traits*, such as flexibility, adaptability, creativity, intelligence, and interpersonal skills?

5. How important is post-MBA *continuing education*?

6. What characteristics of an MBA program *attract corporate recruiting* efforts?

Sampling Plan

A stratified sample of 982 people who hire, manage, or are in some manner involved with MBAs was drawn up (see table 13.6) consisting of the following market segments:

Table 13.6
Sampling plan for survey of business managers

Market Segment	Surveys Sent
Corporate recruiters	406
Simon School alumni	199
Business managers who were not Simon alumni	228
Journalists who write about business education	45
Current Simon School students, randomly selected	59
Simon School faculty members	45
Total	982

To encourage candor on the part of the respondents, the individual responses were anonymous. The response rate of each market segment could be tracked, however, because the outgoing questionnaires were color-coded by segment.

Design of the Questionnaire

Because of the large size of the sample and the length of the questionnaire, it was decided to make this a mail survey. The outgoing survey package consisted of a cover letter on Simon School letterhead signed by all four members of the team, a four-page questionnaire, a postage-paid return envelope and a $1 bill as an expression of appreciation (many of the alumni returned the $1 with their filled-out questionnaires). The questionnaire had six parts:

Part I: *Which skills will be important for your future managers to possess?*

Respondents were asked to rate the importance of twenty-three different skills, ranging from traditional MBA skills like *capital budgeting* and *regression analysis* to soft skills like *leadership* and *creative problem solving,* on a five-point scale from "not valuable" to "very valuable." The skills were listed in alphabetical order, and there was also a "no opinion" rating for respondents who were not sure.

This section also asked respondents whether these skills are best learned in business school or on the job.

Part II: *What are the characteristics of MBA programs from which you would want to hire future managers?*

In this section respondents were asked to answer several questions about inter-disciplinary courses versus specialized courses and the like, and also to rate six factors—ranging from *business school rankings* and *diversity of students* to *quality of the students* and *reputation of the faculty*—on a five-point scale as to their importance in influencing where they recruit.

Part III: Respondents were asked to rate thirteen business schools on the quality of their students.

Part IV: This section dealt with the rate of change in today's organizations.

Respondents were asked about the *rate of change of importance* of business functions ranging from *accounting* and *communications skills* to *legal issues* and *total quality management.*

A second set of questions asked respondents about changes in their organizations, such as the flattening of hierarchy and the use of more multifunctional teams.

Part V: *What are the personal characteristics needed in managers of the mid-'90s?*

In three questions devoted to top management, professional staff, and future MBA recruits, respondents were asked to divide up a constant sum of 100 points to indicate the relative importance in each position of various personal characteristics, such as *vision, specialized functional skills,* and *risk taking.*

Part VI: A few questions at the end of the questionnaire were designed to collect demographic information about the respondents without compromising their anonymity.

Results of the Survey

The overall response rate of 26 percent was less than expected. None of the journalists and only a few of the current Simon School students responded. Almost all of the 253 responses were received from corporate recruiters, alumni, and other managers who were not alumni. Of these, 72 percent said that they influence the hiring of MBAs, so the sample was judged adequate for the objective of the study, which was to explore what business managers want from business schools.

1. Soft skills are most important . . .

a) The *most important skills* for future managers, with average ratings of 4.5 or better on the five-point scale of importance, were found to be:

- Leadership skills (4.6),
- cohesive teamwork skills (4.6),
- interpersonal skills (4.6), and
- creative problem-solving skills (4.5).

b) The *least important skills* for future managers, with average importance ratings in the 2.8 to 3.3 range, were:

- Regression analysis (2.8),
- pricing models (3.0), and
- probability and statistics (3.1).

2. . . . but analytical skills are also important.

It appears that the respondents were sending a message to the school to alter the balance away from emphasis on technical skills like regression towards the softer skills like leadership and teamwork. But business schools were not being asked to drop the teaching of these technical skills; the average importance weights of these technical skills were all rated at about the midpoint of 3.0.[7]

As noted in the Corporate Recruiting Project described earlier in this chapter, business managers may take MBA proficiency in these technical skills as "given." The business schools were now being asked add something that has been lacking— the soft skills of management. It may be that managers are deciding where to recruit using proficiency in these soft skills as a differentiating attribute.

The following "ideal point" attribute preferences were received in response to the question: "Which attributes do you prefer a business school to have?"

- More interdisciplinary than specialized
- Offering state-of-the-art content in the courses
- Equally balanced between quantitative and qualitative material
- Much more applied than theoretical in teaching approach

---

7 Many of the marketing alumni stated in a separate alumni survey that they routinely use regression as part of their daily job, and if they don't use it, they purchase it from consultants. They still have to understand it to be intelligent customers.

3. *Quality of the students* determines where to recruit.

In response to the question "When deciding where to recruit, how important are the following?" these ratings were recorded (on a 1-to-5 scale of importance):

- Quality of students (4.8),[8]
- reputation of the faculty (3.7),
- business school rankings (3.6),
- diversity of the student body (3.5),
- geographic location of the school (3.0), and
- number of alumni currently employed at your company (2.4).

4. Soft skills continue to grow in importance.

With regard to the rate-of-change in skills mix required in business today, skills that were rated as "becoming much more important" were *teamwork, communication, leadership, entrepreneurship/intrapreneurship*, and *total quality management*. Significantly, *none* of the listed skills (including *statistics*) were rated as "becoming less important."

The current organizational trends reported were as expected: Much more emphasis on *teams* and *cross-functional training*, together with *fewer levels* in the organization's hierarchy.

5. The desired mix of skills varies with the manager's level.

For top managers:

- leader (35 percent)
- communicator (27 percent)
- visionary (25 percent)
- educator (8 percent)
- gatherer of information (5 percent)

For management professionals:

- leadership (29 percent)
- cross-functional skills (27 percent)
- creativity (23 percent)
- adaptability (12 percent)
- continuing to learn (9 percent)

For newly-recruited MBAs:

- creative problem-solving (18 percent)
- be proactive (16 percent)

---

8   In appendix B, the quality of incoming students was found to be the most important determinant of the size of a school's MBA Advantage

- work well with other people (12 percent)
- inspire commitment from others (12 percent)
- take risks (10 percent)
- think analytically and quantitatively (8 percent)
- display above-average intelligence (8 percent)
- resolve conflicts (6 percent)
- delegate authority (5 percent)
- develop a specialization (5 percent)

Conclusions about How Corporate Recruiters Choose an MBA Program

Two studies were done to measure how corporate recruiters select the business schools at which to recruit. The results are consistent, not only between the two studies but also with findings reported in chapter 12, appendix B, and elsewhere in this book about the factors that maximize the value of the MBA degree.

In the spring quarter of 1991, a team of Simon School students carried out a national mail survey of 136 corporate recruiters to determine the most important attributes for choosing the business schools at which they recruit. These attributes are:

- The ability of graduates to apply their MBA education in a practical work setting (number one by a wide margin),
- how often I hear or read about the school, and
- admissions standards—a proxy for the quality of the students.

Surprisingly, other factors such as *communications skills* and *analytical skills* are insignificant in choosing among schools, not because they are unimportant, but because recruiters think that all of the top schools are good at teaching these things.

In a follow-up series of personal interviews with corporate recruiters and senior managers who hire MBAs, I heard the same thing: The top business schools are pretty much equal in teaching the basics of analysis and communications. "What we are looking for is evidence of *leadership, teamwork,* and *creativity.*"

A mail survey of 253 recruiters and corporate managers in the spring quarter of 1993 by another team of students asked, "Which abilities and skills will be important for your future managers to possess?" The top four attributes from a list of twenty-two were:

- Creative problem solving,
- cohesive teamwork,
- interpersonal skills, and
- leadership skills.

The newly emerging interest in these "soft skills" offers new opportunities and challenges for business schools, but recruiters still considers *statistics* and other *analytical skills* as essential skills for graduating MBAs.

The optimal amount of pre-MBA work experience is two to four years, according to 70 percent of the recruiters. There is almost no interest in MBAs with no prior work experience.

For recruiters, the most important source of information about schools is the *success of previous graduates.* This is almost twice as important as the *Business Week* rankings and other published information.

In the 1993 study, recruiters and managers reported that the single most important factor in deciding at which business schools to recruit is the *quality of the students* (also the most important factor in determining the size of a school's MBA ADVANTAGE; see appendix B).

The general conclusions of our research were confirmed in a 1993 *Fortune* article reporting on a survey of 202 CEOs of *Fortune* 500 firms. "In 'seeking management talent for your company today,' CEOs cited the following as being 'urgently needed:'"

- Leadership (cited by 53 percent of the CEOs),
- operations management (cited by 28 percent of the CEOs),
- marketing (27 percent),
- finance (13 percent),
- organizational behavior (11 percent), and
- accounting (3 percent)." [9]

The bottom line: Corporate recruiters and senior managers expect business schools to teach the fundamentals, such as finance, marketing, statistics, and business communications, as a matter of course. But when it comes to choosing who they will hire, corporations are increasingly focusing on the *personal* characteristics of graduating MBAs, with evidence of leadership being the most important, followed by teamwork and creativity.

9   Richman, L., "CEOs to Workers: Help Not Wanted," *Fortune*, July 12, 1993, p. 43.

Chapter 14

Teaching Versus Research

Perhaps no topic ignites as much debate in business education as the issue of faculty research. Many critics (and some students) view research as a distraction that compromises teaching quality. Some business schools downplay the importance of research; for example, Dartmouth emphasizes that they have no Ph.D. program. Does faculty research improve or detract from the value of the MBA degree?

The History of the Research University

To understand the role of research in higher education, it is helpful to trace the rise of the modern research university. In nineteenth century America, the primary role of colleges and universities was to teach, passing along knowledge from generation to generation. Research, if it was done at all, was carried out by individual professors to improve the content of their teaching.

In Europe, however, the mission of the university was changing from merely passing along existing knowledge to the creation of new knowledge, the process we know as research. A professor was no longer just a teacher; he was also a scientist. The concept of the research university was born.

In the early twentieth century, the concept of the research university spread to the United States. Johns Hopkins University in Baltimore was one of the first American universities to emphasize the role of research. The Ph.D. degree, for which the candidate is required to carry out original research in the form of a thesis, became the union card for admission to the university faculty. In 1884, only 10 percent of Harvard's 189 professors possessed a Ph.D., but by the early 1900s the Ph.D. was expected at even the less prestigious universities. Increasingly, university teachers were trained as researchers.

During World War II, the research universities made enormous contributions to the war effort. Major breakthroughs were made in radar and servomechanisms at MIT. The first digital computer was constructed at the University of Pennsylvania, and the first nuclear chain reaction took place in a laboratory under the stadium at the University of Chicago. The Los Alamos laboratory for the development of the atomic bomb was staffed by best nuclear physicists from the top research universities. And even small research universities made significant contributions, such as the University of Rochester, which carried out important research projects in optics and nuclear medicine.

In the Cold War era that followed World War II, massive federal spending for university research accelerated. Universities found that research had become an important source of cash flow, and many of the professors who competed for these grants became academic entrepreneurs as well as scholars. The power to access and control this cash flow was concentrated in the hands of the research faculty.

Faculty could generate substantial cash flow through research grants. An engineering professor at a top research university, for example, could bring in $100,000 or more per year in grant money. Given this, university administrators became indifferent as to whether faculty members supported themselves through tuition revenue (i.e., by teaching) or through research grants. From a cash flow standpoint, research became as important to the university as teaching.

But research provided benefits to faculty members that teaching never could. Research was portable. A top researcher could move from school to school and take his research reputation and its cash-generating potential with him. Research professors became more closely associated with their colleagues in the same field in other universities than with faculty members in their own institution. They collaborated on joint papers, evaluated each other's work for publication in the top journals, generated offers of employment to each other, and wrote outside letters recommending (or not recommending) tenure for junior faculty at each other's institutions. A market for research faculty developed, and the offers were determined by a faculty member's research record.[1]

But if university research was good for the professors, it was also good for the country, and for the rest of the world. As we noted earlier, the contributions of the research universities during World War II made a critical difference between winning and losing the war. The strength of American research was a factor in ending the Cold War as well. The former Soviet Union, faced with the prospect of economic bankruptcy trying to keep up with the rapidly improving performance of American military technology, conceded the game after more than forty years of international arms competition.

In the post-war decades, the great scientific and technical research universities like MIT and Stanford became the nuclei of fast-growing and highly productive technical communities such as those around Route 128 in Boston and Silicon Valley in California. They provided not only thousands of jobs, but also a deluge of revolutionary new products. In highly-innovative "design-rich" products where intellectual content counts—such as microprocessor chips, workstations, advanced software, parallel processing supercomputers, medical diagnostic equipment, cellular telephones, fiber optic communications, high performance personal computers, and high definition television—American industry led, and still leads, the world.

Today, American research universities are the best in the world, which is why the most talented graduate students from the rest of the world come to study in America.

The Role of Research in Business Schools

In the 1960s and '70s, while university research was ascending in importance in the physical sciences, the business schools of the time were under attack for being dull and unscientific. Looked upon with disdain by the "real scientists" on campus, business schools were often regarded as little more than trade schools, teaching case histories by telling "war stories" of questionable generalizability to other business situations. Business was for students who couldn't make it in engineering or pre-med.

---

1   Many years ago, a colleague of mine was cautioned by another faculty member not to be openly critical of the dean "because he sets your salary." My colleague replied: "The *market* sets my salary; the dean only determines where I work."

But during this period, a few business schools were taking a hard look at what was being taught, and were designing curricula with sweeping new changes. At MIT and Chicago, research on the random behavior of stock prices led to an entirely new way of teaching about the stock market. At Wharton, an innovative marketing research technique was developed that allowed new product concepts to be scientifically broken down into attributes that could be analyzed individually, much as a chemist breaks down a new compound into its elements. A sophisticated formula for valuing financial options was developed at Stanford. At Rochester, new theories were proposed to explain why corporate managers often make decisions that harm the stockholders. At MIT, research was initiated to better understand the process of innovation in high technology companies, and a systematic study of corporate competitive strategy was undertaken at Harvard.

Much of this work was done by business school professors who had undergraduate degrees in engineering as well as Ph.D.'s in business or economics. They set standards for the same rigorous analysis expected in the physical sciences. (Some of these professors would subsequently make a fortune by applying their mathematical "financial engineering" theories in the stock market.) As in science and engineering, a market for research faculty in business developed.

Not all of this research was useful. Much was excessively arcane and detached from the practice of management. But, as is true of basic research in any field—physics, electrical engineering, medicine—only a very small percentage has significant impact, and it is difficult to predict in advance which research projects will have impact. That small percentage, perhaps only 1 percent, can have such a great impact that it more than justifies the other 99 percent.

Taking Research Into the Classroom

In time, this formal research found its way into the classroom, and the content of business education changed dramatically. As Bill Meckling, the former dean of the Simon School, noted at the time, management education has four components:[2]

1. *Principles or theories.* These are statements about cause and effect. When a manager advertises, he or she has a theory about how the advertising will affect sales. Much of what managers do is based on theories about such cause-and-effect relationships. Sometimes the theories are wrong.

   What business research has tried to do is make these theories explicit, and to test them with actual data from the business community. In this way, faculty have some assurance that when they teach such concepts as the effect of advertising on sales, students will get meaningful results when they apply them on the job.

2. *Techniques and methodology. Techniques* are the tools of analysis. Throughout this book we have used a statistical technique known as regression analysis to examine why the magnitude of THE MBA ADVANTAGE varies from school to school.[3] Why does Harvard offer a higher MBA ADVANTAGE than Indiana? Is it the Harvard name? Is it the quality of the incoming students? Techniques like regression are very useful to

2   Meckling, W. H., "Education for Business and Business Policy," unpublished paper, Graduate School of Management, University of Rochester, August 7, 1973.
3   See appendix B.

marketing managers.[4] Similarly, there is a set of forecasting tools that are very useful to financial managers. With the widespread availability of spreadsheets and user-friendly statistical packages for personal computers, these techniques are inexpensive and powerful, and—believe it or not—they can be fun to use. Graduating MBAs need a toolbox of these techniques of analysis along with a good understanding of their limitations.

Methodology is the application of the scientific method to business problems—that is, hypothesis, test, modified hypothesis, and test some more. Much of this has to do with the structuring of problems, determining what the real problem is, stating the problem in a way that it can be scientifically evaluated, and determining what kind of data or evidence will be needed to get an answer.

If sales are dropping, what's the cause? (There may be many possible causes—a price cut by competitors, quality problems with the product, a lull in the economy, ineffective advertising—just to name a few.) What kind of information do we need to check this out? When we're done, can we be assured that we have the right answer? And what are we going to do to get sales back on track? What evidence do we have that this proposed solution will work? This way of thinking about problems by using a scientific approach with a stubborn insistence on evidence should be second nature to the graduating MBA.

3. *Institutional knowledge.* Like every profession, management has its own jargon. Financial analysts talk about *P/E ratios* and *yield curves*. Advertising managers talk about *reach* and *frequency* and *CPMs*. In the past, much of business education consisted of the teaching of such institutional knowledge. It is still very important; if you don't know what the words mean, your knowledge of regression analysis will be of little help.

In their enthusiasm to make a complete break with the past, some research-oriented business schools de-emphasized the teaching of institutional material to the point where graduating MBAs were illiterate in their chosen field.[5] Many students graduated without the slightest idea of how to write a marketing plan or what the inside of a factory looked like.

Fortunately, the pendulum has swung back. Today, teams of MBA students carry out projects with companies where they run focus groups in shopping malls and analyze production lines on the factory floor. They learn the jargon and the institutional concepts before they graduate, as they should.

---

4   For some reason, a few business school professors like to teach these techniques using lots of Greek letters and subscripts, perhaps so that it will look more like physics. The fact is that the underlying mathematics are really very simple, and if you got through high school algebra, you can handle it. Fortunately, most professors now teach these techniques not as a set of mathematical abstractions but rather as a practical way to attack real business problems, the solutions of which become the focus of their lectures.

5   The argument for not teaching institutional material in business school is that companies can teach this more efficiently after the graduates are hired. This is similar to the argument that General Motors used to make about cars: They would ship cars to the dealers that were half finished, expecting them to correct all the problems because the dealers, guided by customer complaints, were "more efficient" at finishing the cars. This kind of thinking cost General Motors almost half of its market share. Customers today—whether they are buying cars or MBA's—expect a fully functional product from day one. As corporate managers pointed out in the surveys reviewed in chapter 13, new MBA hires are expected to "hit the ground running."

4. *Communications skills.* The ability of managers to communicate orally and in writing remains a critical skill. Recently-hired MBAs, with a toolkit full of advanced analytical techniques, often know more about a particular problem-solving approach than their boss. Much of what the new hire presents will not be fully understood by the boss, who often does not have the benefit of a state-of-the-art MBA degree. Consequently, the quality of what is presented will be judged in part by the quality of its packaging.

Every piece of work must not only be professional, it must *look* professional. This means that the graduating MBA must be articulate and persuasive in oral presentations and lucid in written reports. The newly-hired MBA should also be fully competent in running the latest computerized graphics presentation programs.

Advantages of a Research-Oriented Business School

Business schools vary in the emphasis they place on research. Some, such as Chicago, MIT, and Rochester, take great pride in their research strengths, and this influences the content of what is taught in class. There are advantages to an MBA program that places a high value on research:

1. In some fields, notably finance, the rate of change of knowledge has been very high, resulting in a flood of innovative new financial products. Schools that specialize in teaching finance—Chicago, MIT, Rochester—are among the leading schools in carrying out research in finance, and they have developed great skills in bringing this leading edge knowledge into the classroom.[6]

2. In addition to bringing the freshest material into the classroom, research-oriented schools attract faculty members who are inquisitive, demanding, evidence-oriented, and intolerant of woolly thinking. Interacting with their research colleagues provides the faculty a whetstone for continually sharpening and honing their analytical skills.

3. In small research-oriented schools like Rochester's Simon School, special opportunities exist for cross-functional research and development of course materials. Although I teach primarily in marketing, one of my courses (Strategic Management of Technology) also counts as a "capstone" strategy course, and I frequently call upon my colleagues in both finance and operations for advice on my research projects. With cross-functional teams becoming a significant organizational form in new product development in companies, it makes sense to have a business school faculty that has cross-functional interests and knowledge.

4. Research provides a counterbalance to teaching, a sort of intellectual sandbox for the faculty. Frankly, teaching the same subject over and over can be boring. Research provides the knowledge and the incentive to inject fresh new material into a course every time it is taught. And the challenge of research attracts people to academic life, many of whom are superb teachers, who would be bored if they did nothing but teach.

---

6 In the 1992 edition of the soft-cover *Business Week Guide*, MIT, Rochester and Chicago were rated by their students as the top schools in bringing leading-edge knowledge into the classroom.

Advantages of a Teaching-Oriented Business School

Not every school chooses to emphasize research. A number of top business schools, among them Dartmouth and Virginia, have chosen as a matter of policy to give teaching the top priority in the demands on faculty members' time and energy. This also has advantages:

1. Without the distraction of research deadlines for publications and conferences, faculty are free to concentrate on teaching. And since teaching quality takes priority over research, there are likely to be fewer terrible teachers in a teaching-oriented school. Great research won't compensate for poor teaching.

2. For junior faculty facing a tenure decision, the clear understanding that teaching quality will be given more weight than research productivity encourages them to do an outstanding job in the classroom.

3. In a teaching-oriented school, the composition of the faculty tends to be more stable. There is an active market for research faculty, and top researchers move from school to school. There is not an active market for top-rated teachers (perhaps because over the years their teaching skills become matched to the culture of their particular school). With relatively few offers from other schools, outstanding teachers tend to stay put.

4. Teaching generates cash flow. Unlike sponsored research in engineering and science, which historically attracts large grants, most research programs in business have not attracted significant financial sponsorship.[7] Teaching provides revenue for the business school through tuition; research does not. As universities have come under increasing financial pressure from the concurrent reduction in undergraduate enrollments and the post-Cold War wind-down of federally sponsored research, they have turned to their business schools for more cash flow. Research-oriented business schools, which typically offer lighter teaching loads to offset the increased time spent on research, have found it more difficult to respond.

Which Is Better, a Research-Oriented School or a Teaching-Oriented School?

Having considered the arguments for relative emphasis on research and on teaching, which kind of business school provides more value to the student? Does faculty research improve or detract from the value of the MBA degree?

This is an empirical issue that we can test with actual data. In figure 14.1, I have plotted the value of the MBA degree—as measured by THE MBA ADVANTAGE—against the research activity of the faculty for a number of business schools. Data on the research activity of the faculty is from a separate study done by one of my colleagues, Professor Ross Watts.[8] The schools shown were selected by Watts to demonstrate a wide range of faculty research activity. For his measure of a school's research activity, Watts selected the median number of a times a faculty member's

---

7 An exception is MIT's $50 million Leaders for Manufacturing Program, which involves both the Sloan School of Management and the School of Engineering. The cost is underwritten by thirteen industrial sponsors.

8 Watts, Ross L., "Simon School Research Productivity," unpublished manuscript, William E. Simon Graduate School of Business Administration, November 5, 1992, table 1.

research from that school was cited by other researchers—a measure of the impact of that research on the faculty member's field.

The research citations were from the period 1981–1985, for the following reason: The calculation of the MBA ADVANTAGE for each school necessarily included the 1992 pay of that school's MBA Class of 1987. In order for faculty research to have had an influence on the Class of '87, the students would have had to have been exposed to it during the academic years 1985–86 and 1986–87. The research would have had to have been published by 1985 or before. Therefore, the citations from Watts's study that were used in this analysis were those that occurred in the 1981–1985 period.

Figure 14.1

For most of the schools in this small sample, the value of the MBA degree as measured by THE MBA ADVANTAGE was found to be greater for schools with higher faculty research activity.

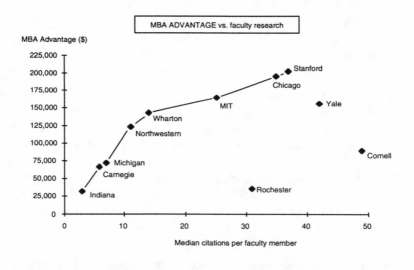

As shown in figure 14.1, when THE MBA ADVANTAGE is plotted against the median number of citations per faculty member for each school, there is a strong positive relationship.[9] High value of the MBA degree to the student and high research activity by the faculty are positively correlated for nine of the eleven schools in the study.

This positive association cannot prove that high research activity by the faculty increases the value of the MBA. But as a minimum, it suggests that high research activity doesn't harm the value of the MBA degree. There is no evidence that a trade-off exists between faculty research and benefits to the student. Quite to the contrary, the evidence suggests that faculty research at a business school enhances the value of the MBA degree from that school.

---

9   For this analysis, THE MBA ADVANTAGE was calculated using a uniform 5 percent annual salary growth rate for all schools for the alternative of not going to business school (Case number 1 in appendix B). It gives a slightly better fit than THE MBA ADVANTAGE data from table 4.1, chapter 4.

Characteristics of THE MBA ADVANTAGE versus Research Curve

There are three features in figure 14.1 that are noteworthy:

1. The relationship is not linear. Rather, there are signs that the benefit of increasing research activity approaches saturation at high levels. An economist would characterize this phenomenon as decreasing marginal returns to scale. It is seen with almost every economic input. For example, in a retail store, as the rate of advertising expenditures is increased, the rate of sales increases—but with decreasing marginal returns and saturation at high levels of advertising. Thus faculty research acts like a classical economic input to the value of the MBA, complete with decreasing marginal returns to scale.[10] This is further evidence that a cause-and-effect relationship may exist between faculty research and the value of the MBA.

2. Three of the schools—Yale, Cornell, and Rochester—are below the curve in figure 14.1. All three are research-intensive schools. Why aren't they on the curve? There are at least three possible explanations:

   - *Young MBA programs*: Both Yale and Rochester have fairly new MBA programs; each is about twenty years old.[11] Both schools are moving up fast, based on the growth of starting salaries between 1988 and 1992; Yale is ranked number 2 and Rochester is number 5 in starting salary growth of Top 20 schools.[12] A young MBA program will have a smaller alumni base, and most of these alumni will not have yet reached their peak managerial positions (CEOs, and so forth), where they can be most influential in hiring graduates of their own schools.

     Furthermore, as noted previously, the way THE MBA ADVANTAGE has to be calculated necessarily discriminates against fast-rising schools. The post-MBA fifth year pay figure in this calculation is based on the 1992 pay of the MBA Class of 1987. But suppose the quality of the current incoming students for these fast-rising schools is better than the Class of '87, and suppose the teaching quality is improving as well. It won't be until the late 1990s before the fifth year pay for these recent classes will be known. Therefore, THE MBA ADVANTAGE is probably understating the current value of MBA degrees from fast-rising schools like Yale and Rochester.

   - *Small size*: The three schools that are below the line in figure 14.1 tend to be smaller than the schools that are on the upper part of the curve. Yale has 210 full-time MBA students in each graduating class, Rochester has 205, and Cornell has 260. In contrast, the schools on the upper part of the curve tend to be large: Northwestern has about 680 in each graduating class, Wharton has 785, Chicago graduates 560, and Stanford has 350. The exception is MIT, which graduates 245 MBAs.

---

10 If THE MBA ADVANTAGE , with Cornell and Rochester omitted, is plotted against the *log* of research activity, the result is a straight line with an R-squared of 0.92.

11 The Yale program was organized in 1975. The MBA program at Rochester dates back to the early 1960s, but recruited most of its research-oriented faculty in the 1970s.

12 Based on a comparison of starting salaries in the 1st and 3rd editions of the *Business Week Guides*. See table 4.2 on page 36.

There may be economies of scale in business schools. According to my research, there is a positive association between school size and post-MBA salary growth (R-squared = 0.324, with a positive coefficient that is significant at the 1 percent level), although the effect is modest; adding another fifty students to the graduating class would increase the five-year post-MBA growth factor by only 4.2 percentage points.[13] The effect may be the result of having more active alumni in the business world to give graduating MBAs an extra boost up the corporate ladder.

- *Proportion of senior faculty:* According to Watts, the great majority of a school's citations are contributed by senior faculty, associate and full professors. Typically, assistant professors have few citations because they have not been publishing long enough to influence the scholarly literature. In the case of Cornell, the proportion of senior faculty in the time period that citations were sampled (1981-1985) was the highest of any of the schools shown in figure 14.1. In a subsequent time period (1987-1991), Cornell's proportion of senior faculty declined, and the median number of citations per faculty member during this period dropped to thirteen. This change would place Cornell almost on the curve in figure 14.1.[14]

3. Harvard has the largest MBA ADVANTAGE of any business school (see table 4.1 on page 30), yet the Harvard Business School is not included in figure 14.1. This is because Harvard was not included in Watts's sample of research schools. The problem is one of defining what constitutes research. Although the Harvard Business School has many faculty engaged in writing cases and books, Harvard's contributions (on a per faculty member basis) to the more specialized refereed scholarly journals are believed to be modest.

But Harvard is the number one *disseminator* of academic material to the business community. The *Harvard Business Review* has a paid circulation of over 200,000 and a claimed readership of 1 million, almost all of whom are senior business managers.[15] While the school's MBA and executive programs generate about $50 million a year in revenue, the school's publishing unit—which produces and markets books, videos, case studies, and the *Harvard Business Review*—was expected to generate about $70 million in revenue in 1993.[16]

Many of the articles that appear in the *Harvard Business Review* are authored by faculty at business schools other than Harvard or by business executives. It may be that by publishing such an enormous volume of material to the business community under the Harvard logo, the Harvard Business School gains many of the reputational benefits that other schools generate by doing original research.[17]

Harvard offers its students the highest MBA ADVANTAGE of any business school. If our definition of research were broadened to include Harvard's total academic out-

---

13 See appendix B.
14 See Watts, table 2.
15 Rate Card number 38 and Subscriber Profiles, *Harvard Business Review*, January 1993.
16 Fuchsberg, G., "Harvard Weighs One-Year Version of MBA Program," The *Wall Street Journal*, October 29, 1993.
17 Recall our research showing that the second most important attribute by which corporate recruiters choose schools at which to recruit is "how often I hear or read about the school." See table 13.3.

put—not just that which appears in refereed scholarly journals—Harvard would undoubtedly appear in the upper right-hand corner of figure 14.1, somewhere above and to the right of Stanford.

The bottom line: The number of schools shown in figure 14.1 is very limited and does not constitute a random sample of business schools. Therefore, any conclusions about the effect of faculty research on the value of the MBA degree are only suggestive. But one tentative conclusion based on this limited sample is that research does not detract from the value of the MBA degree. Rather, it supports the belief that faculty research adds value to the degree.

Chapter 15

The MBA of the Future

How are MBA programs changing? What will the "MBA of the future" look like? I see five major trends in graduate management education that will benefit MBA students of the future.

Trend Number 1: Increasing Specialization in a Mature Industry

The MBA market exhibits the classical symptoms of a mature industry. In the past few years, the leading business schools have constructed magnificent new buildings and hired additional faculty as if the MBA boom would continue forever. But the leading indicator of demand for the MBA degree—the number of students taking the GMAT—dropped 23 percent in the period between 1990 and 1993. For the fall quarter of 1993, the number of business school applicants was down 6 percent from the record 78,700 who earned an MBA in 1991. At Northwestern, the number 1 school in the 1992 *Business Week* Top 20, 1993 applications were down 12 percent from the 1991 peak, and Wharton reported a drop of more than 20 percent in the past three years.[1]

There are other signs of maturity. Business schools are discovering how to market themselves. Public relations firms have been retained, expensive videotapes are being sent to prospective students, and at Cornell the dean personally calls the best applicants.[2] It's not surprising that Northwestern, which has neither the brightest students (as measured by its GMAT scores) nor the highest starting salaries, has nevertheless applied its formidable reputation in marketing to market itself successfully to students and corporate recruiters, ending up three times in succession as number 1 in the *Business Week* Top 20 polls.

Another indication of competitive stress: deans of business schools are quitting in record numbers. Like corporate America, when the organization is not performing well the CEO departs, voluntarily, or otherwise. In the summer of 1993, eighty-four of the nation's 700 business schools were searching for deans.[3]

In a mature market with overcapacity, firms search for a competitive advantage by specialization and innovation. In the late '80s, when American car companies were losing market share to the Japanese, Chrysler survived by specializing in the minivan and in 1993 emerged as America's most profitable car company.

Similarly, business schools are increasingly seeking advantages by specialization. A few examples:

- MIT's Sloan School avoids head-on competition with its neighbor, the Harvard Business School, by conceding the education of general managers to Harvard while building

---

1 Bongiorno, L., "B-Schools are Taking a Crash Course in Hoopla," *Business Week*, April 19, 1993, p. 38.
2 Ibid.
3 Bongiorno, L., "The Dean is Out—and He Isn't Coming Back," *Business Week*, June 7, 1993, p. 36.

strength in manufacturing and information systems, where Harvard is traditionally weak. In this way, the Sloan School leverages the powerful reputation of MIT, a world-class university known for science and engineering. Similarly, Sloan avoids a direct confrontation with Wharton and Chicago in traditional areas of finance by concentrating on "financial engineering," that is, rocket science mathematics applied to Wall Street.[4]

- Chicago, a powerhouse in finance, is conceding the education of marketing managers to its neighbor, Northwestern, which *U.S. News* ranks as the best marketing school in the country.[5] Northwestern, in turn, makes no claims about excellence in finance.

- Dartmouth continues to challenge giant Harvard in the education of general managers, but stresses the advantages of attending a small, collegial school.

- Instead of the MBA, Yale offers a distinctive Master of Public and Private Management degree, which is particularly valuable to those interested in managerial positions in the non-profit sectors of government, health care, and the arts.

In the next few years, specialization will increase. As we saw in chapter 5, the leading schools are all developing areas of specialization, with the possible exception of Stanford which has a *geographic* niche (almost half of its students find jobs in California).

Trend Number 2: Increased Emphasis on Teaching Quality
As we saw in chapter 3, Chicago was one of the first schools to link the importance of good teaching to favorable ratings in the *Business Week* Top 20 rankings. In 1989, Chicago innovated with the LEAD (Leadership Exploration and Development) program, which caused the school's graduate ranking to soar from number 20 in 1988 to number 1 in 1990. Subsequently, Chicago developed a "teaching laboratory" in which faculty members apply the techniques of Total Quality Management to teaching and curriculum development.[6]

A number of Top 20 schools are in the process of making wholesale changes in their MBA curriculum. In the fall semester of 1992, Columbia rolled out a new first year program stressing globalization and ethics along with Total Quality Management. For 1993, following an investment of nearly $2 million in curriculum development, Wharton introduced a substantial revision of its MBA curriculum.[7]

Other business schools have also increased their emphasis on teaching quality. A few, Cornell and NYU among others, have even issued public statements saying that teaching quality will now be weighted equally with research accomplishments in granting tenure to faculty (although faculty insiders say that reality hasn't quite caught up to the expressed policy on this matter).

While part of this emphasis on teaching quality stems from attempts to improve the school's graduate ranking on the *Business Week* Top 20 survey, competitive pressures on universities in general, independent of *Business Week,* have caused schools to pay more attention to the classroom. As we noted in chapter 14, the very concept of the research university, a post-World War II creation nurtured by massive federal spending for research, is now being challenged as federal

---

4 Light, L., "The New Rocket Science: Welcome to the Future of Finance," *Business Week*, November 2, 1992.

5 Lord, M., "The MBA Gets Real," *U.S. News & World Report*, March 22, 1993, p. 59.

6 Lanier, A., "Double Feature: Teaching and Research Share Top Billing among GSB Faculty Priorities," *GSB Chicago Magazine*, Winter 1993.

7 The Wharton School MBA Program Catalog, 1993-1994, The Wharton School of the University of Pennsylvania, 1993.

spending winds down in the aftermath of the collapse of the Eastern Bloc. If colleges and universities are to survive into the next decade, they will have to earn more of their money the old-fashioned way, by teaching. There won't be enough research money to go around.

Fortunately for business schools, teaching has always been the main source of cash flow. The federal government has never funded massive amounts of research on finance and marketing. But as universities lose federal research support for their colleges of engineering and science, they have become more dependent on their business schools as sources of cash flow for the whole university. For business schools, this means more emphasis on teaching. For MBA students, it means a more valuable and more enjoyable two-year educational experience.

Trend Number 3: New MBA Program Options for Students

So far we have seen three options for getting an MBA:

- Full-time two-year programs, which mean giving up the salary and security of a job for two years to get an MBA.

- Part-time programs, which require the student to juggle the responsibilities of both a job and a graduate program at the same time.

- Executive programs, which are very advantageous for students because they allow them to keep their jobs and still complete the MBA in two years, with the company paying the tuition. The main drawback is the tendency to limit attendance to older students who are advanced in their careers.

A New Option: The Company-Sponsored Two-Year "Fast Track" MBA

In the next few years, programs similar to the Executive MBA, but for younger students, will be introduced. Companies will find it increasingly advantageous to have their MBA-seeking professional employees complete their schooling in two years. Stretching a part-time MBA program over three to five years is hard on the student and disruptive to the company. Everyone benefits by getting the program done faster.

Early signs of a trend toward "fast track" programs are already appearing. Chicago has a Weekend MBA program, similar to its Executive MBA but for managers in their twenties. It is offered in a new $44 million facility in downtown Chicago. In Rochester, New York, Kodak allows selected MBA students to take up to sixteen hours a week away from the job to attend courses at the Simon School in the same daytime classes as full-time MBAs. This is a much larger commitment of release time than the typical Executive MBA program, which requires only alternating Fridays and Saturdays, two days a month away from the job. With this amount of release time, most students can complete the MBA in about two years.

Companies might argue that the cost of a fast track program like this is too high. But students would take the same number of courses to complete the degree as they do now, and the total tuition would be the same; they would just pay it faster, in two years instead of three or four.

Another cost to companies is having students on campus rather than in the office for perhaps the equivalent of one day a week. But the increased willingness of many companies to allow professionals to do some of their work at home during normal hours will accommodate this. And if companies are serious about becoming "learning organizations," at least some of that learning will occur in the classroom, whether through short courses for their executives or fast track MBA programs for their young managerial talent.

As in the case of existing part-time programs and executive programs, there is concern about whether such accelerated tuition payments by companies would be counted as income, increasing the students' tax liability. However, if a student could get his or her MBA and start earning a substantially higher salary a year or two earlier, the gains might be more than enough to offset the tax liability.

Another concern of employers is that students would take advantage of the two-year program and then quit right after graduation. This is a potential problem with any employer-sponsored MBA program—part-time, Executive MBA, or proposed "fast track." One way to reduce the impact on the company would be to require fast track students to sign a contract stating that if they quit voluntarily during or immediately after the program, they owe the company the cumulative tuition paid to date up to the time of graduation, after which the amount owed is straight-line-depreciated to zero during a two- or three-year period following graduation.[8]

It is not clear in what format the fast track part-time MBA programs will emerge, whether as special weekend programs like Chicago's or with release time like the Rochester program. But whatever the format, the potential benefits over conventional part-time programs are high for the schools, for the students, and for the employers. For business schools looking for ways to innovate to better serve their customers, the fast track option makes sense.

Trend Number 4: Projects and Internships like Medical Schools

Business schools are unusual among professional schools because traditionally they have not required a professional internship. (Imagine being treated by a doctor who had never interned in a hospital.) But this is changing. For many years the mission of business schools was to transfer the latest knowledge about business research and practice to their students through lectures and exams. (It was as if faculty could unscrew a cap on the student's head and pour in the knowledge.)

While the transfer of such knowledge in the MBA core courses is still absolutely essential as the foundation for the understanding of business practice, it is no longer sufficient to providing a complete professional education. Industry has made it clear that they expect students to be able to *apply* this knowledge. As we saw in table 13.3 on page 220, the number 1 attribute corporate recruiters consider in choosing the schools at which to recruit is the ability to apply the MBA education in a practical work setting.

In chapter 12, we learned about the Product Leadership Laboratory, a second-year MBA course in which my students carry out actual consulting projects for real companies. The objective is to give students the hands-on experience of applying state-of-the-art management methods to real business problems and opportunities. Teams of students work with company managers—many of whom are alumni of the school—to test new product ideas, evaluate distribution channels, interview customers about product quality, and develop strategic plans for growth and profitability.

Almost all of the leading schools reviewed in chapter 5 offer projects courses of this type, and for seven of these top schools the projects courses are *required* for all students. UCLA, for

---

8 According to *The Wall Street Journal*, many companies already require Executive MBAs to repay their tuition costs if they jump ship within a few years of graduation. See Fuchsberg, G. "Managing Your Career," The *Wall Street Journal*, November 17, 1993.

example, has a required two-quarter field study project in the second year in place of the traditional integrative Business Policy course. More than 900 projects have been carried out over the years by UCLA students for companies ranging from Ben & Jerry's to Goldman Sachs. Michigan has an unusual first-year seven-week internship in which teams of students develop plans for re-engineering key business processes at sponsoring companies all over the country.

Projects are appealing to companies that hire MBAs because they give students the chance to demonstrate that they can apply what they've learned to real business situations. My students often take a bound copy of their final project report to interviews to show recruiters the kind of work they can do.

Projects courses are valuable to students because they are required to apply what they have learned in the classroom to actual business problems. The drawback is that projects courses are hard to teach and very labor-intensive for the faculty involved. Projects are full of uncertainty. Managers of the sponsoring companies sometimes have to be reminded of their responsibility to be available to meet with the students on the project. And deans find that projects courses are an expensive use of faculty time. An experienced faculty member may spend more time running a projects course with twelve students than teaching a lecture course with seventy students. If the projects course is required, the logistics of lining up from fifty to one hundred different projects every year can be overwhelming. Nevertheless, wider use of projects courses for MBAs of the 1990s is an idea that makes sense for students and for their future employers. In time, the leading business schools will require all of their students to participate in hands-on projects with real corporate clients, just as medical education requires internships for physicians.

Summer internships are another hands-on opportunity for MBA students. Many students work as professional summer interns in industry between their first and second years, and these jobs often develop into permanent employment upon graduation. These summer internships usually are not supervised by faculty and do not earn academic credit toward the degree, but they can offer solid experience as well as the chance to be considered for permanent employment later. Some students continue to work for the company ten or fifteen hours a week during their second year in school to maintain continuity of interest. In a study of 169 MBA students, those with summer internships had post-MBA starting salaries that averaged $6,000 higher than those who didn't.[9] In the competition to provide more value to their students, many leading schools will take a more active role in finding professional summer internships for their students, and will be able to guarantee a summer internship to every student who wants one.[10]

Trend Number 5: The Use of Computers in Management Education Will Become Even More Pervasive

Computers are revolutionizing the practice of management:[11]

- Computers have leveled the playing field between big businesses and small businesses,

---

9   Daum, M., "Predictors of MBA Starting Salaries," MBA summer research project, William E. Simon Graduate School of Business Administration, University of Rochester, August, 1993. This doesn't prove that getting the internships *caused* the higher starting salaries, however. Perhaps only the better students were able to get internships.

10 Although the goal of finding summer internships for all students may appear impractical, it should be noted that many undergraduate engineering programs manage to find hundreds of co-op positions for their students in industry every year.

11 See Kiechel, W., "How We Will Work in the Year 2000," *Fortune*, May 17, 1993.

and small businesses are thriving. As large companies continue to downsize, all of the growth in the economy is taking place in small companies. The average number of employees per manufacturing company grew until the 1970s, but now it is decreasing. MBAs of the future will not be "business administrators" (maybe it's time to change the name of the degree); rather, they will be entrepreneurs.

* Hierarchical organizations are giving way to flat organizations. These may evolve into networks of specialists since computers can provide everyone in the organization with all the information they need. Because of computers, there is no longer any need for layers of middle managers to collect and report information upwards, or to carry orders of top management downward.

  If companies do eventually evolve into computerized networks of specialists, they will resemble many large professional organizations of today, such as law firms, hospitals, and consulting firms. Groupware, the latest networking software for linking professionals, may revolutionize the shape of the organization of the future.[12] The success of individuals in such organizations will be increasingly determined not by their position in the hierarchy, but by their education, skills, and credentials. In time, the MBA may not be enough; should business schools consider offering a doctorate in business administration—a DBA?

* With services, many of which are now organized around high-speed computer networks, now accounting for 75 percent of the gross domestic product, manufacturing will employ fewer and fewer MBAs (or anyone else for that matter). Coursework will be less concerned with optimizing manufacturing processes and more concerned with information technology and with human resource management of organizations made up of professional specialists.

* Business schools will be slower to forsake the narrow vertical "stovepipe" functional organizational structures than industry (because faculty will continue to define themselves by their functional research specializations). Although business schools will emphasize their specializations in functional fields such as finance, marketing or information technology, second-year MBA courses will begin to focus more on multifunctional tasks such as new product development, and less on the traditional concentrations of finance, marketing, and operations.

* Because of the continuing rapid growth of knowledge, largely as the result of improved computing power, learning will be a life-long process for professionals. Continuing education offers vast new market opportunities for business schools that are able to stay out in front of the changes. For many professionals, the MBA will be just one of many educational experiences undertaken during their lifetime to maintain their competitive edge.

The bottom line: Over the next few years, graduate business education will change rapidly as the result of competitive market forces, and all of these changes will make the MBA of the future an even greater value for students.

---

12 Kirkpatrick, D., "Here Comes the Payoff from PCs," *Fortune*, March 23, 1992.

Chapter 16

Should You Get an MBA?

The time has never been better to get an MBA. Business schools are competing vigorously for good students, and like the factory rebates in the automotive market of the '80s, they're cutting prices and offering very good deals on financial aid. Many schools have state-of-the-art classroom buildings and fresh new curricula. The quality of business school teaching is the best it has ever been, and it's getting better.

Is this a good time for *you* to get an MBA? Here's a checklist to consider:

- ☐ Do you see yourself as a manager some day? If so, are you going to wing it? Wouldn't you do better with some professional training?

- ☐ Are you willing to make the commitment? Earning an MBA from a good school involves a lot of hard work and long hours. Whether you go full-time to a Top 20 school or part time to a regional school, you'll work harder than you have in a long time. But in a good program the learning experience will be invigorating, and with bright classmates it can be a great deal of fun as well.

- ☐ Have you had at least two or three years of work experience since getting your under-graduate degree? Work experience helps make the MBA classroom material a lot more relevant, and you'll also earn more when you graduate. A recent study of 169 graduating MBAs showed that *each* year of work experience added $1,400 to post-MBA starting salaries.[1]

  In chapter 1 we met Anne, who is in her early twenties and has just completed her bachelor's and master's degree in early childhood development. Anne has no in-terest in being a business manager, but she has the talent to run her own preschool some day. An MBA would be a valuable asset if she still feels that way in two or three years. She might even go to Yale, which specializes in management for the non-profit sector. But in the meantime, she needs to get some work experience in her profession.

- ☐ Will your finances and your family situation allow you to return full time, or should you be considering a part-time program? Would you be able to qualify for an Executive MBA program in the near future?

  You'll remember David from chapter 1. He has a family and an excellent job with a major electronics firm. For him, the choice was easy: a part-time MBA program at a good regional school with the tuition paid by his employer. He was already on a fast

1   Daum, M., "Predictors of MBA Starting Salaries," MBA summer research project, William E. Simon Graduate School of Business Ad-ministration, University of Rochester, August, 1993.

track with his company and it didn't make sense to leave his job, putting his young family through a difficult financial struggle, to go back to school full time. He's more than half way through the degree now, and he increasingly finds that he can apply what he is learning in class to his job as a marketing product manager. For David, the part-time MBA program was the right decision.

☐ Is this the best time for you to begin your MBA program?

Jodie, the associate editor of a national magazine who we also met in chapter 1, has decided to hold off on pursuing an MBA for a while. Her husband, Eric, who is halfway through medical school, is putting in eighteen-hour days between his duties at the hospital and studying for exams. For both of them to be deeply involved in getting advanced degrees is more than they would like to take on right now. So Jodie continues to advance and undertake new responsibilities in her job, although the possibility of going for an MBA at sometime in the future remains a definite option.

☐ Remember that there are several reasons for considering an MBA. Financial gain is only one. Others include the enhancement of your knowledge for its own sake, the opportunity to learn how to structure and critically analyze complex problems, the security of adding an MBA to your professional credentials, and the fun of meeting and working with outstanding young professionals.

☐ Finally, remember the point that was made early in this book: Changes that are occurring in the 1990s will affect you whether or not you have an MBA. The relevant question is whether you will be better equipped to deal with these changes *with* an MBA than without one. What are your professional options if you choose not to get an MBA?

The bottom line: The decision to invest time and money in an MBA is a very personal one. Is it worth it? Consider the three options that we have examined—full-time programs, part-time programs, and Executive MBA programs. Talk to your family and friends about this decision. Order some business school catalogs and placement reports. Visit a leading business school and sit in on some classes. Fill out the Personal MBA Advantage worksheet in appendix C. Then think about it for a while, and trust your intuition on this major decision. And whatever your decision, good luck with your career!

One final note: Susan, who first posed the question to me about the value of the MBA, is married now, and her husband, Juan, is developing a new software product for the transportation industry. Susan continues to advance in her job at the publishing company, and last fall her company sponsored her to enroll in the Executive MBA program at Rollins College, a fine regional school in Orlando, Florida. Last week she called and I asked her whether it's worth it. With great enthusiasm, she said that it is.

Appendix A

How the Magazine Rankings Work

The *Business Week* Top 20 Ranking Method

The *Business Week* Top 20 ranking is the most widely-quoted ranking of business schools and has had a substantial impact on graduate business education in the United States (see table A.1). In the following pages we'll examine the strengths and weaknesses of the *Business Week* Top 20 ranking method.

Table A.1

The *Business Week* Top 20 rankings for 1992, 1990, and 1988

	1992 Rank	1990 Rank	1988 Rank
Northwestern	1	1	1
Chicago	2	4	11
Harvard	3	3	2
Wharton	4	2	4
Michigan	5	7	6
Dartmouth	6	6	3
Stanford	7	5	9
Indiana	8	15	12
Columbia	9	8	14
North Carolina	10	12	8
Virginia	11	14	7
Duke	12	13	10
MIT	13	11	15
Cornell	14	16	5
NYU	15	17	18
UCLA	16	10	16
Carnegie Mellon	17	9	13
Berkeley	18	19	17
Vanderbilt	19	(NR)	(NR)
Washington U.	20	(NR)	(NR)

As noted in chapter 3, the *Business Week* Top 20 rankings are a statistical combination of separate surveys of graduating MBA students (graduate rankings) and corporate recruiters (corporate rankings). According to the 1993 edition of the *Guide*, the 1992 survey was compiled from 4,712 questionnaires returned by graduates (a 78 percent response rate) and 199 questionnaires returned by corporate recruiters (a 57 percent response rate).[1]

---

1   Byrne, J., *A Business Week Guide: The Best Business Schools*, 3rd edition, McGraw-Hill, 1993, pp. 345, 347.

Since the *Guide* publishes the individual graduate and corporate rankings for each school as well as the overall business school ranking, it is possible to ascertain the formula by which *Business Week* combines these two components. (*Business Week* does not publicize how it weights the various components of its survey to get the overall rankings.)

A statistical regression analysis of the 1992 Top 20 rankings shows that the corporate component is weighted twice as heavily as the graduate component in determining the overall ranking.[2] According to my analysis, the equation for combining these components is:

Overall 1992 *Business Week* Rank = 0.724 Corporate Rank + 0.357 Graduate Rank – 1.20

For the most part, the published overall ranks follow this formula quite closely.[3,4] If you know the corporate rank and the graduate rank of a school, you can plug these values into the formula to get an index number for each school. The rank order of these index numbers is a very close fit to the published *Business Week* Top 20 ranking. However, because *Business Week* apparently does some fine tuning of the final overall rankings, in a few cases the formula does not exactly reproduce the published overall ranks for all the schools.

As we shall see, the graduate rankings and the corporate rankings affect the Overall *Business Week* Top 20 rankings in different ways. Furthermore, both of these components appear to be strongly influenced by the school's size and location.

Limitations of the Business Week *Survey Method*

If business schools are to survive and prosper in the '90s, they must satisfy their student and corporate customers. There is no disagreement on this.

Questionnaires similar to those used in the *Business Week* surveys are often used to measure customer satisfaction. Such questionnaires can be useful to measure *short-term* satisfaction. But because of their short-term emphasis, the results from such questionnaires can be volatile over time. Opinions of graduating students from a given business school have been found to vary sharply from year to year, depending on short-term phenomena, such as problems in the local job market or transient annoyances with the school's administration.

This is what has happened to the graduate rankings component of the *Business Week* survey. For example, using the *actual* 1992 survey data collected from the graduates, Carnegie Mellon received a 1992 graduate ranking of number 31—a disastrous drop from number 4 in 1990—because the students were having a dispute with the school's administration. It was enough to knock Carnegie Mellon, which in 1990 had been ranked the ninth best business school in the country in the overall Top 20 rankings, right off the Top 20 list.[5]

---

2 Technically, it is inappropriate to run regressions on rank-ordered data because the distances between the ranks might not be equal. For example, the distance between number 1 and number 2 might not be the same as the distance between number 2 and number 3. However, we will make the assumption that these distances are about equal.

3 The t-statistic on the corporate rank coefficient is 11.4 and on the graduate rank coefficient is 5.6. The R-squared, which measures the goodness of fit, is 0.917.

4 Subsequent to my analysis, Professor Morris Holbrook of Columbia University published a regression equation for the 1992 *Business Week* rankings with very similar coefficients. See Holbrook, M.B., "Gratitudes and Latitudes in M.B.A. Attitudes: Customer Orientation and the Business Week Poll," *Marketing Letters* 4:3, (1993): pp. 267-278, particularly table 1, B.

5 Prati, R., and Greenstein, M., "The Man Behind the Ranking: an Exclusive Interview with John A. Byrne," *The World According to Simon*, October, 1992, p. 15.

This obviously was inappropriate. Carnegie Mellon is an excellent school and deserves to be on any list of the Top 20.

Smoothing the Data

In an attempt to fix the problem by reducing the volatility, the *published* 1992 graduate rankings were "smoothed" by adding in old data from previous surveys. For the 1992 Top 20 article, *Business Week* "smoothed" the actual survey data for 1992 by adding in graduate ranking data from the 1990 and 1988 surveys, with the following weights: 50 percent for 1992 data, 25 percent for 1990 data, and 25 percent for 1988 data. This old data, of course, describes what the school was like in 1988 and 1990, not how it was in the survey year of 1992. So the 1992 graduate ranking was not really a clean measure of how each business school was satisfying its students *in 1992*.

Even with this smoothing, Carnegie Mellon dropped in overall ranking from ninth in 1990 to seventeenth in 1992 (see table A.1). In the past, Chicago, Indiana, Cornell, and Virginia have experienced similar wide swings in overall ranking (table A.1) due to volatile graduate rankings (table A.2).

Table A.2
Business Week graduate rankings for 1992, 1990, and 1988

	1992 Rank*	Rankings by *Graduates* 1990 Rank	1988 Rank
Northwestern	3	7	5
Chicago	10	1	20
Harvard	12	9	6
Wharton	15	11	13
Michigan	9	14	12
Dartmouth	1	5	1
Stanford	5	3	8
Indiana	6	23	11
Columbia	18	10	19
North Carolina	8	6	2
Virginia	2	16	4
Duke	7	12	7
MIT	14	13	10
Cornell	4	15	3
NYU	16	18	22
UCLA	11	2	16
Carnegie Mellon	23	4	9
Berkeley	13	19	14
Vanderbilt	19	(NR)	(NR)
Washington U.	24	(NR)	(NR)

*Because of excessive volatility in the *actual* 1992 graduate ranking survey results, *Business Week* "smoothed" the *published* data for 1992 shown above by adding in graduate ranking data from the 1990 and 1988 surveys, with the following weights: 50 percent 1992 data, 25 percent 1990 data, and 25 percent 1988 data.

A statistical comparison of the graduate rankings for the years 1988, 1990, and 1992 shows little consistency from survey to survey. The rank order correlation between the 1988 and the

1990 graduate rankings for the *Business Week* Top 20 schools is only 0.137, and between 1990 and 1992 is a miniscule 0.027. (A correlation of 1.000 means perfect agreement from year-to-year, whereas a correlation of 0.000 means no agreement whatsoever from year-to-year.)[6]

To compound the problem, a statistical analysis shows that almost all of the survey-to-survey changes in the overall *Business Week* Top 20 rankings of business schools (table A.1) are driven by these volatile changes in the graduate rankings from survey to survey (table A.2). (As we shall see later in this appendix, the corporate rankings have almost no effect on survey-to-survey changes in the overall Top 20 rankings.)

If *Business Week* publicized the graduate rankings separately as a periodic business school student satisfaction ranking, this volatility wouldn't be a problem; in fact, it would be interesting to know how well each school satisfied its current crop of students while they were in school. But one should be cautious about the use of these volatile numbers as the basis for an overall comprehensive ranking of the value of an MBA from these Top 20 schools, as suggested by the survey's title, "The Best Business Schools."

Besides Volatile Survey Data, What Else Affects the Graduate Rankings?

In figure A.1 (known in marketing circles as a perceptual map), the 1992 graduate rankings are plotted against school size (defined as the size of the full-time MBA student body). Some interesting relationships emerge. The individual graduate rankings appear to be grouped in clusters:

- *The size factor:* In the upper right quadrant is a cluster of small schools (Dartmouth, Virginia, Cornell, etc.) that are ranked highest by graduates. Small size (as defined by the size of the full-time MBA class) and high graduate rankings appear to go together. With the exception of Northwestern, which is ranked third by graduates, none of the large urban schools is ranked higher than tenth by the graduates. It may be that small schools, like small companies, are more fun and more fulfilling.

    This confirms what we found from the GMAT-takers survey described in chapter 12: MBA students (and prospective students) prefer small schools.

- *The quant factor:* In the lower right quadrant is a handful of small schools that are often characterized as "quantitative" schools because of their emphasis on mathematical analysis rather than the "soft skills" of management. Although the math used in business schools can be handled by anyone able to pass high school algebra, some "quant school" professors dress up their equations in Greek letters with multiple subscripts and superscripts, and the math looks intimidating. Some students prefer not to deal with this approach to business education.

There are other concerns about the use of these graduate rankings as a major factor in determining overall business school rankings:

---

6   The reader might ask at this point, "If the *Business Week* Graduate Rankings are this volatile, what assurance do you have that the *Business Week* salary data that forms the basis for THE MBA ADVANTAGE calculations is not also volatile from survey to survey?" The answer is that reported salary data *ought* to be more objective than customer satisfaction opinion data, which is inherently volatile for the reasons described above. But since the salary data was published only once, in the *1993 Business Week Guide*, we won't know for sure until the 1995 *Guide* appears.

Figure A.1
1992 business school rankings by graduating MBA students

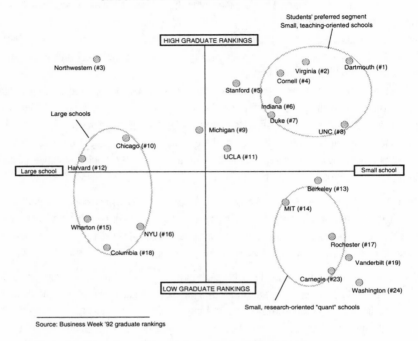

GRADUATES' PERCEPTUAL MAP OF MBA SCHOOLS

Source: Business Week '92 graduate rankings

- *Short-term versus long-term customer satisfaction: Business Week* points out that the graduate rankings are customer satisfaction surveys like the J. D. Power surveys of automobile owners. However, the graduate rankings measure short-term satisfaction. Asking MBA students at the time of graduation about satisfaction with their business school is like asking new car owners how they like the car on the day they drive it home. J. D. Power asks consumers to rate their new car after they have owned it for a while. Similarly, it would seem more relevant to ask graduates of these business schools to rate the quality of their education after they have been on the job for a year or two.[7]

- *The cheerleading factor:* The graduate rankings are susceptible to a certain amount of cheerleading by business school deans who are quick to point out to graduating MBAs that the value of their degree is influenced by the *Business Week* ranking of the school. Whatever their frustrations with the school, graduates are reminded that it is in their own interest to give the school a high rating when the *Business Week* questionnaire is mailed to them.

---

7 In the 1993 edition of the *Guide*, a separate poll of 1,553 graduates who have been out of school for five years asked whether they would choose the same business school again if they had the chance to do it over. Unfortunately, the results of this very important question were not used in computing the *Business Week* Top 20 rankings.

The Dependable Corporate Rankings

Unlike the volatile graduate rankings, changes in the corporate rankings from year to year have virtually no effect on the overall rankings. This is because survey-to-survey changes in corporate rankings are small. Corporate recruiters tend to stay with their favorite schools and the average corporate survey-to survey change (1990 to 1992) is less than two positions in the ranking (see table A.3). In contrast, the average 1990-to-1992 change in the published graduate rankings, even after smoothing by adding in 1990 and 1988 data, is seven positions, almost four times as volatile (see table A.2).

This is not to imply that the corporate rankings are unimportant. As noted previously, the corporate rankings are weighted twice as heavily as the graduate rankings. In fact, using our estimated formula, if a school is not ranked at least in the top 28 by recruiters, it cannot be in the overall Top 20, even if it is ranked number 1 by its graduates. The corporate rankings are very important; they are just slow to change.

The bottom line: If a business school wants to make a fast improvement in its Top 20 position, it should concentrate on the volatile graduate rankings. (Chicago did just that in 1990 by going all out to improve the satisfaction of its graduates, jacking up its graduate ranking from twentieth to first place, and raising its overall ranking from eleventh to fourth.)

Table A.3
Business Week corporate recruiter rankings for 1992, 1990, and 1988

| | Rankings by *Corporate Recruiters* | | |
	1992 Rank	1990 Rank	1988 Rank
Northwestern	1	2	1
Chicago	4	5	4
Harvard	3	3	3
Wharton	2	1	2
Michigan	6	4	5
Dartmouth	12	8	15
Stanford	7	7	7
Indiana	8	9	9
Columbia	5	6	6
North Carolina	11	14	19
Virginia	15	12	14
Duke	14	13	10
MIT	10	10	17
Cornell	17	19	11
NYU	13	20	13
UCLA	16	16	8
Carnegie Mellon	9	11	12
Berkeley	19	23	16
Vanderbilt	20	(NR)	(NR)
Washington U.	18	(NR)	(NR)

What Affects the Corporate Rankings?

Figure A.2 is a perceptual map of the 1992 corporate rankings versus school size (again, defined as the number of students in the full-time MBA program). Two interesting effects are worth highlighting:

- *The supermarket factor:* The Top 10 corporate rankings correlate very closely with school size. Large schools in the upper left quadrant (Northwestern, Wharton, Harvard, Chicago, Columbia) are more highly rated than smaller schools (Michigan, Stanford, Indiana, Carnegie Mellon, MIT). In fact, the "R-squared" of the downward-sloping regression line on the map relating corporate rankings of the ten highest-rated schools to school size is 0.853 (an R-squared of 1.000 would be a perfect fit). Could it be that recruiters prefer to go to large schools because of a "supermarket effect?" Isn't it reasonable that a *Fortune* 500 recruiter seeking to hire a total of ten financial analysts would prefer to go to a large school where he or she could select from 100 candidates rather than a small school with only twenty candidates?

  On the surface, it would appear that students would have a big advantage going to a large school that attracts more recruiters. But remember, at the large school you'll also have a lot more competition; there were ninety-nine other candidates for our *Fortune* 500 recruiter to interview for those financial analyst positions.

Figure A.2
1992 business school rankings by corporate recruiters

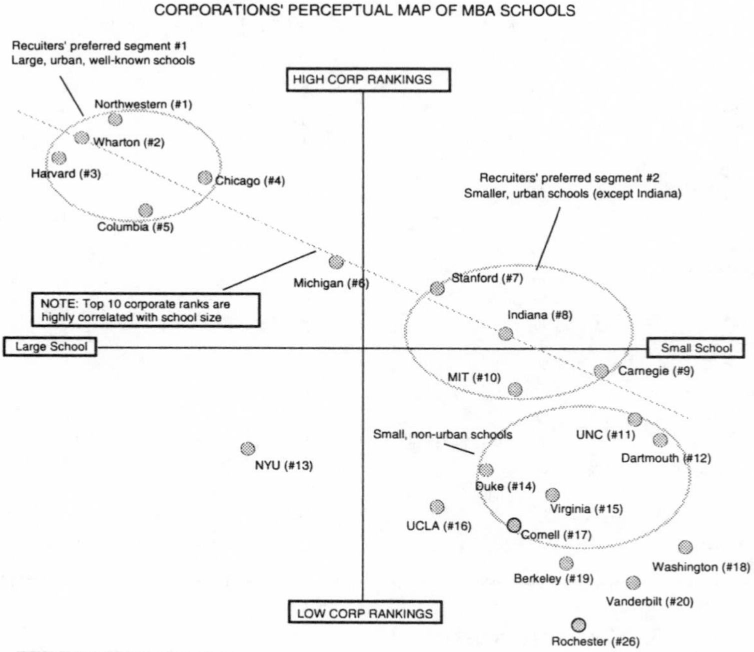

CORPORATIONS' PERCEPTUAL MAP OF MBA SCHOOLS

Source: Business Week '92 corporate rankings

- *The convenience factor:* Note also that the most preferred schools are located in large cities. Even among the smaller schools, those located in urban areas (Stanford, MIT, Carnegie Mellon) are preferred over those located in more rural places (Dartmouth, Duke, Virginia, Cornell). Is this because the urban schools are easier to get to? Certainly it is easier to reach schools like Harvard or MIT than Dartmouth (in Hanover, NH) or Cornell (in Ithaca, NY), particularly during the winter recruiting season.

These observations raise an important question: Are the corporate rankings a true measure of the perceived quality of the graduates of these schools, or are these preference rankings more an index of the selection and the convenience experienced by recruiters when they have to travel to these schools?

The relevance of the corporate rankings shown in figure A.2 can be questioned on other grounds as well:

- *Selecting the recruiters:* The corporate rankings are based on the responses of 199 corporate recruiters who were asked to rank any ten of the thirty-six schools listed in the questionnaire that they had knowledge of, in terms of overall preference. This is a rather small sample to be evaluating thirty-six schools. But the more important question is the basis on which the individual recruiters were selected. According to the 1993 edition of the *Guide*, the companies selected were not a random sample from *all* companies that recruit MBAs, but rather were "a set of 353 organizations with established histories of recruiting at business schools."[8] Established histories of recruiting at *which* business schools? Are there inadvertent biases in the selection process that would favor some schools over others?

- *Large firms only?* As noted in chapter 1, most large firms are continuing to downsize while millions of new jobs are being created by small businesses. Further, the previously cited survey of the Harvard MBA Class of 1970 showed that for every Harvard Business School alum working for a *Business Week* 1,000 firm, there were eight alums working for small companies or for themselves.

    Yet when the *Business Week* corporate ranking poll was established in 1988, it was designed to be similar to the 1985 *Wall Street Journal* corporate survey mentioned in chapter 3—a survey of "the *largest* industrial and service companies in the country."[9,10] As a Stanford spokesman noted in commenting on this '85 *Wall Street Journal* ranking, " . . . Many (Stanford) graduates may choose to work for small Silicon Valley companies. Such companies may lack the national base and size necessary to be included in the survey."[11] If the decade of the '90s belongs to small- and medium-size business, is it appropriate to survey the business school preferences of only large firms?

- *Off-campus recruiting:* Large companies that are downsizing are unlikely to do much recruiting on campus, and experience has shown that small companies are also unlikely

8   Byrne, J., *A Business Week Guide: The Best Business Schools*, 3rd edition, McGraw-Hill, 1993, p. 347.
9   MacKay-Smith, A., "Survey Says Top Business Schools May Not Be Top Business Schools," The *Wall Street Journal*, October 11, 1985.
10 Byrne, J., "The Best B-Schools," *Business Week*, November 28, 1988, p. 78.
11 MacKay-Smith, A., "Survey Says Top Business Schools May Not Be Top Business Schools," *The Wall Street Journal*, October 11, 1985.

to recruit on campus. More and more MBAs are going off campus to uncover great jobs with companies and organizations that typically don't recruit on campus. If most graduating MBAs will be pursuing job opportunities by means other than on-campus interviewing, how relevant will the "convenience factor"—the preference of corporate recruiters for large schools located in cities—be in the future?

Finally, there is the intriguing question of just what these corporate recruiter surveys are measuring:

- *The brand name effect:* How much of a Top 20 business school's reputation is really a "halo effect" from its parent university? Is it more than coincidence that seventeen of the *Business Week* Top 20 Business Schools are affiliated with internationally known universities listed among the Top 25 most distinguished universities, as ranked by *U.S. News and World Report*? (see table A.4).[12, 13]

Table A.4
Correlation between Top 20 ranking and university reputation

Business Week Top 20 Business School	*U.S. News* Top 25 University
Northwestern	✓
Chicago	✓
Harvard	✓
Wharton	✓
Michigan	✓
Dartmouth	✓
Stanford	✓
Indiana	
Columbia	✓
North Carolina	
Virginia	✓
Duke	✓
MIT	✓
Cornell	✓
NYU	
UCLA	✓
Carnegie Mellon	✓
Berkeley	✓
Vanderbilt	✓
Washington U.	✓

- *No agreement on "the best" schools:* A casual inspection of the perceptual maps shows

---

12 "America's Best Colleges," *U.S. News & World Report*, 1993 edition, pp. 26-27.

13 As will be shown in appendix B, table B.5, the highest ranked business schools in terms of THE MBA ADVANTAGE—Harvard, Chicago, Stanford, MIT and Yale—are affiliated with the highest ranked universities, as ranked in the *U.S. News and World Report* poll of the Top 25 universities. The highest starting salaries for MBAs are typically in consulting, which also tends to be the number one job choice for graduates of these top schools. Management consulting is an image-conscious business, and consulting firms may prefer having members of the firm with degrees from the best universities. ("I would like to introduce Ms. Smith from Harvard.") If so, the "halo effect" from these top universities—by attracting high-paying consulting job opportunities to their business schools—could affect the value of a degree from these business schools in a very real way.

that a number of the small schools most highly ranked by graduates in figure A.1 (e.g., Dartmouth, Virginia, Cornell) are among the *least* preferred by corporate recruiters in figure A.2. Moreover, a statistical check of the 1992 rankings shows that there is only a 0.23 correlation between "the best" schools as ranked by graduates versus "the best" schools as ranked by corporate recruiters. Is the excellence of business schools so elusive that graduates and recruiters cannot agree on which schools are best? Or is there a problem with the methodology?

An Example of Size-Related Biases in the Corporate Survey

Business Week's writeup on Stanford illustrates how this excellent school is ranked well down the list due to both the small size of the school and the small size of the companies that recruit there, as noted on page 115 of the 1993 edition of the *Guide* (emphasis added):

> "So why doesn't Stanford do better than seventh in *Business Week's* corporate poll? School officials theorize that the *small size* of the graduating class makes it a more competitive hunting ground for recruiters, who sometimes return to headquarters empty-handed because job offers outnumber Stanford MBAs. They may be particularly bothered because *43 percent of the class accepts jobs with Silicon Valley startups and smaller firms that employ fewer than 1,000 workers. Many of these companies are not surveyed by [Business Week] magazine* because they do not hire significant numbers of MBAs and can't compare Stanford's candidates against those from other institutions."[14]

What Do the Business Week *Rankings Tell about Business Schools?*

By focusing attention on the quality of MBA programs as perceived by students and corporate recruiters, the *Business Week* Top 20 surveys of business schools have had a significant impact on graduate business education in the United States. *Business Week* Associate Editor John Byrne and his staff deserve the thanks of hundreds of thousands of future business students who will benefit from the improvements that have resulted from their turning the spotlight on customer satisfaction of MBA students.

However, the *Business Week* Top 20 is basically an opinion survey. The methodology suffers from the inherent shortcomings of all opinion surveys, such as concerns about unrepresentative samples of respondents, and about their limited knowledge, biases, and motivations. The survey-to-survey volatility of the graduate survey results diminishes the credibility of the graduate rankings as a true measure of the value of an MBA from these fine schools. Graduating students may be less than candid in reporting dissatisfaction with their program because it might compromise the value of their degree if the school receives a lower ranking. The rankings by recruiters may in large part be measures of school size and location. The selection of the small non-random sample of corporate recruiters may be unintentionally biased for or against some schools.

The biennial *Business Week* survey is certainly worth reviewing to compare business schools. The soft cover *Business Week Guide* is a very valuable reference for getting a sense of what it would be like to be a student at each of the major business schools. Read separately, the individual graduate rankings and corporate rankings are useful input for a prospective MBA student once the limitations are understood. But when these two independent surveys are statisti-

---

14 Byrne, J., *A Business Week Guide: The Best Business Schools*, 3rd edition, McGraw-Hill, 1993, p. 115.

cally combined into a single comprehensive ranking of "the best business schools," the resulting overall *Business Week* Top 20 ranking is on shaky ground.

The bottom line: Read the stories in the *Guide* and note the individual graduate and corporate rankings of each school, but don't base your choice of business school entirely on the overall *Business Week* Top 20 Ranking.

U.S. News & World Report: A Different Approach to Ranking Business Schools

U.S. News & World Report takes a very different approach than *Business Week* to ranking business schools. Once a year, in late March, *U.S. News* devotes most of an issue to a cover article on "America's Best Graduate Schools."

U.S. News describes its ranking of graduate schools as " . . . offering prospective students and their families vital data about the comparative merits and professional reputations of hundreds of business, law and medical schools . . ."[15] As shown in table A.5, the upper reaches of the *U.S. News* rankings are fairly stable from year to year. Many of the same schools appear in about the same relative positions on both the *Business Week* and *U.S. News* rankings. In fact, there is a high 0.72 correlation between the 1993 *U.S. News* ranking and the 1992 *Business Week* ranking.

The *U.S. News* ranks are produced by an entirely different methodology than the *Business Week* rankings, however. Under the direction of Senior Editor Robert J. Morse, the *U.S. News* rankings are compiled from a complex formula that includes:

- *Student selectivity* (weighted as 25 percent of the total ranking), made up of average GMAT scores (which is weighted as 65 percent of the student selectivity category total), undergraduate GPAs (30 percent of the category) and the percentage of applicants accepted (5 percent).

- *Placement success* (30 percent of the total ranking), a mix of the percent of the class employed at graduation (30 percent of this category), the percent employed three months after graduation (25 percent), the median starting salaries less bonuses (40 percent), and the ratio of the number of last year's on-campus MBA recruiters to the number of last year's MBA graduates (5 percent).

- *Graduation rate* (5 percent of the total ranking), which represents the percentage of MBA students in the past two classes who earned their MBA degree within two years of starting.

- *Reputation* (40 percent of the total ranking), a combination of results from two independent surveys about business school reputations: one a survey of the deans and MBA directors of all 268 accredited business school (50 percent of the category), and the second a survey of 2,000 CEOs representing a "cross section of the largest U.S. corporations" (50 percent).[16]

---

15 Morse, R. J., "America's Best Graduate Schools," *U.S. News & World Report*, March 22, 1993, p. 51.
16 Ibid., p. 59.

Table A.5
The *U.S. News* Top 25 rankings for 1993, 1992, 1991, and 1990

	1993 Rank	1992 Rank	1991 Rank	1990 Rank
Harvard	1	2	1	2
Stanford	2	1	2	1
Wharton	3	3	3	3
Northwestern	4	4	4	4
Michigan	5	7	10	7
MIT	6	5	5	5
Duke	7	9	7	9
Dartmouth	8	10	8	6
Chicago	9	6	6	8
Columbia	10	8	11	10
Virginia	11	11	9	11
Cornell	12	12	12	12
Carnegie Mellon	13	15	13	14
Berkeley	14	13	15	13
UCLA	15	14	16	15
NYU	16	18	19	18
Yale	17	16	(NR)	(NR)
Texas	18	20	17	24
North Carolina	19	17	14	17
Indiana	20	19	18	16
USC	21	21	21	(NR)
Georgetown	22	(NR)	22	(NR)
Purdue	23	23	20	19
Rochester	24	22	25	23
Vanderbilt	25	25	(NR)	(NR)
Pittsburgh	(NR)	24	22	(NR)
Maryland	(NR)	(NR)	24	(NR)
Penn State	(NR)	(NR)	(NR)	20
Illinois	(NR)	(NR)	(NR)	21
Wisconsin	(NR)	(NR)	(NR)	22
Ohio State	(NR)	(NR)	(NR)	25

(NR = not rated)

Limitations of the U.S. News & World Report *Top 25 Rankings*

Like the *Business Week* rankings, the *U.S. News* method has some limitations:

- *Are the inputs meaningful?* The *U.S. News* ranking is compiled from a weighted mix of ten different inputs—GMAT scores, starting salaries, graduation rates, opinion surveys of deans and CEOs, and so on. Is there solid evidence that these inputs are relevant to the value of an MBA degree from these schools?

- *Are the formula weights meaningful?* How were the formula weights determined? Why, for example, is the GMAT score weighted as 16.3 percent of the total score, while the ratio of recruiters on campus, the corporate customers of the schools, is weighted as only 1.5 percent of the total score, less than one-tenth as much?

- *Are the schools always honest?* Editor Robert Morse believes that his *U.S. News* ranking is a better measure of the excellence of the schools because 60 percent is determined from objective data (starting salaries, GMAT scores, placement rates) and only 40 percent is based on opinion surveys.

In criticizing the *U.S. News* approach, *Business Week* notes that this objective data is supplied by schools who have an incentive to selectively edit the numbers. *Business Week*, on the other hand, gets its starting salaries and other numbers directly from the graduates rather than requesting data from the schools.

- *Is it measuring the halo effect?* The *U.S. News* reputational opinion surveys of the deans and CEOs (which together are weighted as 40 percent of the rankings) may be biased by the same "halo effect" from the prestige of their affiliated universities that we saw previously in table A.4. A statistical evaluation of this halo effect shows a relatively high 0.65 correlation between the rankings of the 1993 *U.S. News* Top 25 business schools and a separate 1993 *U.S. News* ranking of the top universities.[17] (The halo effect correlation between the 1992 *Business Week* Top 20 business school ranking and the 1992 *U.S. News* ranking of the top universities is somewhat less, at 0.49.)

  Given that the 268 deans and 2,000 CEOs are asked to rate the reputation of all 268 accredited business schools, most of which they never heard of, it's plausible that they tend to give high marks to the business schools associated with universities they are familiar with. (As I noted in chapter 3, one of my colleagues, Professor Shlomo Kalish, asked 128 corporate recruiters to rate a list of fifteen business schools. As expected, Harvard and Stanford got the highest ratings. Princeton also got a good rating, but Princeton doesn't have a business school.)

- *Are the respondents knowledgeable?* A more subtle criticism of the *U.S. News* ranking methodology comes from some of the Top 25 schools. They claim that the 268 deans who are surveyed include more than 200 deans and administrators of schools below the top 50 who are not in serious competition with the top schools for either students or faculty, and do not have an incentive to keep up on changes taking place at the top schools.

  Because there are so many of them, these 200 or more deans from the regional schools dominate the deans' survey and they each have the same vote as deans from the top 50 schools, who supposedly are much more knowledgeable about the programs of the top business schools. It has been suggested that ranking the Top 25 business schools should be done only by the top 50 deans, not by all 268.

- *Are only big companies represented?* The reputational survey of 2,000 CEOs represents "a cross section of the largest U.S. corporations." But as we saw earlier, almost all of the growth in the economy is in small companies, while large corporations are expected to continue to downsize for the next several years. Shouldn't small and medium-size companies also be represented in the CEO survey?

The bottom line: The *U.S. News & World Report* business school survey is compiled from a set of objective inputs with various weightings, plus a pair of reputational opinion surveys of

---

17 "America's Best Colleges," *U.S. News & World Report*, 1993 edition, pp. 26-27.

deans and CEOs. As with the *Business Week* survey, this is useful information for the prospective student once the limitations of the methodology are understood.

In Closing, a Word of Appreciation

It is easy to criticize the approaches of others, particularly those who pioneered the evaluation of business schools by published surveys. There is always room for improvement in any kind of survey work.

But it is important to close with a note of appreciation to John Byrne at *Business Week* and Robert Morse at *U.S. News & World Report*. Without their leadership in developing and publishing these surveys, it's doubtful that business schools would have been as quick to improve the quality of their MBA programs. The MBA students of the future and the employers who hire these students will benefit greatly from the pioneering work of these two innovators.

Appendix B

How THE MBA ADVANTAGE *Rankings Work*

Part I: THE MBA ADVANTAGE: A Market-Based Method for Comparing Business Schools

From a financial standpoint, is it worth it to go to business school? The best way to answer that question is to estimate how much you will make over the next several years if you go to business school, less the cost of tuition and fees (leaving out room and board, because you will have living expenses whether or not you go to business school). Then make an estimate of how much you will make over the same period if you don't go to business school. The difference is the additional value acquired by getting the MBA. I call this difference THE MBA ADVANTAGE.

The advantage of THE MBA ADVANTAGE method is that it does not involve surveys of opinions about which business schools are best. Rather, it is a measure of what employers are willing to pay the graduates of these schools, not only at the time of graduation, but also during the first five years on the job following graduation. These are market-based measures, reflecting thousands of hiring and promotion decisions by large and small companies, and therefore are much less likely to be biased than opinion surveys.

In this section, we will calculate THE MBA ADVANTAGE using a variety of assumptions, and we'll see that the rank order of the best business schools doesn't change very much, regardless of the assumptions.[1] (Academics say that an analysis with this kind of consistency is "robust," meaning that no matter which assumptions we use, Harvard, Chicago, Stanford, MIT, and Yale are at the top of the ranking, and so on.)

For convenience, THE MBA ADVANTAGE will be calculated over a seven-year period of two years in school followed by five years on the job. Since the benefits of an MBA from a top school accrue over one's professional lifetime, this is a conservative calculation that understates the true value of the MBA.

Next, we'll show that on average, the quality of incoming students is the major factor in determining each school's MBA ADVANTAGE.

Finally, we'll look at a variety of other factors, such as the halo effect from the parent university's reputation, mix of functional concentrations, regional cost of living, school size, and faculty research to see which of these also affect a school's MBA ADVANTAGE.

---

[1] These calculations use data from Byrne, J., *A Business Week Guide: The Best Business Schools*, 1st edition, 1990, and 3rd edition, 1993, McGraw-Hill.

THE MBA ADVANTAGE is defined as the estimated average cumulative post-MBA pay after five years on the job (after subtracting the cost of going to business school), less what incoming students for that school *would* have made in their pre-MBA jobs with nominal pay increases every year (see figure B.1). This is the best measure of the additional payoff of getting an MBA degree versus staying in the pre-MBA job with nominal pay increases.

Figure B.1

THE MBA ADVANTAGE, as estimated for the Harvard Business School Class of 1992, is the cumulative difference in annual pay with and without the MBA through the fifth year after graduation. In this illustration, annual pay without the MBA is assumed to grow at five percent per year (see case 1 which follows).

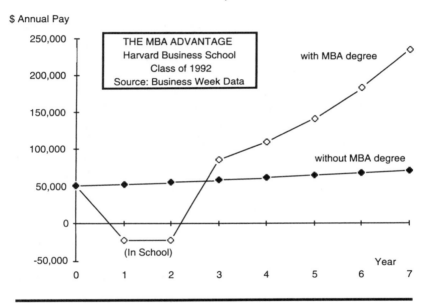

How THE MBA ADVANTAGE Was Calculated For Each School

The data for the Class of '92 pre-MBA pay and post-MBA starting pay for the top schools was obtained from the third edition of the *Business Week Guide*, pages 56 and 57. According to *Business Week*, these numbers were acquired in the spring of 1992 from a direct mail survey of the graduates of the top business schools. A total of 4,712 surveys were returned. The response rate across schools ranged from 54 percent to 89 percent and averaged 78 percent, which is exceptional for a mail survey. (*Business Week* is to be commended for achieving such a high response rate and for making this information available.)

Tuition and fees for each school were also obtained from the third edition of the *Guide*. Living expenses were not included in this analysis because they are incurred to some extent whether or not one goes to business school.

The pay for the fifth year following graduation was estimated as follows: The actual 1988 starting pay for each of the Top 20 schools (from the first edition of the *Business Week Guide*) was reduced by 5 percent to approximate the 1987 starting pay for each school (MBA starting salaries grew about 5 percent per year during the 1980s). The actual 1992 current (fifth year) pay for each school's Class of 1987 (from the third edition, page 17) was then divided by the estimated 1987 starting pay to get a five year post-MBA growth factor for each school, which we call the post-MBA FAST TRACK (It varies from about 1.5 to 2.5.). Finally, the actual 1992 starting pay for each school was multiplied by this growth factor to obtain an estimated post-MBA fifth year pay for the year 1997 for each school (see table 4.6 on page 40).

Using these four numbers—pre-MBA pay, tuition and fees, post-MBA starting pay, and fifth year pay—it is possible to calculate two cash flows for each school for the seven year period, one with the MBA and the other without the MBA (see figure B.1). The difference in these cash flows is the school's MBA ADVANTAGE for the Class of '92.

In calculating THE MBA ADVANTAGE for each school, an important question is: What growth rate in annual pay should we use for the alternative of *not* going to business school? We'll run cases with three different sets of assumptions to see how much difference it makes.

CASE 1: THE UNIFORM 5 PERCENT ASSUMPTION

We'll begin by assuming a nominal growth rate of 5 percent per year salary growth for the alternative of not going to business school, and we'll use this 5 percent assumption uniformly for all the schools. (In reality, this is not a particularly good assumption. As we shall see later in this appendix, the quality of incoming students, as measured by pre-MBA pay and by GMATs, varies substantially across the Top 20 schools. The students that would be accepted at the best schools like Harvard and Chicago would probably see their pay grow faster than 5 percent per year even if they didn't go to business school.)

The results for this calculation of THE MBA ADVANTAGE are shown in table B.1.

THE MBA ADVANTAGE for the Top Business Schools (Uniform 5 Percent Assumption)

In table B.1, THE MBA ADVANTAGE has been calculated for the Class of 1992 from each of the Top 20[2] business schools, in the manner shown in figure B.1. This was done using each school's average pre-MBA pay, tuition and fees, average post-MBA starting pay, and average pay after five years on the job.

- Even among the Top 20 Business Schools comprising the top 3 percent of all the business schools in the United States major differences exist in the average payoff for getting the MBA. At the end of five years on the job, the difference in the average payoff be-

---

2 The *Business Week Guides* did not publish complete information needed for these calculations on all of the schools in the 1992 *Business Week* Top 20. There was no published information on pay after five years on the job for Columbia, Vanderbilt, or Washington University, so it was not possible to calculate THE MBA ADVANTAGE for these schools. There was complete information in the *Guides*, however, for Rochester, Texas, and Yale, which had been on the *Business Week* Top 20 in 1988 and/or 1990, so these three schools were included in these calculations.

Table B.1

THE MBA ADVANTAGE is the estimated average cumulative post-MBA pay after five years on the job (after subtracting the cost of going to business school), less what the average incoming students for that school *would* have made in their pre-MBA jobs *with pay increases of 5 percent per year.*

	THE MBA ADVANTAGE	Years to Breakeven	The Best Business Schools MBA ADVANTAGE Rank	*Business Week* Top 20 Rank
Harvard	$277,525	3	1	3
Stanford	201,906	4	2	7
Chicago	195,862	4	3	2
MIT	164,758	4	4	13
Yale	156,244	4	5	(NR)
Wharton	141,835	4	6	4
UCLA	134,636	4	7	16
Northwestern	122,665	4	8	1
Berkeley	118,543	4	9	18
Dartmouth	96,894	4	10	6
Cornell	89,314	4	11	14
Virginia	78,579	4	12	11
Michigan	71,024	4	13	5
Carnegie Mellon	66,269	4	14	17
Texas	64,214	4	15	(NR)
NYU	55,084	5	16	15
North Carolina	39,974	5	17	10
Rochester	35,162	5	18	(NR)
Indiana	30,734	5	19	8
Duke	4,762	5	20	12

tween attending Harvard and the lowest ranked schools on this list is about a quarter of a million dollars.

- The ranking of schools based on THE MBA ADVANTAGE is quite different from the *Business Week* Top 20 ranking. Harvard leads, followed by Stanford (number 7 in the *Business Week* rankings). MIT—ranked number 13 by *Business Week*—is fourth, while Indiana (ranked number 8 by *Business Week*) drops to nineteenth place. Yale, not included at all in *Business Week*'s Top 20, ranks fifth. *Business Week*'s number 1 school, Northwestern, is eighth in this MBA ADVANTAGE ranking.

- Within five years of graduation, the investment in the MBA, namely tuition and two years without salary, has been recovered at all of the Top 20 schools. (For Harvard, breakeven occurs in three years, and for many of the rest it occurs within four years.)

- The calculation in table B.1 was done using pretax salaries. If estimated federal and state income taxes are factored in (20 percent on pay without the MBA; 30 percent on post-MBA pay) it takes an additional year to break even at most of the schools. If present value calculations are made by discounting the future *after-tax* cash flows by 6 percent per year (to recognize the time value of money), Harvard breaks even within four years, and all but the lowest four schools break even within six years.

In table B.1, THE MBA ADVANTAGE was estimated only for the first five years following graduation. As we mentioned earlier, this understates the true lifetime value of getting an MBA.

CASE 2: THE VARIABLE RATE ASSUMPTION

In table B.1, it was assumed that pay without the MBA would grow at only 5 percent per year. As noted earlier, it can be argued that since the post-MBA salary growth rate is influenced by the average quality of students as well by the quality of the MBA education, the assumption of a 5 percent annual growth in salary without the MBA for *all* schools is inappropriate. Presumably, Harvard-quality students would see their pre-MBA pay increase faster than 5 percent even without an MBA.

Therefore, in table B.2 we'll take a different approach to calculating THE MBA ADVANTAGE. For each school, we'll assume that pay without the MBA would grow at *half the rate* it would grow with the MBA, illustrated as in figure B.2, which should be compared with figure B.1. In the first five years following graduation, the annual growth rates in post-MBA pay range from 28.8 percent for Harvard to 9.4 percent for Duke. Accordingly, in table B.2, the growth rates for pay without the MBA will range from 14.4 percent for Harvard students to 4.7 percent for Duke students. (This is the method used in chapter 4.)

Figure B.2
THE MBA ADVANTAGE is estimated for the Harvard Business School Class of 1992, assuming that pay *without* the MBA would grow at half the rate it grows *with* the MBA (see Case number 2). Because it takes into account the differences in quality of incoming students, we have adopted the variable rate method illustrated in figure B.2 as the standard method for calculating THE MBA ADVANTAGE throughout this book.

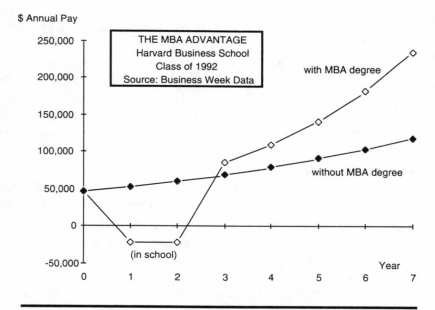

THE MBA ADVANTAGE (Variable Rate Assumption)

Table B.2

In this table, THE MBA ADVANTAGE is the estimated average cumulative post-MBA pay after five years on the job (after subtracting the cost of going to business school), less what the average incoming students for that school *would* have made in their pre-MBA jobs *with annual pay increases equal to half the growth rate of their post-MBA pay.*

Rank		Post-MBA Pay Growth Rate	Est. 5th Year Pay (in 1997)	MBA ADVANTAGE (5 years post-MBA)	Years to Breakeven
			For the Class of 1992		
1	Harvard	28.8%	$233,985	$133,647	4
2	Chicago	25.1	167,896	110,294	4
3	Stanford	23.6	193,429	104,337	4
4	MIT	20.7	154,976	102,989	4
5	Yale	20.9	142,651	99,882	4
6	Northwestern	18.8	139,705	72,500	4
7	Berkeley	18.7	129,811	71,298	4
8	Wharton	21.4	156,716	70,912	5
9	UCLA	22.6	145,656	60,809	5
10	Virginia	14.7	112,900	54,200	4
11	Cornell	18.6	118,730	45,866	5
12	Michigan	16.6	107,381	39,663	5
13	Dartmouth	19.0	148,877	37,258	5
14	Carnegie Mellon	16.3	104,303	36,782	5
15	Texas	18.2	95,372	27,466	5
16	Rochester	13.8	89,411	18,683	5
17	Indiana	14.4	84,256	11,543	5
18	North Carolina	16.2	101,084	7,844	5
19	Duke	9.4	85,881	7,506	5
20	NYU	19.5	115,618	4,121	5

The bottom line: Even under these more conservative assumptions, the MBA at a Top 20 school is still an excellent investment.

It is interesting to compare the results in table B.2 with those in table B.1:

- THE MBA ADVANTAGE calculated the new way for each school drops to about half the value shown previously in table B.1, which assumed that pay without the MBA grows at only 5 percent. This is because we are now assuming that students good enough to get into these top schools would do well even without an MBA. Therefore, the marginal contribution of investing in an MBA under this new assumption is lower.

- The ranking under the new assumption changes for some schools. Chicago replaces Stanford as the number 2 school, and Northwestern, Berkeley, Virginia, Rochester, and Indiana each move up two positions. Dartmouth drops three positions to number 13, and NYU plunges four positions to last place on the ranking. It should be underscored, however, that NYU and the other schools near the bottom of the list are very good schools; they are still in the top 3 percent of all the business schools in the country. But they are somewhat less effective in creating additional value beyond what their excellent students would be able to accomplish without the MBA.

- It may not be obvious why a school like NYU, with an estimated 1997 fifth year pay of $115,618, ranks below Indiana, with an estimated 1997 fifth year pay of $84,256. The answer is that NYU combines higher tuition ($18,000 versus $12,300 for Indiana), higher opportunity costs of foregone salary ($41,000 versus $34,000) and the second lowest two-year salary STEP UP upon graduation (41 percent versus 47 percent for Indiana and about 60 percent for most other schools). So although NYU graduates are paid more than Indiana graduates, their costs are much higher. Since THE MBA ADVANTAGE measures the difference between what graduates are paid and what it costs to attain the degree, the Indiana graduates come out ahead on this comparison, at least for the first five years post-MBA.

- Intuitively, the rankings in table B.2, adjusted for the quality of incoming students, would seem to be more appropriate than those with the uniform 5 percent assumption (table B.1). Because it takes into account these differences in quality of incoming students, we have adopted the variable rate method as the standard method for calculating THE MBA ADVANTAGE throughout this book. As we shall see in the next section, the quality of incoming students is the most important determinant of a school's MBA ADVANTAGE.

CASE 3: THE SLOWER GROWTH ASSUMPTION

Although calculated from *Business Week* survey data, the post-MBA pay growth rates of 15 to 25 percent per year shown in table B.2 may seem high in a period of low inflation and moderate economic growth. As previously described, these post-MBA FAST TRACK growth rates were derived using the actual post-MBA starting pay for the Class of 1988 and the actual fifth year pay for the Class of 1987, as published in the first and third editions of the *Business Week Guide*. There may be concern that the post-MBA FAST TRACK growth rates and the fifth year pay (actual and estimated) are "just too high."

Are the fifth year pay estimates in table B.2 unrealistic? About 40 percent of the Harvard graduates pursue consulting and investment banking, both of which are high paying fields. How high? A 1993 *Fortune* article disclosed that McKinsey & Co. pays its junior partners—a position typically achieved within seven years—about $250,000.[3] McKinsey concentrates its MBA recruiting at Chicago, Harvard, Stanford, MIT, Northwestern, Wharton, and Insead in France. With a 17 percent annual attrition rate, this elite consulting organization of 3,100 professionals has a voracious appetite for top quality MBAs. Investment banking pays even more for outstanding performers. Therefore, the actual fifth year pay figures for the Class of '87 used as the basis for this analysis—$167,740 for Harvard, $144,540 for Stanford, $127,350 for Chicago, etc.—may not be "too high."

Nevertheless, there is the possibility that the respondents who provided the *Business Week* data on fifth year pay were not representative of the entire Class of '87. According to the third edition of the *Guide*, a questionnaire was sent to 3,683 members of the Class of 1987 from the 21 schools that made the *Business Week* Top 20 in 1988 and/or 1990, and 1,553 responded.[4] Assuming there are about 6,300 Class of '87 alumni of these schools (21 schools times an average

---

3   Huey, J., "How McKinsey Does It," *Fortune*, November 1, 1993, p. 81.
4   Byrne, 3rd Edition, pp. 12-13.

of about 300 graduates per school), the responding sample represented about 25 percent of the '87 alumni.

It is possible that this 25 percent was the most successful segment of the Class of '87 and its pay is therefore biased on the high side. This could mean that the post-MBA FAST TRACK growth rates and the fifth year pay are overstated in tables B.1 and B.2.

For the next case, we'll use a much more conservative assumption about post-MBA pay growth rates. What if the post-MBA salary growth rates were only half of those used to calculate the previous tables? Would it still pay to get an MBA from a top school?

To test the sensitivity of THE MBA ADVANTAGE to slower growth rates of post-MBA pay, calculations were made in which the post-MBA growth rates were cut in half (Harvard's was cut from 28.8 percent to 14.4 percent, Chicago's from 25.1 percent to 12.5 percent, etc.). As in Case number 2, the growth rates without the MBA were half those with the MBA (Harvard's was 7.2 percent, Chicago's was 6.3 percent, etc.). THE MBA ADVANTAGE was extended to six years post-MBA so that all of the schools would achieve breakeven. The results are illustrated in figure B.3 and listed in table B.3.

Figure B.3

THE MBA ADVANTAGE is estimated for the Harvard Business School Class of 1992, assuming that pay with and without the MBA would grow at half the rates shown in figure B.2. Under this assumption, pay with the MBA would grow at 14.4 percent annually, and without the MBA would grow at 7.2 percent annually, as described in case 3.

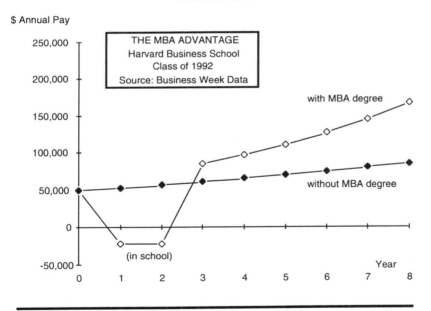

THE MBA ADVANTAGE with Salary Growth Rates Cut in Half

Table B.3

THE MBA ADVANTAGE (for the first *six* years following graduation) was calculated *with pay growth rates that are half of those used in table B.2.*

Rank		Reduced Post-MBA Pay Growth Rate	Est. 5th Year Pay (in 1997)	MBA ADVANTAGE (6 years Post-MBA)	Years to Breakeven
		For the Class of 1992			
1	Harvard	14.4%	$145,576	$143,436	5
2	Chicago	12.5	110,024	121,462	4
3	Stanford	11.8	129,458	120,214	5
4	MIT	10.4	108,263	119,632	5
5	Yale	10.5	99,312	114,876	5
6	Northwestern	9.4	100,504	90,088	5
7	Berkeley	9.3	93,584	87,664	5
8	Wharton	10.7	108,410	86,759	5
9	UCLA	11.3	98,986	74,263	5
10	Virginia	7.3	86,645	73,141	5
11	Cornell	9.3	85,604	60,812	5
12	Michigan	8.3	79,931	55,395	5
13	Dartmouth	9.5	106,751	55,153	5
14	Carnegie Mellon	8.2	77,988	52,338	5
15	Texas	9.1	69,256	39,371	5
16	Rochester	6.9	69,666	34,100	5
17	Duke	4.7	71,986	26,205	6
18	Indiana	7.2	64,888	24,778	6
19	North Carolina	8.1	75,739	21,614	6
20	NYU	9.7	82,278	17,362	6

The bottom line: Even with pay growth rates cut in half, the MBA from a top school still pays for itself in four to six years.

Arbitrarily cutting the post-MBA pay growth rates in half (see table B.3) increases the time to breakeven by about one year. Note that under this assumption, the *estimated* fifth year pay for the Class of *1997* (see table B.3) is now generally less than the reported *actual* fifth year pay for the Class of *1992* (see table 4.6 on page 40). Thus the assumptions for table B.3 are considered to be very conservative.

A comparison of the rankings in table B.3 with those in table B.2 shows only one change— Duke has moved ahead of Indiana and North Carolina.

THE MBA ADVANTAGE Method May Understate the Value of Current Graduates

As noted in chapter 4, some schools seem to have more *momentum*—their starting pay is moving up faster (see table 4.2). If in fact these schools are gaining on their competitors, THE MBA ADVANTAGE rankings in tables B.1, B.2, and B.3 may understate the quality of their *current* graduates. The fifth year pay used to calculate THE MBA ADVANTAGE is based on the actual fifth year pay of the Class of 1987, as surveyed in 1992. If the current crop of students and/or the quality of teaching at these schools has improved disproportionately since 1987, the post-MBA FAST TRACK growth rates of these schools in table 4.4 on page 38 might be too low, and

THE MBA ADVANTAGE rankings in tables B.1, B.2, and B.3 could understate the true value of the current graduates of these schools. The converse is also a possibility for schools that are falling behind.

The MBA Degree Is a Good Investment over a Wide Range of Assumptions

Tables B.1 through B.3 have presented THE MBA ADVANTAGE for the Top 20 schools calculated under three sets of assumptions, ranging from optimistic to conservative. In all three cases, the MBA paid for itself within four to six years. And despite wide variations in the assumptions, THE MBA ADVANTAGE ranking of the Top 20 business schools remains about the same. THE MBA ADVANTAGE is a stable market-based method for comparing the best business schools. It provides a powerful analytical tool for gaining understanding about how the top business schools can better serve their customers, the MBA students.

Part II: What Causes the Variation in THE MBA ADVANTAGE across Schools?

Why is one school able to provide its students a higher MBA ADVANTAGE than another? Why do Harvard and Chicago consistently outperform North Carolina and Duke on this measure of value to the student? In the following pages we will examine a number of possible causes:[5]

1. *The quality of the incoming students.* Is a high MBA ADVANTAGE mostly the result of what students learn in their MBA programs or is it heavily dependent on intelligence and other personal characteristics of the students themselves?

2. *The halo effect of the parent university's "brand name."* To what extent is the success of a business school caused by the halo effect of its affiliation with a prestigious university? Do good students choose the Harvard Business School mainly because it is affiliated with Harvard University? Do they choose Wharton because its is part of the University of Pennsylvania? Or do the best business schools enjoy reputations of their own that are independent of their parent university?

3. *The reputational effects from the* Business Week *Top 20 published rankings.* To what extent do the periodic business school ratings by *Business Week* tend to be self-fulfilling prophecies, in the sense that they help attract corporate recruiters and top quality students, thus increasing THE MBA ADVANTAGE for the schools that are highly ranked?

4. *The research activity of the faculty.* Many of the best business schools emphasize the research activity of their faculty in the belief that excellence in research leads to excellence in teaching. Do the schools that stress faculty research provide a higher MBA ADVANTAGE to their students than schools that don't emphasize research?

5. *The regional cost of living.* The cost of living varies from one region of the country to another. Would the ranking of the best schools by their MBA ADVANTAGE change

---

5 In the sections that follow, a number of statistical tests of association will be discussed—correlations, regressions, etc. It is important to bear in mind that such tests, even if statistically significant, do not by themselves prove cause and effect. Furthermore, because of the limited amount of data, these results must be viewed as suggestive rather than conclusive.

significantly if regional cost-of-living adjustments were made in the salary levels used to calculate the MBA ADVANTAGE?

6. *The functional mix of the school's placements.* On average, jobs in consulting pay more than jobs in marketing. Do schools that place a higher percentage of their graduates in consulting and other high paying functions have a higher MBA ADVANTAGE?

7. *The size of the business school (number of full-time MBA students).* Evidence from appendix A about the preferences of corporate recruiters suggests that they favor large schools where they can interview many students for each opening. Do large schools provide a higher MBA ADVANTAGE to their students?

8. *The size of the metropolitan area in which the school is located.* Corporate recruiters also appear to prefer schools located in large metropolitan areas that are easy to reach on recruiting trips. Do schools located in large metropolitan areas (e.g., Harvard, MIT, NYU) tend to provide a higher MBA ADVANTAGE than those located in rural communities (e.g., Dartmouth, Cornell)?

These are important questions. Understanding the factors that influence the economic value of a school's MBA degree, as measured by its MBA ADVANTAGE, contributes to improving the quality and value of management education. Although definitive answers to these questions are not possible with the limited data available, it is possible to shed some light on these matters, with the hope of encouraging further research.[6]

A complete set of simple regressions were run to test the association between each of these variables and THE MBA ADVANTAGE, along with its two components, STEP UP and FAST TRACK. The results are summarized in table B.4. Because of the limited amount of data available, it was not feasible to use multiple regression to test the combined effects of all of the variables simultaneously.

1. The Effect of Incoming Student Quality on THE MBA ADVANTAGE

Our statistical analysis (summarized in table B.4) shows that incoming student quality, measured by either GMAT scores or pre-MBA pay, is an important factor in explaining school-to-school variations in THE MBA ADVANTAGE.[7] In general, schools that offer a high MBA ADVANTAGE tend to have brighter students (as measured by their GMAT scores) and/or students who have achieved more before coming to business school (as measured by their pre-MBA pay). Not surprisingly, on a school-by-school basis, these two measures are themselves highly correlated (R = 0.69).

A graph of THE MBA ADVANTAGE versus average GMAT for the top schools is shown in figure B.4. The diagonal line across each graph is a *regression line* that gives the best fit of all the points relating the THE MBA ADVANTAGE to this measure of student quality. The line shows

---

6 Other variables that conceivably could help explain school-to-school variations in THE MBA ADVANTAGE are the average age of incoming students and average years of work experience (which would be expected to correlate closely with age). As it turns out, however, all of the top schools have about the same average age for incoming students (27±1 years) and the same work experience (4±1 years)—see chapter 5. Also, there were no significant correlations between THE MBA ADVANTAGE of each school and the percentage women, minorities, or international students in its graduating class.

7 See the discussion in chapter 4 about the relative merits of using each of these variables to measure incoming student quality.

Table B.4

Summary of individual *simple* regressions proposed to explain school-to-school variations in THE MBA ADVANTAGE and its two components, the two-year STEP UP and the and five-year post-MBA FAST TRACK. The associations marked with +++ are highly significant, while those marked with ++ and + are somewhat less strong. (In formal terms, the indicated coefficients of the regression equations have the appropriate signs and the null hypothesis is rejected at the following levels: +++ = 1%; ++ = 5%; + = 10%.)

	STEP UP	FAST TRACK	MBA ADVANTAGE
1. Quality of incoming students			
GMAT		++	+++
pre-MBA pay		+++	+++
2. Halo effect from parent university			++
3. *Business Week* rankings			
4. Faculty research intensity			
5. Cost of living		+++	+
6. Placement mix (percent consulting)	++	+++	+++
7. Size of school (full-time MBAs)		+++	+
8. Size of metro area		+	

how the "average" business school's MBA ADVANTAGE increases with GMAT and with pre-MBA pay. Note that only a few of the actual schools are approximately "average." Most are above or below the line.[8]

THE MBA ADVANTAGE is Highly Related to Student Quality

The slope of the regression line in figure B.4 is 1884.3, which means that on average every ten point increase in a school's average GMAT translates into almost $19,000 more in its MBA ADVANTAGE. The R-squared of 0.501 means that 50 percent of the variation in MBA ADVANTAGE across schools can be explained by the differences in average GMAT.[9]

Similarly, THE MBA ADVANTAGE versus average pre-MBA pay, as graphed in figure B.5, has a slope of 4.238, which means that on average every $1,000 increase in a school's average pre-MBA pay is associated with $4,238 in its MBA ADVANTAGE. The R-squared of 0.364 indicates that 36 percent of the variation in MBA ADVANTAGE across schools can be explained by differences in pre-MBA pay.

As noted above, since average GMATs and average pre-MBA pay are highly correlated on a school-by-school basis, there's a lot of overlap in these two measures of student quality, and we can't just add the 50 percent and the 36 percent to claim that these two measures explain 86 percent of the variation in THE MBA ADVANTAGE across schools.

---

8   Average GMAT scores for Harvard, Stanford, and Northwestern are *Business Week* estimates.

9   Although a school's average GMAT scores correlate well with THE MBA ADVANTAGE, the GMAT does not predict post-MBA starting pay of individual students within a school's graduating class. This was observed in a study of 150 Simon School graduates carried out by Michael Daum in the summer of 1993 and was confirmed by information received from the Graduate Management Admissions Council, which administers the GMAT. The GMAT has been shown to predict individual students' grades in the first year of the MBA program, however.

Figure B.4

THE MBA ADVANTAGE as a function of each school's average GMAT score. (Schools that are above the line are outperforming the "average" Top 20 school at each level of student quality, and vice versa.)

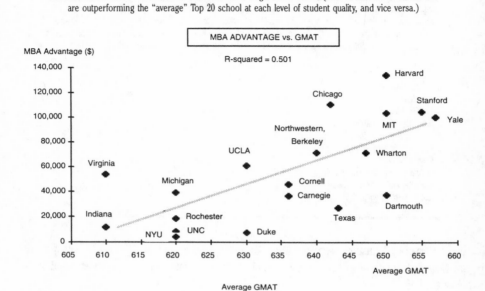

Figure B.5

THE MBA ADVANTAGE as a function of each school's pre-MBA pay.

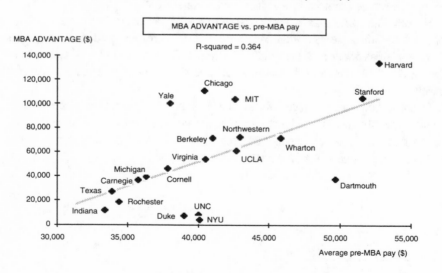

The reason for examining both measures of student quality is that on a school-by-school basis they have somewhat different patterns of interaction with the various schools. For example, in figure B.4, Stanford has high GMATs and its students have very high pre-MBA pay (see figure B.5). But Yale, Chicago, and MIT students, also with high GMATs, have only average pre-MBA pay. And Virginia, with the same pre-MBA pay as Chicago, has low GMATs.

What is the significance of schools lying above or below the regression line? The vertical distance from the school to the line is called a *residual*, and it is a measure of whether an individual school is outperforming or underperforming the "average" school *for a given level of student quality*. For example, in figure B.4, Chicago, Harvard, and Virginia are well above the line, meaning that their MBA ADVANTAGE is higher than would be expected given the GMATs of their students. On the other hand, Texas, Dartmouth, Duke, North Carolina, and NYU are well below the line, indicating that their MBA ADVANTAGE is below what would be expected given the GMATs of their students.

Similarly, in figure B.5, Harvard, MIT, Chicago, and Yale have a higher MBA ADVANTAGE than would be expected based on the pre-MBA pay of their students, while Dartmouth, North Carolina, Duke, and NYU are below average.

The MBA STEP UP: Unrelated to Student Quality

These residuals suggest that there is something besides student quality that affects THE MBA ADVANTAGE of these schools. We can get some insight into this by separating THE MBA ADVANTAGE for each school into its two components: the two-year STEP UP (which is the ratio of post-MBA starting pay to pre-MBA pay) and the five-year post-MBA FAST TRACK (which is the ratio of post-MBA fifth year pay to post-MBA starting pay). The STEP UP measures how much more a student gets at the time of graduation, typically 50 to 60 percent above pre-MBA pay. The FAST TRACK measures how fast pay increases in the first five years following graduation, typically by a factor of about two times.

Intuitively, we would expect that student quality, measured either by GMAT or by pre-MBA pay, would affect both the STEP UP and the FAST TRACK. In fact, however, this is not the case. In figure B.6, the STEP UP is plotted against GMATs. Although the STEP UP ranges from about 40 percent for North Carolina and NYU to about 70 percent for Yale, MIT, Chicago, and Vanderbilt, the R-squared of 0.119 indicates that only about 12 percent of the variation in STEP UP is related to the school's average GMAT. Similarly in figure B.7, the R-squared of 0.003 means that the STEP UP is completely unrelated to pre-MBA pay. These two regressions imply that the size of the STEP UP is essentially unrelated to student quality.

Figure B.6
MBA STEP UP as a function of each school's average GMAT score.

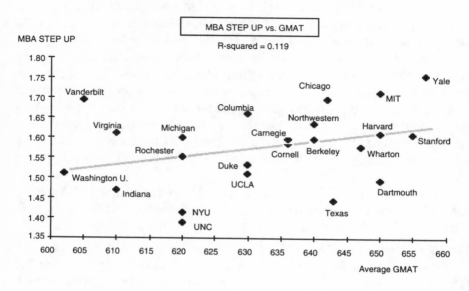

Figure B.7
MBA STEP UP as a function of each school's average pre-MBA pay.

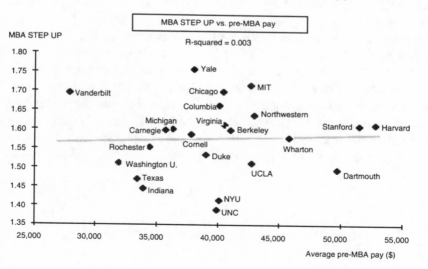

Further analysis shows that the size of a school's STEP UP is unrelated to its post-MBA starting pay (R-squared = 0.162). Schools that are lagging in either pre-MBA pay or starting pay are not systematically "catching up" by means of larger STEP UPS.[10] Nor is there any association between a school's STEP UP and the school's size (R-squared = 0.009).

If the size of the STEP UP is not related to any of these variables, then what might cause the large school-to-school variations in STEP UP (from 40 percent to more than 75 percent) observed in figures B.6 and B.7? Are we are seeing a "labelling" or "branding" effect that encourages the managerial employment market to pay more for the graduates of schools like Yale and MIT over and above what the incoming quality of the students might otherwise justify?

Since there is no way for corporate recruiters to extensively test the individual quality of graduating students other than through brief interviews, it appears that there is a significant amount of business school "brand equity" affecting the size of the STEP UP. The question is, does this brand equity originate from a halo effect from the parent university's prestige, or is it the result of the recruiters having good prior experience with graduates of these schools? Do recruiters go to Yale because of the Yale University name, or because they have had good experience with Yale business school graduates in the past? We'll return to this important question following the next section, where we examine the relationship between the FAST TRACK and student quality.

FAST TRACK: Highly Related to Student Quality

The FAST TRACK measures the rate of salary growth through the first five years following graduation. During this five-year period, pay typically grows by a factor of 2 to 2.5 times. One would expect that this salary growth would be a function of two components:

- The inherent personal qualities of the graduates—intelligence, talent, ambition, etc.
- The quality of the education received from the business schools from which they graduated.

Figures B.8 and B.9 show that this is the case. In figure B.8, there is a moderately strong correlation between salary growth and GMAT (R-squared = 0.397, suggesting that about 40 percent of this growth relates to student quality.) A typical school with an average GMAT of 610 has a FAST TRACK multiplier of 1.7, whereas a typical school with an average GMAT of 650 has a FAST TRACK multiplier of 2.2 times.

In figure B.9, the R-squared between salary growth and pre-MBA pay is 0.447, suggesting that 45 percent of the salary growth is associated with this alternative measure of student quality. A typical school with an average pre-MBA pay of $35,000 has a FAST TRACK multiplier of 1.8; a typical school with an average pre-MBA pay of $46,000 has a FAST TRACK multiplier of 2.2 times.

The bottom line: From these statements it is clear that the quality of incoming students, whether measured by GMATs or pre-MBA pay, appears to have a substantial effect on the value of the MBA, as measured by THE MBA ADVANTAGE.

---

10 A possible exception is Vanderbilt, which has a high STEP UP from a very low average pre-MBA pay.

Figure B.8
MBA FAST TRACK as a function of each school's average GMAT score.

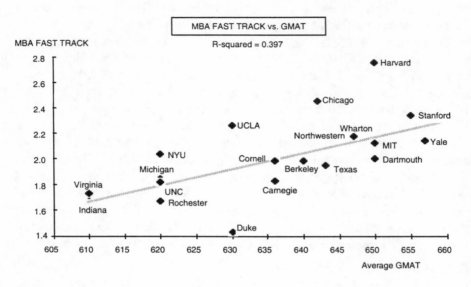

Figure B.9
MBA FAST TRACK as a function of each school's average pre-MBA pay.

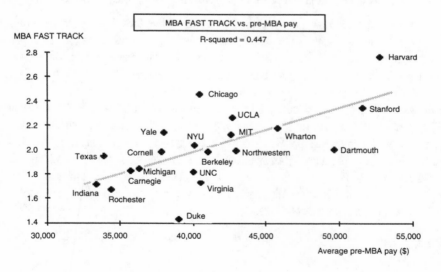

The residuals from these curves show sizeable variations from school to school. Harvard and Chicago graduates appear to outperform graduates from other schools even after adjusting for the effect of their high student quality. Similarly, graduates of Dartmouth and Duke do less well than would be expected based on the quality of their students. Is this related to the quality of the instruction they received, or is it associated with other variables, such as the size and location of the schools (Dartmouth and Duke are small schools located away from large metropolitan areas) or perhaps the brand image of the parent universities?

2. Does the "Brand Name" of the Parent University Affect THE MBA ADVANTAGE?

To what extent does the halo effect of the parent university's reputation affect THE MBA ADVANTAGE? As shown in table B.5, all but five of THE MBA ADVANTAGE Top 20 schools are associated with universities that are ranked in the Top 25 universities by *U.S. News & World Report.*[11]

Table B.5
Correlation between business school and university rankings

MBA ADVANTAGE Top Business School Rank		U.S. News Top 25 University Rank
1	Harvard	1
2	Chicago	9
3	Stanford	4
4	MIT	5
5	Yale	3
6	Northwestern	13
7	Berkeley	16
8	Wharton	14
9	UCLA	23
10	Virginia	22
11	Cornell	11
12	Michigan	24
13	Dartmouth	7
14	Carnegie Mellon	19
15	Texas	(not rated)
16	Rochester	(not rated)
17	Indiana	(not rated)
18	North Carolina	(not rated)
19	Duke	7
20	NYU	(not rated)
(not rated)	Vanderbilt	25
(not rated)	Washington U.	20

Looking at table B.5, there appears to be some association between the Top 20 business schools and the top-ranked universities. The top five business schools are associated with top ten universities. Business schools ranked from sixth to fourteenth are all affiliated with Top 25 universities, while only one of the business schools in the bottom six (Duke) is associated with a

11 "America's Best Colleges," *U.S. News & World Report*, 1993 edition, pp. 26-27.

Top 25 university. If we plot the magnitude of THE MBA ADVANTAGE of the top business schools against the *U.S. News* rank of the parent universities, there is a moderate correlation (R-squared = 0.278).

But the ranks of the universities are also likely to be associated with the quality of students in their respective business schools. The association between a Top 20 business school's average GMAT and the *U.S. News* rank of its parent university is very strong (R-squared = 0.646). Similarly, there is a fairly strong relationship between a school's average pre-MBA pay and its parent university's rank (R-squared = 0.404). A "brand name" university may attract high quality students to its business school.[12]

Recall the residuals in figures B.4 and B.5 that show the extra value individual schools offer relative to the "average" top business school for a given level of student quality. If we plot these residuals from the regressions of THE MBA ADVANTAGE on GMAT and pre-MBA pay against the ranks of the universities (to remove the effects of student quality), there is no association whatsoever. (GMAT residuals versus university ranks gives an R-squared of 0.003; pre-MBA pay residuals versus university ranks gives an R-squared of 0.048.)

Regressing STEP UP directly against university ranks shows little association of this component of THE MBA ADVANTAGE with the ranks of the universities (R-squared = 0.068). Similarly, FAST TRACK has an insignificant association with the ranks of the universities (R-squared = 0.177).

The bottom line: It is difficult to build a case that the "brand name" of the parent universities has an effect on the value of the MBA degree from their respective business schools *beyond that of helping attract high quality students to these business schools.*

3. Do the *Business Week* Rankings Affect THE MBA ADVANTAGE?

Do the periodic *Business Week* rankings of the Top 20 business schools affect THE MBA ADVANTAGE? Are corporate recruiters and top quality students attracted to schools that are highly ranked by *Business Week*, thus raising THE MBA ADVANTAGE of these schools?

The regressions summarized in table B.4 provide little support for this hypothesis. For a *Business Week* ranking to influence the quality of incoming students, the survey must be published before the date at which these students enroll in their MBA programs. Since the biennial survey is published in October, it cannot influence students who begin their MBA classes in September of that year. The October 1990 *Business Week* rankings could not influence the school selection of the Class of '92, which began taking classes in September, 1990.

The only *Business Week* survey that could influence the school choice of the Class of '92 is the one that was published in October 1988. Furthermore, it could only affect the STEP UP component of THE MBA ADVANTAGE. (The FAST TRACK component is based on fifth year pay data from the Class of '87, which had already graduated before the 1988 survey was published.) As shown in table B.4, there is no significant association between the 1988 *Business Week* ranking and the STEP UP or any of the components of THE MBA ADVANTAGE.

Similarly, corporate recruiters choosing schools to recruit MBAs from the Class of '92 could only have been influenced by the *Business Week* surveys of 1988 and 1990, and again this would have affected only the STEP UP component of THE MBA ADVANTAGE. There is, however, no sig-

---

12 An outstanding business school also helps the reputation of the parent university.

nificant correlation between the STEP UP and either the 1988 *Business Week* ranking (R-squared = 0.110) or the 1990 ranking (R-squared = 0.149).

The bottom line: There is little evidence that the *Business Week* rankings have influenced THE MBA ADVANTAGE of the top business schools.

4. Faculty Research Intensity

Is there a trade-off between teaching and research? Do schools that emphasize teaching over research provide a higher MBA ADVANTAGE?

Faculty research is sometimes viewed as a distraction that compromises teaching quality. Some business schools downplay the importance of research. For example, Dartmouth emphasizes in their catalog that they have no Ph.D. program, which is an important component of a school's research activity.

As described in chapter 14, I have discovered something interesting about the relationship between research and teaching. One of my colleagues, Professor Ross Watts, recently completed a research citation study of several of the Top 20 schools.[13] If THE MBA ADVANTAGE is plotted against the median number of citations per faculty member (from Watts's study), there is a positive relationship for most of the schools studied (see figure 14.1). High value of the MBA degree to the student and high research activity by the faculty go together. (Citation studies of this kind are a good measure of the importance of a faculty member's research because they show how frequently his or her research has been cited by others.) But not all schools have been successful in leveraging their research activities into higher value in the teaching arena. The possible reasons for this are discussed in chapter 14.

When all the schools for which we have research citation data are included in the analysis, the correlation of research intensity with the value of THE MBA ADVANTAGE just misses being significant at the 10 percent level that is the cutoff for listing in table B.4 (the correlation is positive and significant at the 14 percent level). Research intensity does not correlate at all with the STEP UP component; being a research intensive school does not add value at the time of graduation. But in the five years of post-MBA work experience, there is a correlation between pay increases (as measured by FAST TRACK) and the research orientation of the graduate's business school that is significant at the 13 percent level. The implication is that research intensive schools give students better analytical tools and problem solving approaches that help them progress more rapidly on the job.

The bottom line: There is no evidence whatsoever that the research activity of the faculty detracts from the value of the MBA degree. To the contrary, there is evidence that it adds value.

5. Does the Regional Cost-of-Living Affect THE MBA ADVANTAGE?

Various regions of the country differ in the cost-of-living that can influence average starting pay, depending on where each school's graduates accept employment. An unpublished paper by Joseph Tracy and Joel Waldfogel estimates that the cost-of-living for MBA graduates can range from about minus 9 percent to plus 13 percent, relative to the average cost-of-living for the coun-

---

13 Watts, Ross L., "Simon School Research Productivity," unpublished manuscript, William E. Simon Graduate School of Business Administration, November 5, 1992, table 1.

try.[14] For large schools with national admissions and placements, these regional cost-of-living differences should tend to wash out in the averages. For regional schools that both accept and place students mostly in the same region, the cost-of-living for that region should be reflected in the average pre-MBA pay, the average starting pay and the average fifth year pay. Since our comparative analysis across schools is based on the ratios of these numbers, the regional cost-of-living index will cancel out. Many schools in the Top 20 serve a mix of national and regional markets, however, and cost-of-living factors could affect the magnitude of their MBA ADVANTAGE.

To test the sensitivity of THE MBA ADVANTAGE to regional cost-of-living differences, the STEP UP and the FAST TRACK were regressed against school-specific cost-of-living salary deflators developed by Tracy and Waldfogel.[15] These deflators were developed for seventeen of the twenty schools ranked in tables B.1, B.2 and B.3, and their values ranged from 1.01 for North Carolina to 1.14 for Harvard and Dartmouth.

The size of the STEP UP was found to be completely unrelated to these cost-of-living deflators (R-squared = 0.034). The regression between the post-MBA FAST TRACK salary growth rate was found to be highly significant, however (R-squared = 0.363, significant at the 1 percent level). Schools with deflators of 1.01 had FAST TRACK multipliers of about 1.8, while those with deflators of 1.10 or more had FAST TRACK multipliers of between 2.0 and 2.7. This makes sense—post-MBA salary growth is higher in regions that have a high cost-of-living.

To test the possibility that regional cost-of-living differences would alter THE MBA ADVANTAGE rankings, the values of THE MBA ADVANTAGE in table B.2 were divided by these school-specific salary deflators.

While the absolute values of THE MBA ADVANTAGE in table B.2 were reduced slightly by the deflators, the effects on the rankings were minimal:

- Yale moved up one position to number 4 while MIT slipped down one position to number 5.

- Carnegie Mellon moved up one position to number 13 while Dartmouth dropped one position to number 14.

The bottom line: While the effects of regional differences in the cost-of-living should be kept in mind when comparing the absolute values of THE MBA ADVANTAGE across schools, the rankings of the top businesses schools as shown in table B.2 were virtually unaffected.

6. Does the Mix of Functional Placements Affect THE MBA ADVANTAGE?

Do schools that place a high percentage of their students into high paying jobs like consulting have a higher MBA ADVANTAGE? Data is not available for pre-MBA pay and post-MBA fifth year pay sorted by functional concentration, so it is not possible to directly calculate a school's MBA ADVANTAGE for consulting majors or finance majors. It is possible, however, to use the data we have to shed some light on the relationship between a school's MBA ADVANTAGE and its mix of functional concentrations.

---

14 Tracy, J. and Waldfogel, J., "The Best Business Schools: A Market Based Approach," unpublished manuscript, Columbia University Department of Economics and Yale University Department of Economics, October, 1993.
15 Ibid., table 1. These deflators also contain factors designed to adjust for occupational and public/private sector placement differences.

Limited data from Top 20 business school catalogs for the Class of '92 shows that the average post-MBA starting pay for consulting is about $10,000 higher than the starting pay for finance and marketing, which are about equal (see figures 5.1–5.3 in chapter 5 for the range of Class of '93 starting pay for each concentration). As one might expect, there is a strong association between a school's MBA ADVANTAGE and the percentage of its graduating class that enters consulting (R-squared = 0.538). Each additional one percent of the graduating class that enters consulting adds almost $5,000 to the average school's MBA ADVANTAGE. Schools with high average GMATs (e.g., MIT) tend to have a higher percentage of placements into consulting (R-squared = 0.439). Overall, about 17 percent of the Class of '92 entered consulting, varying from 9 percent at Duke to 28 percent at MIT.

Conversely, schools with a high percentage of marketing placements tend to do less well. The relationship between THE MBA ADVANTAGE and the percentage entering marketing is negative, with an R-squared of 0.477. Each additional one percent of the graduating class that enters marketing subtracts almost $3,400 from the average school's MBA ADVANTAGE. There is a weak negative correlation between average GMATs and a school's percentage of marketing placements (R-squared = 0.235). Marketing accounted for 20 percent of the placements of the Class of '92, ranging from 8 percent at MIT to 31 percent at Cornell and Duke.

Finance is the most popular concentration, averaging 33 percent of the Top 20 placements in 1992. Stanford placed only 13 percent of its graduates in finance, compared with Chicago (43 percent), NYU (44 percent), and Rochester (58 percent) at the high end. There is no significant association between THE MBA ADVANTAGE and the percentage of finance placements (R-squared = 0.174), nor is there a significant association between average GMATs and the percentage of finance placements (R-squared = 0.109).

Therefore, a school's MBA ADVANTAGE is affected by the mix of functional concentrations. Schools with relatively high consulting placements have a higher MBA ADVANTAGE than those with high marketing placements.

This evaluation goes beyond merely comparing the average functional starting salaries across schools. The calculation of THE MBA ADVANTAGE also includes the growth of pay in the five years following graduation, it deducts the cost of going to business school, and it subtracts the opportunity cost of staying in the pre-MBA job with nominal pay increases.

The relationship between a school's placement mix (as measured by the percent of students who take jobs in consulting) and the school's overall MBA ADVANTAGE is fairly strong (R-squared = 0.538, significant at the 1 percent level). This is also true for both components of THE MBA ADVANTAGE, STEP UP and FAST TRACK. The association between placement mix and STEP UP has an R-squared = 0.247, significant at the 5 percent level; the association between placement mix and FAST TRACK has an R-squared = 0.372, significant at the 1 percent level.

The bottom line: Schools that place a higher-than-average proportion of graduates into consulting have a higher-than-average two-year STEP UP at the time of graduation and higher-than-average Fast TRACK salary growth in the five years following graduation.

7. Size of the School

In the perceptual map shown in figure A.2, appendix A, it was observed that corporate recruiters seem to prefer large schools where they have the opportunity to interview many students for each opening (the "supermarket effect"). Does this translate into a higher MBA AD-VANTAGE for large schools?

There is no correlation between school size (as measured by the number of its full-time MBA students) and STEP UP (R-squared = 0.009). There is no advantage for large schools in terms of achieving high percentage gains in pay at the time of graduation.

As shown in table B.4, there is a moderately strong positive association between school size and post-MBA salary growth, as measured by the FAST TRACK (R-squared = 0.324). The slope of the regression (which is significant at the 1 percent level) indicates that adding one hundred students—fifty in the first year class and fifty in the second year class—would increase the five-year FAST TRACK growth factor of a business school by 4.2 percentage points. This would cause a student with a starting salary of $50,000 to earn an extra $2,000 a year by his or her fifth year on the job.

The reasons for this are unclear. There is no correlation between school size and the mix of placements. Large schools do not tend to place more students in consulting jobs. They do not have brighter students, as measured by GMATs, although pre-MBA pay at the largest schools tends to be about $7,000 higher than at the smallest schools (significant at the 4 percent level). This higher average pay on entering business school may reflect more years of pre-MBA work experience, and this greater work experience could help those graduates progress more rapidly once they are employed.

Large schools tend to have more active alumni in the business world, and the "old boy network" may give fledgling MBAs from large schools an extra boost up the corporate ladder.

There could also be reputational effects. Large business schools are ranked significantly higher by both *U.S. News* (significant at the 1 percent level for the 1993 ranking) and *Business Week* (significant at the 1 percent level in both 1990 and 1992 surveys).

The bottom line: For whatever reasons, the post-MBA pay of graduates from the largest schools tends to grow significantly faster than those from the smallest schools, although the effect is modest (less than 1 percent per year).

8. Size of the Metropolitan Area

The perceptual map of recruiters' perceptions of business schools (see figure A.2 in appendix A) suggests a correlation between a recruiter's preference for recruiting at a business school and the size of the metropolitan area in which the school is located. The interpretation is that recruiters prefer to travel to large cities like New York, Boston, and Chicago, which have convenient air service.

A statistical analysis shows that there is no association whatsoever between the size of the metropolitan area and the STEP UP (R-squared = 0.001).[16] Attending a business school in a large city does not lead to higher percentage salary increases at the time of graduation.

There is a small positive correlation between post-MBA salary growth and the size of a school's metropolitan area (R-squared = 0.146, with a coefficient that is positive and significant

---

16 Metro sizes were obtained from Labich, K., "The Best Cities for Knowledge Workers," *Fortune*, November 15, 1993, p. 50; and *Rand McNally Atlas*, 1993 Edition.

at the 10 percent level), although the effect is small (adding one million to the metropolitan area increases a school's five-year FAST TRACK factor by only 2.67 percentage points). This effect cannot be explained by higher GMATs, higher pre-MBA pay, or a higher percent of placements in consulting, all of which are completely uncorrelated with metropolitan size. Perhaps, instead, it is related to the higher cost of living in large cities (cost of living and post-MBA pay growth rates were shown above to be positively correlated).

The bottom line: The post-MBA pay of graduates of business schools located in large cities tends to grow faster than that of graduates of schools located in small towns, but the effect is small.

CONCLUSIONS ABOUT THE MBA ADVANTAGE

1. THE MBA ADVANTAGE is a robust market-based method for evaluating business schools. The rank order of schools compared by THE MBA ADVANTAGE method is stable over a wide range of assumptions.

2. THE MBA ADVANTAGE is made up of two components: the two-year STEP UP in pay that occurs upon graduation and the post-MBA five-year FAST TRACK salary growth. Each of these components can be analyzed separately to determine which factors influence the observed differences in THE MBA ADVANTAGE across various schools.

3. The two-year STEP UP ranges from 40 percent to 75 percent. It is unrelated to student quality, the halo effect of the parent university, *Business Week* rankings, regional cost-of-living, the size of the school, or the size of the metropolitan area in which the school is located. About 25 percent of the variation of the STEP UP across schools can be explained by the mix of occupations into which the schools' students are placed. The rest appears to be a school-specific factor based on the school's reputation for producing quality graduates.

4. The five year post-MBA FAST TRACK salary growth factor ranges from 1.4 times to 2.8 times the post-MBA starting salary. About 40 to 45 percent of the variation in the FAST TRACK growth factor can be explained by differences in incoming student quality. This post-MBA growth factor also appears to be influenced by the placement mix of graduates (higher with more placements into consulting), the regional cost-of-living index, and the size of the school (higher for larger schools).

5. There is no evidence of a trade-off between faculty research activity and the value of the MBA degree. Quite to the contrary, evidence was presented in chapter 14 that suggests a strong positive association between faculty research intensity and the magnitude of a school's MBA ADVANTAGE.

6. The two most important factors in explaining differences in THE MBA ADVANTAGE across business schools are *incoming student quality* and *mix of placements*. There is also a moderate halo effect from the prestige of the parent university, but this can be completely explained by the strength of the parent university's prestige in attracting high quality students.

Appendix C

A Worksheet for Calculating Your Personal MBA ADVANTAGE

Using the approach illustrated in figure B.1 in appendix B, let's see how you can calculate your own estimated PERSONAL MBA ADVANTAGE.[1] We'll provide a worksheet that can be used whether you are considering a full-time program or a part-time program.

First, let's make a list of the information you will need, as shown in table C.1:

Table C.1

Information needed to calculate your PERSONAL MBA ADVANTAGE

1.	Your pay (pre-MBA pay) in the year before you start school ("year 0"):	$ _____
2.	The expected annual growth rate in your pay if you *don't* get an MBA:	_____ %
3.	The annual tuition and fees you will pay at the school of your choice:	$ _____
4.	Your expected post-MBA pay increase in percent (MBA STEP UP):	_____ %
5.	Your expected post-MBA pay annual growth rate (post-MBA FAST TRACK):	_____ %

Example 1: Suppose you decide that you would like to attend Cornell's Johnson School. Your pay in the year before you start your program will be $35,000 and you estimate that if you don't get an MBA this pay will grow at an annual rate of 5 percent. From chapter 5 you find that the annual tuition and fees at Cornell are $19,500. From chapter 4, table 4.3, you find that the average MBA STEP UP at Cornell is 58.5 percent, and from table 4.4, the average post-MBA FAST TRACK growth rate for Cornell is 18.64 percent.

Filling in the blanks in table C.1, we have:

Information Needed for Example 1

1. Your pay (pre-MBA pay) in the year before you start school ("year 0"):	$ 35,000
2. The expected annual growth rate in your pay if you *don't* get an MBA:	5%
3. The annual tuition and fees you will pay at the school of your choice:	$ 19,500
4. Your expected post-MBA pay increase in percent (MBA STEP UP):	58.5%
5. Your expected post-MBA pay annual growth rate (post-MBA FAST TRACK):	18.64%

Next, let's lay out a worksheet (table C.2) to calculate your PERSONAL MBA ADVANTAGE:

---

[1] In the examples shown, these calculations are made with estimated pre-tax pay. The calculations could be made with after-tax pay estimates if the appropriate tax rates are known.

Table C.2
Worksheet for calculating your PERSONAL MBA ADVANTAGE

	Column A Pay without MBA	Column B Pay with MBA	Column C Difference (B–A)	Column D Cum. Difference
Year 0				
Year 1*				
Year 2*				
Year 3				
Year 4				
Year 5				
Year 6				
Year 7				

* = years in school

1. Column A will be your estimated annual pay if you choose not to go on for your MBA.

2. Column B will be your estimated annual cash flow if you decide to go full time for your MBA. You will be in school during years 1 and 2, so your income goes to zero during these two years and your school expenses are equal to the tuition and fees. (We are not including living expenses at school on the assumption that you will have the same living expenses whether you go to school or not. But if you expect your living expenses to be higher at school, then this extra amount should be added to your tuition and fees for years 1 and 2.)

3. For column B, year 3, enter your post-MBA starting pay. To estimate this, increase your pre-MBA pay by the MBA STEP UP percentage for your school. Then increase this amount in each of the remaining years by your expected post-MBA FAST TRACK growth rate.

4. Column C is the difference in your expected cash flow between these two alternatives, so for each year subtract the entries in column A from column B.

5. Finally, column D is the cumulative value of column C for each year. When this value turns positive, you will have reached "breakeven" on your investment. The value in year 7 (which is your fifth year of post-MBA employment) is your estimated PERSONAL MBA ADVANTAGE.

For example 1, let's fill in the values and calculate your PERSONAL MBA ADVANTAGE:

1. For column A, enter your pre-MBA pay ($35,000) at year 0, and then increase it each year by the expected growth rate in your pay (5 percent) if you don't get an MBA.

2. For column B, years 0–2, enter your pre-MBA pay ($35,000) at year 0, and your annual tuition (–$19,500) at year 1 and year 2, the two years you'll be in school.

3. For column B, year 3, increase your pre-MBA pay by your MBA STEP UP ($35,000 plus 58.5 percent = $55,475) to get the amount you expect to be paid the first year

following graduation. Then increase this amount in each of the remaining years by your expected post-MBA FAST TRACK growth rate (18.64 percent per year).

4. Column C is the difference in your expected cash flow between these two alternatives, so for each year subtract the entries in column A from column B.

5. Finally, column D is the cumulative value of column C for each year. Note that at the end of year 2, when you graduate, you are $114,337 "in the hole" on your investment. Note also that the value turns positive in year 6, which is the fourth year of work following graduation. This means you break even on your investment in the MBA in the fourth year. At the end of five years, your estimated PERSONAL MBA ADVANTAGE for attending Cornell would be plus $63,703.

Worksheet for Example Number 1

	Column A Pay without MBA	Column B Pay with MBA	Column C Difference (B-A)	Column D Cum Difference
Year 0	$35,000	$35,000	$0	$0
Year 1*	36,750	–19,500	–56,250	–56,250
Year 2*	38,588	–19,500	–58,087	–114,337
Year 3	40,517	55,475	14,958	–99,379
Year 4	42,543	65,816	23,273	–76,106
Year 5	44,670	78,084	33,414	–42,692
Year 6	46,903	92,639	45,736	3,044
Year 7	49,248	109,907	60,659	63,703

* = years in school

Example 2: The first example shown was for attending the Johnson School at Cornell, where we had estimates in chapter 4 of Cornell's MBA STEP UP and post-MBA FAST TRACK growth rates based on historical data. But what if you are interested in a school for which the STEP UP and FAST TRACK growth rates are unknown?

In this case, you'll have to make some estimates. Your post-MBA starting pay (which is entered in column B for year 3) can be estimated from the school's most recent placement report. The growth rate in post-MBA pay is more difficult, and it's best to be conservative. As can be seen by reviewing table 4.4 in chapter 4, a value of 10 percent per year would be a conservative estimate.

Example 3: Suppose you are considering a part-time MBA program for which you will have to pay the tuition, although you will continue in your job while you are in school. Let's assume that your present job is the same as that described in Example 1: $35,000 with 5 percent expected pay increases. Assume also that your part-time tuition payments will be $10,000 per year for the three years it will take you to complete the program. Finally, assume that your Step Up will be $10,000 when you finish your degree and your post-MBA salary growth rate will be 10 percent annually.

In example 3, you would break even in year 6 and your PERSONAL MBA ADVANTAGE for this part-time program would be plus $21,086. Your worksheet would look like this:

Worksheet for Example Number 3

	Column A Pay without MBA	Column B Pay with MBA	Column C Difference (B–A)	Column D Cum Difference
Year 0	$35,000	$35,000	$0	$0
Year 1*	36,750	26,750**	–10,000	–10,000
Year 2*	38,588	28,588**	–10,000	–20,000
Year 3*	40,517	30,517**	–10,000	–30,000
Year 4	42,543	50,517	7,974	–22,026
Year 5	44,670	55,569	10,899	–11,127
Year 6	46,903	61,126	14,223	3,096
Year 7	49,248	67,238	17,990	21,086
* = years in school		** $10,000 tuition is subtracted from pay		

Blank worksheets for evaluating your personal options are provided on the following pages.

Case 1: Your PERSONAL MBA ADVANTAGE Calculation (table C.3)
for Option number 1: _____

Table C.3

Information needed to calculate your PERSONAL MBA ADVANTAGE for Option 1

1. Your pay (pre-MBA pay) in the year before you start school ("year 0"): $ _____
2. The expected annual growth rate in your pay if you *don't* get an MBA: _____ %
3. The annual tuition and fees you will pay at the school of your choice: $ _____
4. Your expected post-MBA pay increase in percent (MBA STEP UP):   _____ %
5. Your expected post-MBA pay annual growth rate (post-MBA FAST TRACK):   _____ %

Worksheet for Calculating Your PERSONAL MBA ADVANTAGE for Option 1

	Column A Pay without MBA	Column B Pay with MBA	Column C Difference (B–A)	Column D Cum. Difference
Year 0				
Year 1*				
Year 2*				
Year 3				
Year 4				
Year 5				
Year 6				
Year 7				

* = years in school

Notes:

Case 2: Your PERSONAL MBA ADVANTAGE Calculation (table C.4)
    for Option number 2: _____

Table C.4
Information needed to calculate your PERSONAL MBA ADVANTAGE for Option 2

1. Your pay (pre-MBA pay) in the year before you start school ("year 0"):	$ _____
2. The expected annual growth rate in your pay if you *don't* get an MBA:	_____ %
3. The annual tuition and fees you will pay at the school of your choice:	$ _____
4. Your expected post-MBA pay increase in percent (MBA STEP UP):	_____ %
5. Your expected post-MBA pay annual growth rate (post-MBA FAST TRACK):	_____ %

Worksheet for Calculating Your PERSONAL MBA ADVANTAGE for Option 2

	Column A Pay without MBA	Column B Pay with MBA	Column C Difference (B–A)	Column D Cum. Difference
Year 0	_____	_____	_____	_____
Year 1*	_____	_____	_____	_____
Year 2*	_____	_____	_____	_____
Year 3	_____	_____	_____	_____
Year 4	_____	_____	_____	_____
Year 5	_____	_____	_____	_____
Year 6	_____	_____	_____	_____
Year 7	_____	_____	_____	_____

* = years in school

Notes:

Case 3: Your PERSONAL MBA ADVANTAGE Calculation (table C.5)
for Option number 3: _____

Table C.5
Information needed to calculate your PERSONAL MBA ADVANTAGE for Option 3

1. Your pay (pre-MBA pay) in the year before you start school ("year 0"): $ _____
2. The expected annual growth rate in your pay if you *don't* get an MBA: _____ %
3. The annual tuition and fees you will pay at the school of your choice: $ _____
4. Your expected post-MBA pay increase in percent (MBA STEP UP):   _____ %
5. Your expected post-MBA pay annual growth rate (post-MBA FAST TRACK):   _____ %

Worksheet for Calculating Your PERSONAL MBA ADVANTAGE for Option 3

	Column A Pay without MBA	Column B Pay with MBA	Column C Difference (B–A)	Column D Cum. Difference
Year 0				
Year 1*				
Year 2*				
Year 3				
Year 4				
Year 5				
Year 6				
Year 7				

* = years in school

Notes:

Further Reading

For more information on graduate business education and career planning, here are some books you might find helpful:

Business school guides
Byrne, John A., *A Business Week Guide: The Best Business Schools*, third edition, McGraw-Hill, 1993, $14.95. The most widely quoted book on MBA programs, with in-depth profiles of over fifty business schools. A "must read" for every prospective MBA student.

Fischgrund, Tom, *The Insider's Guide to the Top 10 Business Schools*, fifth edition, Little, Brown and Company, 1993, $11.95. If you have your heart set on attending one of the very top business schools, this book contains twenty or more pages of facts, stories, and student essays on each school.

Krasna, Jodi Z., editor, *The Official Guide to MBA Programs*, 1992–1994 edition, published by The Graduate Management Admissions Council, P.O. Box 6106, Princeton, NJ 08541-6106, $13.95. Full page descriptions and key facts about more than 550 graduate management programs worldwide, by the organization that administers the GMAT exam.

Schatz, Dr. Martin, *The MBA Guidebook: The Authoritative Guide to Accredited MBA Programs*, Unicorn Research Corporation, 4621 North Landmark Drive, Orlando, FL 32617-1235, 1993, $29.95 for the book and a diskette with a computerized database on all the accredited MBA programs. Developed by a former business school dean, this 568-page sourcebook comes with a PC-compatible diskette that can be searched on eighteen different business school attributes using your own personal preference weightings to prepare a rank-ordered list of the best schools for your personal requirements. Telephone (407) 657-4974 or fax (407) 657-6149 for more information.

Career planning
The best guide I know of for doing a personal strengths and weaknesses analysis is Richard Nelson Bolles' classic, *What Color Is Your Parachute*, Ten Speed Press, 1994 edition, $14.95. Pay particular attention to chapters 9, 10, and 11. This manual for career development has been in print since 1970 and is now in its 22nd edition. This book takes the reader through a highly-structured method for determining his or her special skills and interests, and it is full of practical and inspirational advice for the job seeker.

Entrepreneurship
Stolze, William J., *Startup: An Entrepreneur's Guide to Launching and Managing a New Venture*, second edition, Rock Beach Press, 1255 University Avenue, Rochester, NY 14607, 1992, $14.95. Bill Stolze is a very successful entrepreneur who started a company in 1961 that now

has annual sales in excess of $150 million. To learn how to cope with the opportunities and the uncertainties faced by an entrepreneur, you should obtain a copy of Bill's book, which can be ordered from Career Press, Inc., 180 Fifth Avenue, P.O. Box 34, Hawthorne, NJ 07507, or by calling toll-free 1-800-CAREER-1.

Rich, S. and Gumpert, D., *Business Plans that Win $$$: Lessons from the MIT Enterprise Forum*, Harper & Row, 1985. Developed by a panel of MIT alumni, this book offers many solid tips on writing a business plan that will answer the questions most frequently asked by sources of venture capital.

Executive MBA programs

Byrne, John A., and Cynthia Greene, *Business Week's Guide to the Best Executive Education Programs*, McGraw-Hill, 1993, $14.95. A comprehensive review of the top twenty Executive MBA programs in the country, with facts, insights, and program rankings by deans and former students.

Fertig, Kevin, editor, *Directory of Executive MBA Programs*, available by mail from American Assembly of Collegiate Schools of Business, 600 Emerson Road, Suite 300, St. Louis, MO 63141-67623, 1993, $10.00. One-page descriptions of 126 Executive MBA programs offered in the United States and Canada. Call (314) 872-8481 for more information.

Job interviewing

Yate, Martin, *Knock 'em Dead: The Ultimate Job Seeker's Handbook*, Bob Adams, Inc., 260 Center Street, Holbrook, MA 02343, 1994, $8.95. An outstanding source of advice on how to succeed in the job market, including how to respond to the toughest interviewers. Now in its seventh edition, with over one million copies in print. For more information call (617) 767-8100.

Index